Studia Fennica
Linguistica 19

THE FINNISH LITERATURE SOCIETY (SKS) was founded in 1831 and has, from the very beginning, engaged in publishing operations. It nowadays publishes literature in the fields of ethnology and folkloristics, linguistics, literary research and cultural history.

The first volume of the Studia Fennica series appeared in 1933. Since 1992, the series has been divided into three thematic subseries: Ethnologica, Folkloristica and Linguistica. Two additional subseries were formed in 2002, Historica and Litteraria. The subseries Anthropologica was formed in 2007.

In addition to its publishing activities, the Finnish Literature Society maintains research activities and infrastructures, an archive containing folklore and literary collections, a research library and promotes Finnish literature abroad.

STUDIA FENNICA EDITORIAL BOARD
Pasi Ihalainen, Professor, University of Jyväskylä, Finland
Timo Kaartinen, Title of Docent, Lecturer, University of Helsinki, Finland
Taru Nordlund, Title of Docent, Lecturer, University of Helsinki, Finland
Riikka Rossi, Title of Docent, Researcher, University of Helsinki, Finland
Katriina Siivonen, Substitute Professor, University of Helsinki, Finland
Lotte Tarkka, Professor, University of Helsinki, Finland
Tuomas M. S. Lehtonen, Secretary General, Dr. Phil., Finnish Literature Society, Finland
Tero Norkola, Publishing Director, Finnish Literature Society, Finland
Kati Romppanen, Secretary of the Board, Finnish Literature Society, Finland

Editorial Office
SKS
P.O. Box 259
FI-00171 Helsinki
www.finlit.fi

Kaisa Häkkinen

Spreading the Written Word

Mikael Agricola and the Birth of Literary Finnish

Translated by Leonard Pearl

Finnish Literature Society · SKS · Helsinki

Studia Fennica Linguistica 19

The publication has undergone a peer review.

The open access publication of this volume has received part funding via Helsinki University Library.

© 2015 Kaisa Häkkinen and SKS
License CC-BY-NC-ND 4.0 International

A digital edition of a printed book first published in 2015 by the Finnish Literature Society.
Cover Design: Timo Numminen
EPUB: Tero Salmén

ISBN 978-952-222-674-7 (Print)
ISBN 978-952-222-755-3 (PDF)
ISBN 978-952-222-754-6 (EPUB)

ISSN 0085-6835 (Studia Fennica)
ISSN 1235-1938 (Studia Fennica Linguistica)

DOI: http://dx.doi.org/10.21435/sflin.19

This work is licensed under a Creative Commons CC-BY-NC-ND 4.0 International License.
To view a copy of the license, please visit http://creativecommons.org/licenses/by-nc-nd/4.0/

A free open access version of the book is available at http://dx.doi.org/10.21435/sflin.19 or by scanning this QR code with your mobile device.

Contents

Preface 8
Abbreviations and Symbols 11

1. **From a Pre-Literary to a Literary Culture** 13
    1.1 Mediaeval Heritage 13
        1.1.1 A Literary Culture Arrives in Finland 13
        1.1.2 Finnish in Texts of Other Languages 17
        1.1.3 Finnish in the Middle Ages 18
    1.2 The Reformation Progresses to Finland 21
        1.2.1 New Teachings in Wittenberg 21
        1.2.2 The Reformation Expands to Scandinavia 23
        1.2.3 The First Reformation Messengers and Strongholds in Finland 25
    1.3 The First Finnish Manuscripts 27

2. **The Life of Mikael Agricola** 31
    2.1 Family Background and Early Schooling 31
    2.2 A Schoolboy in Vyborg 34
    2.3 Work as Secretary to the Bishop 35
    2.4 A Student in Wittenberg 37
    2.5 A Cathedral School Headmaster 41
    2.6 From a Bishop's Assistant to Bishop 46

3. **The Finnish Works of Mikael Agricola** 53
    3.1 Agricola's Primer / *Abckiria* 53
    3.2 Agricola's Prayer Book / *Rucouskiria Bibliasta* 58
    3.3 Agricola's New Testament / *Se Wsi Testamenti* 60
    3.4 Agricola's Agenda / *Käsikiria Castesta ia muista Christikunnan Menoista* 63
    3.5 Agricola's Missal / *Messu eli Herran Echtolinen* 66
    3.6 Agricola's Passion / *Se meiden Herran Jesusen Christusen Pina* 68
    3.7 Agricola's Psalter / *Dauidin Psaltari* 70
    3.8 Agricola's Collection of Canticles and Prophecies / *Weisut ia Ennustoxet Mosesen Laista ia Prophetista Wloshaetut* 73
    3.9 Agricola's Three Minor Prophets / *Ne Prophetat Haggai SacharJa Maleachi* 74

4. Finnish in the Works of Mikael Agricola 76
    4.1 Agricola's Alphabet and its Characters 76
    4.2 Phonetic Length 80
    4.3 Individual Characters by Phonetic Class 82
        4.3.1 Stops 82
        4.3.2 Fricatives Not Known in Contemporary Finnish 83
        4.3.3 Semivowels *j* and *v* 84
        4.3.4 Other Consonants 85
        4.3.5 Vowel Quality 85
        4.3.6 Phonetic Phenomenon and Inflectional Forms 87
    4.4 Nominal Inflection 89
        4.4.1 Declension: Case Inflection 90
        4.4.2 Pronouns 93
    4.5 Conjugation: Finite Verbal Inflection 96
        4.5.1 Main Classes 96
        4.5.2 Moods 97
        4.5.3 Tenses 98
        4.5.4 Personal Inflection 98
        4.5.5 Two Important Features 100
    4.6 Infinitive Verbal Forms 103
    4.7 Possessive Suffixes 107
    4.8 Special Syntactic Features in Agricola 108
        4.8.1 Word Order 108
        4.8.2 Passive Constructions and Reflexive Expressions 110
        4.8.3 Congruency 111
        4.8.4 Conjunctions 113
        4.8.5 Non-Finite Clauses 117
    4.9 Vocabulary in the Works of Agricola 120
        4.9.1 Statistics on Agricola's Vocabulary 120
        4.9.2 Basic Vocabulary 122
        4.9.3 Word Formation 123
        4.9.4 Dialectical Vocabulary 125
        4.9.5 Loanwords and Calques 126
        4.9.6 Remnants of the Past in Agricola's Vocabulary 127
        4.9.7 Cultural-Historical Evidence 128

5. Mikael Agricola's Networks in Finland and Abroad 130
    5.1 Agricola's Teachers, Assistants and Supporters 130
    5.2 Agricola as a Representative of Finland 135
    5.3 Agricola as a Provider of Information and Influence from Abroad 139

6. The Legacy of Mikael Agricola 144
    6.1 The Literary Legacy of Mikael Agricola 144
    6.2 Research on Michael Agricola and His Life's Work 148
    6.3 Mikael Agricola as a National Figure 157

Timeline of Events in the Life of Mikael Agricola 163
Bibliography 164
    Source Materials 164
    Literature 165
Historical Personal Names 174
Place Names in Past and Present Finland 176
    Naming in Finland 176
    Historical Provinces 177
Inflectional Paradigms in Finnish 178
    Nominal Inflection 178
    Possessive Suffixes 178
    Nominal Inflection with Possessive Suffixes 179
    Personal Pronoun Inflection 179
    Verbal Inflection 180
    Infinitive (Non-Finite) Forms 184
Abstract 186
Index 187
The most important places throughout Mikael Agricola's life

Preface

Finnish culture has ancient roots, but it was not until the 16th century that Finnish had begun to be written down. The Protestant Reformation began in Germany in 1517, and the expansion of Lutheranism was the decisive impetus for literary development. The principle was that the people had to get to hear and read the word of God in their own mother tongue. If there previously was no literary language, it had to be created.

The first Finnish books were produced by Mikael Agricola. He was born an ordinary son of a farmer, but his dedication to his studies and subsequent work in the office of the Bishop of Turku opened up the road to leading roles in the Finnish Church. Agricola became a respected headmaster of the cathedral school in Turku, a Finnish Reformer and finally Bishop of Turku. He was able to bring a total of nine works in Finnish to print, which became the foundation of literary Finnish.

Finnish in Agricola's time was, in many respects, different than it is today. There still was no standard language because the Finns were scattered throughout a vast, scarcely settled country and spoke local dialects. For their whole lives, many of them interacted only with the inhabitants in their own home regions. Literary Finnish became a connective thread between the different dialects. A standard language independent from these regional dialects began to develop on the basis of the works of Agricola.

In practice, literary Finnish was essentially created through the translation of Latin, Swedish and German spiritual literature. In translating scripture, it was important for the original content of the text to remain unchanged, and for this reason, translating was done verbatim as accurately as possible. There were structural features that came into literary Finnish through translations that were not in the true vernacular. Furthermore, the literary language required a great amount of new vocabulary because its subject matter was different from that of the ordinary, everyday language. The lands and events found in the Bible were alien to Finnish culture as well. In describing these phenomena, Finnish means of expression had to be developed to be more diverse than before.

We divided *Spreading the Written Word: Mikael Agricola and the Birth of Literary Finnish* into six chapters. The first chapter outlines the historical background necessary to understand the life's work of Mikael Agricola and its importance. The second chapter describes Agricola's life in chronological order. Chapter three presents the Finnish works published by Agricola and their most important non-Finnish exemplars. The fourth and most extensive chapter is a depiction of Agricola's Finnish: we divided it into sections according to linguistic level, starting with an examination of his orthographic system and its relation to phonetics, then describing nominal and verbal inflection, syntax, vocabulary and word formation. Agricola carried out his life's work as part of a Finnish and non-Finnish network of influential connections, which is described in chapter five. The sixth and final chapter examines the importance of Agricola's work, research on Agricola and his life's work and Agricola's role in contemporary Finnish culture.

Our book is not a translation of a previously published work in Finnish. We wrote it specifically with an international audience in mind. There has indeed been a depiction of Mikael Agricola, his literary work and his Finnish in published studies, but a majority of them has been released only in Finnish. Therefore, reading them requires prior knowledge on both Finnish history and culture, in addition to Finnish language skills. We provided background information on both history and language so that it will be possible for the international reader to understand the core content of the book. However, it is not possible to introduce analyses in great detail in a non-academic book. Nevertheless, the bibliography can provide the reader with the possibility to find further information.

Chapter four on the language in Agricola also introduces the main features of the structure of contemporary Finnish. This way, it will be possible to concretely highlight the differences between Agricola and contemporary Finnish. As a compliment to this, we provided paradigm tables of nominal and verbal inflection at the end of the book. There is also a list of historical figures at the end of the book, whose names in Finnish literature are found in different forms than those in international contexts. It is customary in Finnish to use Fennicised personal names adapted for historical persons, which is why it can be difficult to recognise a figure in Finnish literature on the basis of his or her internationally known name. Furthermore, as there is a bilingual tradition of place names in past and present Finland, we also provided a short guide to explain their use and nature.

Not all Finnish inflected words on their own can or could be translated without context. In this case, we used glosses in chapter four to clarify the morphological content of those words, striving to keep them as clear and simple as possible. On the other hand, we occasionally used glosses with a regular translation for clarification or to show a comparison. We provided a list of glossing abbreviations along with other symbols on pages 11 and 12 to help the reader become familiar with the nature of Finnish words.

Because Agricola's Finnish-language works are liturgical books, many of the linguistic samples in chapter four are from the Bible. The Bible in English and its many versions are conveniently and readily available online. We found the easiest portal to navigate through to be *www.biblegateway.com*. The website can display the different versions of a biblical line in a list, easily comparing them to each other on one page. Our goal was to select the linguistically closest English equivalent to the passage taken from Agricola. Thus, multiple Bibles were used for these samples. Passages not from the books of the Bible – a biblical gloss or an excerpt from a poem, for example – have been provided in English with their source by the translator of our book. Unless otherwise noted, the author provided all other samples or selected individual words or phrases from Agricola and the translator provided their English equivalents.

We would like to praise the book *Mikael Agricola: Suomen uskonpuhdistaja* (1985) by Viljo and Kari Tarkiainen and the biography *Mikael Agricola: Elämä ja teokset* (2007) by Simo Heininen as particularly noteworthy sources in the sphere of previous studies on Agricola. Moreover, Viljo Tarkiainen's and Simo Heininen's research have provided an excellent foundation to this general overview. We also wish to highlight the work of those scholars who are no longer with us and who provided multiple works on Agricola's Finnish: Heikki Ojansuu, Martti Rapola, Osmo Nikkilä and Silva Kiuru. Others who have carried out research on Agricola can be found in chapter six. We provided the bibliography with English translations of all the Finnish works noted in this book to help the reader get acquainted with these studies.

Finland observed the anniversary of the 450th year of Agricola's death in 2007 as a national commemorative year. There were various projects under way for the anniversary year, including a variety of new studies and multidisciplinary research co-operation as well as a great deal of books and articles on Agricola and his life's work. There has continually been active research even after 2007, and as the bibliography shows, we used new information produced by these studies in the creation of our book.

This overview of Mikael Agricola's life's work and the beginning stages of literary Finnish is especially geared towards researchers and students. It provides information required on the development of Finnish language and literary culture and the features that have influenced them upon the meeting of the Middle Ages and the modern era. The book mainly focuses on language, history and cultural history, but in terms of theology and Church history, it also provides an excellent review on the progression and arrival of the Reformation and Lutheranism to Finland. It was written with a broad audience in mind, as a work of non-fiction for anyone interested in these subjects.

The author of the book is Professor Kaisa Häkkinen, PhD, a Finnish language researcher of the University of Turku whose areas of expertise are the history of Finnish and the Finno-Ugric languages, etymology and old literary Finnish. She has written many scholarly and non-academic books and articles, as well as participated in various projects on Mikael Agricola. The translator is Leonard Pearl, MA, a linguist specialised in Finnish and who has previously translated a book on Finnish onomastics into English. We would like to thank the Varsinais-Suomi Regional Fund of the Finnish Cultural Foundation for funding the translation of our book, as well as our publisher, the Finnish Literature Society, for committing to support the project.

Kaisa Häkkinen and Leonard Pearl
Turku
May 2015

Abbreviations and Symbols

The following is a list of the most frequently used abbreviations and symbols in this book. While abbreviations and symbols have been used to indicate the morphological structure and elements in certain words that cannot be translated without context, our goal was to make them as simple as possible, so no strict glossing convention has been used. International Phonetic Alphabet (IPA) characters are not listed here.

Agr. = Agricola
Fin. = Finnish
Std. = Standard contemporary Finnish
Swe. = Swedish

Morphological symbols:
+ = Morphological affixations, e.g. *kala-a* 'fish+PART'
| = Compounding marker, e.g. *esi|kuva* 'fore|image'
- = Morphological affixation marker in regular orthography e.g. *las-ta* 'child+PART'

Capital letter = Morphophoneme showing apophony in inflection and allomorphic information, e.g. *V* is a vowel in the illative case (see inflectional suffixes below) that employs the same vowel in the stem (e.g. *kala-an* 'fish+ILL', *käte-en* 'hand+ILL', *talo-on* 'house+ILL'); e.g. U in NUT can either be /u/ or /y/, depending on the other vowels in the stem (e.g. *anta-nut* 'given' and *men-nyt* 'gone')

Other symbols
: = Morphological change or stem, starting with the root form e.g. *mies* : *miehe-* : *miehe-n* 'man+GEN'; translation after a gloss e.g. *Isämme* 'father+1PL.PX': 'our father'
* = Unaccepted form e.g. **henkki*; archaic or proto-form (not attested) e.g. **sano-pa*
← = Morphologically or and/or historically derived e.g. *näiden* 'these+GEN' ← *nämä* 'these'

Inflectional suffixes:

ABE	=	Abessive (*tta* or *ttä*) e.g *vaimotta* 'wife+ABE'
ABL	=	Ablative (*lta* or *ltä*) e.g. *keskeltä* 'middle+ABL'
ADE	=	Adessive (*lla* or *llä*) e.g. *kivellä* 'stone+ADE'
ALL	=	Allative (*lle*) e.g. *puolelle* 'side+ALL'
COM	=	Comitative (*ine*) e.g. *kauniine* 'beautiful+COM'
ELA	=	Elative (*sta* or *stä*) e.g. *ahkerasta* 'diligent+ELA'
ESS	=	Essive (*na* or *nä*) e.g. *kolmantena* 'third+ESS'
GEN	=	Genitive (*n*), e.g. *miehen* 'man+GEN'
ILL	=	Illative (*Vn*, *hVn* or *seen*), e.g. *kalaan* 'fish+ILL'
INE	=	Inessive (*ssa* or *ssä*), e.g. *rakentamassa* 'build+AGT+INE'
INSTR	=	Instructive (*n*), e.g. *sanoman* 'say+INF3+INSTR'
PART	=	Partitive (*a* or *ä*, *ta* or *tä*), e.g. *miestä* 'man+PART'
TRANSL	=	Translative (*ksi*), e.g. *pojaksi* 'boy+TRANSL'

Additional grammatical abbreviations:

1, 2, 3	=	First, second, third (person, infinitive, participle)
ADV	=	Adverbial suffix
AGT	=	Agent participle
CLT	=	Clitic
IMP	=	Imperative
INF	=	Infinitive
NEG	=	Negative verb
PL	=	Plural
PASS	=	Passive
PCP	=	Participle
POT	=	Potential
PX	=	Possessive suffix
SG	=	Singular

1. From a Pre-Literary to a Literary Culture

This chapter describes Finland in the Middle Ages and the arrival of a literary culture to Finland, which began with Latin and Swedish. Finland was a part of the Swedish Realm and it belonged to the Roman Catholic Church. The most important sources of livelihood were agriculture, hunting and fishing. There were only six cities and they all were located on the coast. The capital was Turku, situated in Southwest Finland. Education was arranged solely by the Church, and the language used was Latin. There were no universities in Finland but some Finns went to study in Central Europe, such as in Paris and Rostock. As a consequence of the Protestant Reformation and the spread of Lutheranism, Finnish began to be used for the Church. Since there previously was no literary language, it had to be developed.

1.1 Mediaeval Heritage

1.1.1 A LITERARY CULTURE ARRIVES IN FINLAND

In the first half of the Middle Ages, Finland and the other northernmost parts of Europe were such unfamiliar territories to the inhabitants of Central and Southern Europe, that they could not be illustrated, even on maps. Only a few merchants and explorers dared to go and see with their own eyes what kinds of regions and peoples could be found in the North, and when they returned, they relayed unbelievable stories about a snow- and ice-covered expanse, a frozen sea, whirlpools and sea monsters that threaten sailors as well as a sun that does not set at all in the summer.

At the end of the first millennium CE, the situation began to change. At that time, the Finns' western neighbours – the Scandinavian Vikings – actively began to sail the seas and go on trade and pillaging missions to the British Isles and the shores of Central Europe. Routes from the Swedish territory in particular were orientated toward the East as well, along the great rivers of Russia all the way until the rich and famous city of Constantinople. Judging from archaeological evidence, Finns also participated to some extent in these travels, although the actual Vikings were northern Germanic peoples, that is, the forefathers of the contemporary Swedes, Norwegians, Danes and Icelanders. In any case, Finland was on the important trade routes and became known as an area where priceless furs could be acquired for selling in Central and Southern Europe. (Lavery 2006; Meinander 2011.)

There was also a great change in spiritual culture during the Viking Age as Christianity began to extend to the North. The Scandinavians were first converted, and through them, information on a new faith began to permeate the trading centres located in the region of Finland. Christian influences also came into Finland from the Slavs who inhabited the East, judging from the fact that a few fundamental Finnish words pertaining to Christianity, such as *risti* ('cross'), *pappi* ('priest') and *pakana* ('pagan'), were borrowed from Old East Slavic. The proselytism carried out by the Swedish rulers was, however, more effective, and with the support of the secular authority, the Roman Catholic Church began to establish its position, starting from the 12th century, in the southwestern part of the country – that is, in the region that had historically been called *Suomi* ('Finland') – and also in the northern neighbouring region of Satakunta.

The first actual document in which there was some mention of conditions in Finland was a papal bull from 1171, entitled *Gravis admodum* ('Greatly laborious') after its incipit. In it, the Pope bemoans to the Archbishop of Uppsala how difficult it is to permanently convert the Finns to Christianity. Indeed, they accepted being baptised but when the converters left, they went to wash the baptism away and returned to their previous way of life. (Heininen & Heikkilä 1996.) In any case, proselytism produced results and parishes began to be established in the more densely populated areas of the country, above all in Finland Proper (today known as Southwest Finland) and Satakunta.

The first episcopal church was constructed in the municipality of Nousiainen, 25 kilometres north of Turku, but after 1229, the episcopal see was moved first to the district of Koroinen in Turku, located close to the city centre, and then by the end of the 13th century, it was moved to its current location in the city. Thus, Turku established itself as the spiritual and administrative heart of Finland where both a castle and a cathedral were erected.

Another significant stronghold was Vyborg, in Karelia, which was directly bordered with Russia at the back end of the Gulf of Finland. The mainland Häme region of Western Finland remained a more isolated area where old customs and pagan beliefs were here and there preserved for centuries. On the other hand, however, the castle erected in Häme and the roads from it leading to Turku and Vyborg strengthened the connections to the cultural and educational centres of Finland.

From the beginning, books played a key role in the undertakings of the Christian Church. Books were feverously written, copied, used and interpreted, and because of this, the Church arranged education for young men who intended to work for the Church. The common language of the Roman Catholic Church was Latin which was also the language of the institution of university that emerged in the Middle Ages. Accessing the road to learning and to an ecclesiastical career undoubtedly required Latin skills, whereupon Latin grammar, Latin rhetoric and debating skills were crucial subjects in mediaeval schools. Moreover, at the very least mathematics and song were also studied. Mathematical knowledge was required, for example, in chronology, and singing was a crucial part of ecclesiastical ceremonies. There were at least three schools in mediaeval Finland: in Turku, in Vyborg and in Rauma. Of these, the cathedral school of Turku, Katedralskolan i Åbo, was the best and most distinguished.

Along with the Catholic Church, monasticism also came to Finland. The Dominican and Franciscan monks circulated amongst the people and took care of providing religious primary education. The monasteries and convents also became centres of literary activity for which foreign literature was acquired and also where new books were written and copied. Books were rigorously produced especially in the Birgittine monastery church established in Naantali in 1443, and the monk Jöns Budde who worked there has traditionally been named as the first Finnish writer. However, he wrote in his mother tongue, which was Swedish, and did not use any Finnish in his books. The abbey of the Birgittine Order in Vadstena, Sweden was in those times known as a central site of the development and use of literary Swedish. The vernacular played an important role in the Birgittine Order because education arranged by the Roman Catholic Church was usually planned for men only, and proficiency in Latin was not quite as common amongst the nuns as it was amidst the monks. Within the Birgittine Order, however, women had the opportunity to study and work, for example, as scribes.

Since Antiquity, papyrus and parchment were used as the material for books, but upon entering the Middle Ages, fragile and difficult to acquire papyrus became replaced by firm and easier to handle parchment. Books were originally scrolls but it was more practical to put more extensive manuscripts together in the form of book-shaped codices compiled from separate sheets. The Latin word *codex* originally referred to a tree trunk and subsequently a tablet of wood used as a writing board. It gradually became a term for a whole compilation of wooden tablets, and later a manuscript bound into a book prepared even from other materials.

Starting from the 13th century, paper came into use alongside parchment. Paper was made out of rags by hand, and each papermaker had his own watermark which allowed the papers to later be identified and dated. This rag paper was sturdy and durable so that even the old manuscripts were surprisingly well intact as long as they were properly preserved.

Manuscripts were at best priceless works of art. The handwriting in them was clear and consistent. The most popular lettering style was originally Carolingian minuscule with rounded shapes, but starting from the 12th century, more narrow and angular Gothic fonts began to become standard, the oldest of which was textualis, also known as textura. The name *textualis* stems from the fact that a page filled with condensedly written letters looks as if it were woven fabric. Sparing no expense with regard to time or effort, the manuscripts were illuminated with miniature paintings and decorative initials. Real gold and expensive pigmentation were used in these decorative illustrations. Such manuscripts were not within the reach of the common person. They were treasures for churches, monasteries, rulers and wealthy individuals.

The first definite acknowledgment of a Finnish library was in found in the monastery in Sigtuna, Sweden (Heikkilä 2009). Tuomas, Bishop of Finland who died in 1248, donated a manuscript to the monastery which included a list from his own library. It altogether had 58 books. The second acknowledgment concerning a library pertains to Turku Cathedral which received a gift of 22 books from Bishop Hemming, Roman Catholic Bishop of Turku, in the mid-14th century and, in addition, some books from a Katedralskolan i Åbo schoolmaster. The cathedral chapter and the Bishop of Turku, the Birgittine Monastery of Naantali and the Turku Convent of St Olav were in possession of the largest mediaeval collections of books in Finland. There was local mediaeval book production in Turku and Naantali, possibly also in Vyborg. It is estimated that there were approximately a total of 1,000 to 1,500 books in Finland during the Middle Ages. (Heikkilä 2009.)

Notes and writing exercises were also done in a more modest manner, for example on wooden or wax boards or strips of birch bark. A great deal of mediaeval birch bark letters from Novgorod, Russia is known, verifying an active literary culture, and they include notes and notices of common city dwellers. The first birch bark letter in Finland was just recently found, and actually quite by accident, as one birch bark roll found in mediaeval city excavations was opened up (Harjula 2012a). Coiled up pieces of birch bark were found in the excavations in large amounts. The writing was originally done on the lighter, outer surface of the bark, but it later curled up inside itself and it could not reveal if they included writing or not. As no one knew to search for the birch bark letters and birch bark was not as such considered to be an archaeological finding, a valuable set of materials possibly got lost along with the landmass removed from the excavations.

In the Middle Ages, books were brought in to Finland from abroad. They were not only brought over by clerics, but also by students who went to Central European universities, such as the University of Paris. Books were copied in Finland, and circles of scribes emerged at least in Turku and Naantali. It is possible to identify their production on the basis of handwriting and images used in the ornamentation. Only a small part of mediaeval books have however been preserved whole. During the Reformation era, several books were taken apart and their parchment pages were reused as the covers of ledgers. The National Library of Finland in Helsinki has a collection of approximately 10,000 fragments of these kinds of loose pages, a part of which could later be identified and pinpointed to its original context. There is a digital collection available online so anyone today has the possibility to easily browse through mediaeval Finnish manuscripts.

Since around the mid-15th century, printed literature began to emerge alongside and in place of manuscripts. The first book printed for Finland was the Dominican missal *Missale Aboense* which was printed in Lübeck in 1488. The book contains a calendar of saints of the Turku diocese and a special cover page which shows English-born Bishop Henry, patron saint of Finland, and his murderer, the peasant Lalli. Moreover, the picture shows high-ranking Finnish clerics, as well as the printer Bartholomeus Ghotan off-centre. However, the content of the book consists of materials for mass appropriate for a more general purpose, which has no special connection to Finland or Turku.

The *Missale Aboense* is the only incunable – that is, a book printed before the year 1500 – printed especially for Finland. There are a total of eight copies of this book in the National Library of Finland, which are also available digitally on the Internet.

1.1.2 Finnish in Texts of Other Languages

In the Middle Ages, Finnish in written form was only randomly used. The organisation and activity of secular administration were carried out in Swedish, and a large part of administrative vocabulary was thus borrowed from Swedish. The country was divided into provinces, and castles were built as the headquarters and administrative strongholds of these provinces. As the region of Finland officially became a part of Sweden in the Treaty of Nöteborg (also known as the Treaty of Oreshek) in 1323, Swedish law came into force in Finland. Local administration was primarily run by parishes and their priests. (Meinander 2011.) Documents were drawn up in Swedish and Latin, and Finnish was only used as needed in the names of people and places.

Sometimes, there were sentence fragments that found their way into documents when, for example, describing the boundary line that ran in the terrain. From these fragments, we can deduce that Finnish was used in boundary discussions, but the languages were switched when the outcome of this process was transferred to written form. For example, there are several names and passages in Finnish found in the Swedish designation of boundaries completed in 1477 in the former municipality of Perniö:

"…Emillan Huctis och *Melkila* j från *Taluitien sw* och til *Rieckopaiun nemin*, thedan j f[rån] Reickon och til *Vähä Kangaren pähen* och tedhan och til almande [v]äghen, j fro almande vägen och til *Mylly oia*… j fron *Kiuilan nityn päst* och til Varnanummen, thedan och til *Sannasten oia, Sannasten oiast* och till almende väghen…"

> *Melkila* (a homestead name)
> *Taluitien sw* (Std. *Talvitien suu* 'the beginning of Talvitie ('winter road')')
> *Rieckopaiun nemin* (Std. *Riekkopajun niemeen* 'to Riekkopaju cape')
> *Vähä Kangaren pähen* (Std. *Vähä Kankaren päähän* 'to the end of Vähä Kankare ('small Kankare')')
> *Mylly oia* (Std. *Myllyoja* 'mill ditch')
> *Kiuilan nityn päst* (Std. *Kivilän niityn päästä* 'from the Kivilä meadow')
> *Sannasten oia* (Std. *Sannasten oja* 'Sannanen ditch')
> *Sannasten oiast* (Std. *Sannasten ojasta* 'out from the Sannanen ditch')

The Church in mediaeval Finland did not systematically keep records on those who were born baptised, married or died, as it has done since early modern history. Mediaeval names can be found, for example, in the minutes of city council meetings or judicial proceedings. The most important source concerning the Finnish Middle Ages is a registrum – a register – known as the *Black Book of Åbo Cathedral* (Fin. *Turun tuomiokirkon Mustakirja*).

Copies of documents concerning primarily the Church and the spaces under its ownership were compiled for the registrum. The documents are from early 1229 and there are a total of 727 of them. The only mediaeval ledger is the church accounts of Kalliala (today known as the town of Sastamala) which was in safekeeping from 1469 to 1524.

The first Finnish sentences can be found in a travelogue of a German clergyman (Wulf 1982). He was getting to know the ecclesiastical circumstances of Scandinavia, and upon arrival in Finland, he encountered an old bishop who taught him the following words: *Mÿnna thachton gernast spuho somen gelen Emÿna dayda* (Std. *Minä tahdon kernaasti puhua suomen kielen. En minä taida.* 'I would like to speak the Finnish language. I do not know how.'). The name of the bishop was not noted in the account, but judging from the other information in the travelogue, it was probably one of the most powerful 15th century Finnish bishops, Magnus II Tavast. Bishop Magnus erected a large number of stone churches in Finland and in many ways increased the influence and wealth of the Church. The 15th century specifically was thus the heyday of the Roman Catholic Church and ecclesiastical culture. The situation changed dramatically in the early 16th century when the Protestant Reformation and Lutheranism spread to Sweden through which it came to Finland as well.

1.1.3 Finnish in the Middle Ages

It is actually misleading to speak about Finnish in the Middle Ages because there still was no common and homogenous Finnish language in existence at that time. The language spoken by the indigenous habitants of the Finnish region existed in oral form only and it varied all throughout the country. The country was expansive and sparsely inhabited, and mutual communication was not close enough for any common language form to emerge. Some kind of mixing and balancing of dialects happened perhaps in cities, but only a few cities existed during the Middle Ages and their linguistic influence did not extend to the countryside.

The name *Suomi* ('Finland') originally referred to the country's southwestern region only. Nowadays, the specified name *Varsinais-Suomi* ('Finland Proper' in a historic and 'Southwest Finland' in a modern context) is used for this area. The name *Suomi* expanded to refer to the entire country based on the fact that Turku, located in Southwest Finland, has long been the country's heart of spiritual and secular administration. All of mediaeval Finland formed a single diocese in the ecclesiastical province of Uppsala, and the Bishop of Turku was the representative of the whole diocese in both spiritual and governmental matters. Finland Proper is also one of those areas where Finnish-language settlement has been going on for the longest time.

At the end of the Iron Age – in other words, in the Viking Age from the Scandinavian perspective, approximately around the 11th century – Finnish settlement was concentrated in the southern and central parts of the country. The old tribal areas, which became the historical provinces of Finland – their historic names in English based on the Latin variants – were Tavastia (Swe. *Tavastland,* Fin. *Häme*), Finland Proper and Karelia (Swe. *Karelen,* Fin. *Karjala*). The heart of the tribal area of Savonia (Swe. *Savolax,*

Fin. *Savo*) emerged on the boarder of Tavastia and Karelia in the region of the current city of Mikkeli (located in eastern Finland), and its linguistic basis was acquired from Old Karelian.

Satakunta was established in the area where the northern part of Finland Proper, so-called Northern Finland, and Häme met. According to historical sources, this area was in close connection with Sweden and had adopted Christianity before the rest of Finland. Over the Middle Ages, settlement from Satakunta and Häme spread out to the shore of the Gulf of Bothnia which became its own tribal area, Ostrobothnia. Water routes ran right to the back end of the Gulf of Bothnia via the mainland, and it was also possible to sail along the sea. The Karelians took advantage of these opportunities, and it was their way of speaking that especially influenced the Northern Ostrobothnian and Peräpohja dialects.

The foundation for the five main sets of Finnish dialects emerged in the Middle Ages (Lehtinen 2007). Of these, the western ones included the southwestern, Häme and northern dialects and the eastern ones included the Karelian and Savo dialects. Today, instead of the Karelian dialects, we can speak of southeastern dialects so that they would not accidentally be confused with Karelian, a language counted as a close relative of Finnish.

There were mixed dialects that emerged on the boundaries of the old tribal areas. Moreover, dialect boundaries were not strict or permanent. This was especially the case in southeastern Finland. The marking of the eastern border along Russia had greatly changed over the centuries and where to place Karelian in its development into a closely related language to Finnish had been quite indistinct. The boundary of the main sets of dialects, that is, the western and eastern dialects, had been defined in the 19th century according to what equivalents the standard *d* phoneme has in the consonant gradation of words of Finnic origin (for example, in standard Finnish *pata* 'cauldron' : *padan* 'cauldron+GEN'). The equivalents in the western dialects include an *r* or *l* (*paran* or *palan*), however the equivalent in the eastern dialects is either a weaker consonant (*pajan*) or none at all (*paan* [pɑːn] or [pɑ.ɑn]).

In addition to Finnish dialects, there were other languages spoken in mediaeval Finland. There was a Sámi settlement in Häme and in the mainland areas north of it. From the late 12th century or no later than the beginning of the 13th century, a Swedish-speaking population began to migrate to the western and southwestern coasts of Finland (K. Tarkiainen 2008). All of the mediaeval Finnish towns had emerged on the coasts, and from the start, they were international trade centres where people from elsewhere lived, in addition to Finns. More detailed information on the population base of the towns is not available, but on the basis of nomenclature, it has been deduced that a large part of the inhabitants that came from elsewhere were Swedish and German. Baltic trade in the Middle Ages was governed by the Hanseatic League and thus by Low German merchants. Notably in the 14th century, there was a significant percentage of Low German merchants in the Turku and Vyborg bourgeoisie.

Language contacts made their own marks in the development of Finnish dialects. There had already been a significant amount of Swedish influence in the Middle Ages, particularly in Finland Proper, and to some extent it can be felt in the costal Ostrobothnian dialects. However, the Häme and Savo dialects for a long time were left alone without any close, outside contacts. The southeastern dialects were influenced by Russian, but many Russian loanwords did not reach standard Finnish until later on, when eastern elements began to be consciously favoured in the development of the language. Traditionally, cities had been completely excluded from the study of regional dialects because they were not uniform dialectical areas but rather places where different languages and cultures encountered one another.

It is possible – and even probable – that as a result of the contacts between and the assimilation of different languages, some kind of new, general dialect was born in the Middle Ages in cities especially for the needs of religion and the Church (Rapola 1969). The Christian world view included a great amount of previously unknown concepts which in some way had to be transferred from the conceptual system of other languages to Finnish. This was also the case with secular power. Both spiritual and secular authorities and order were of foreign origin and brought to the people from outside. At least a part of the vocabulary reflecting this organisation must have been generally known, and the vocabulary must also have been partly of foreign origin because the words in question were cultural. Rulers or their representatives must have at least, to some extent, used the language of the majority of the population alongside their own mother tongues. Through power, the language they used that deviated from the vernacular of the ordinary people probably gained the same reverence which the language users themselves, on the basis of their status, enjoyed, and the general dialect became a certain kind of language of prestige for public use.

In addition to an oral, general dialect, some written Finnish was probably in existence. In the provincial synod of Söderköping, Sweden, an ordinance was given in 1441 stating that in connection with Sunday services, the priests had to read certain catechetical texts – that is, texts concerning religious primary education – in the vernacular, for example the Lord's Prayer, a creed and Ave Maria (Pirinen 1988). The ordinance was revised in the Turku diocesan synod in 1492, and no later than that time, it was understood that it would apply to Finland as well. The texts always had to be read in the same way in order for the people to learn them by heart, which is why they had to be written down. However, not a single written note has been preserved to this day. As we examine the forms of the aforementioned texts in the earliest literary Finnish, we can make out clear differences between them. There was thus still no standard form used in the texts in all of Finland in the Middle Ages. Instead, each parish may have had its own version, slightly differing from others.

Song has always played an important role in spiritual life. In the Catholic Church of the Middle Ages, clerics, schoolchildren and trained choirs were responsible for the singing parts of the services. However, it may be considered possible that the ordinary people were also able to participate in singing in ecclesiastical processions and other, more informal occasions. There are a few refrains in the oldest manuscripts of congregational singing which were regularly written without musical notation. These refrains have been suggested to be mediaeval songs in the vernacular. Such a song was known as a *leisi* in Finnish. This term stems from the refrain's closing plea in Greek *Kyrie eleison* ('Lord, have mercy'). Mediaeval exemplars in other languages can be noted as models for the leisis in Finland but there is no actual proof that they would have also been sung in Finnish in the Middle Ages.

1.2 The Reformation Progresses to Finland

1.2.1 NEW TEACHINGS IN WITTENBERG

The Protestant Reformation began in Wittenberg, Germany in 1517 when Augustinian monk Martin Luther grew weary of secularisation, the selling of papal indulgences and other questionable practices of the Catholic Church and nailed his *Ninety-Five Theses* to the door of All Saints' Church (commonly known as *Schloßkirche*, the "castle church"). (Marshall 2009.) It was easy to spread the word on the new teachings because book printing had been developed around the mid-15th century and had already begun to become common, and this allowed leaflets and other literature to be copied and distributed more quickly and inexpensively than ever before. Luther wrote his original theses in Latin but they were translated into German, printed and distributed to the public in a form that even the common people could understand.

The Reformation took place against the backdrop of the humanism movement which started to develop in Europe at the end of the Middle Ages. Humanism demanded a return to the roots of knowledge and thinking in Ancient Greece and Rome, studying true history and reading the works of great teachers and thinkers in their original languages in their original form and in their purest state, not through translations and later explanations, as had been done during the Middle Ages. The demands of the humanists did not solely concern church teachings but the arts and sciences more generally. However, as the Church and canonised literature held a transcendent position in mediaeval Europe in matters concerning intellectual and spiritual life, these demands were geared rather strongly and specifically towards the Church.

Included amongst the leading humanist figures was Desiderius Erasmus Roterodamus, also known as Erasmus of Rotterdam, (e.g. Huizinga 1953) who published the New Testament in the original Greek and made a revised Latin translation based on this. He appended explanations and notes to his translations, creating a foundation to a new kind of critical study of the Bible. Erasmus concretely highlighted the substantial difference between the original text and translation. The Latin translation of the Bible known as the *Vulgate* by Church Father St Jerome and his collaborators was the version most often read in the Middle Ages. Now, Erasmus showed that the *Vulgate*, which had been raised to the status of a standard translation, had shortcomings and even blatant errors.

Erasmus published a great deal of other types of literature as well, such as ancient literature, proverbs, works on moral philosophy, and popular guidebooks on life skills, which were read all around Europe. He did not permanently commit to any university or other institution. Instead, he was an independent researcher and a non-fiction writer who lived off of his scholarly work and publications.

Martin Luther himself was not a humanist, although the humanists were, from the start, his followers and supporters. He respected Erasmus' translations of the Bible and used them as a source for his own works, but strictly disagreed on many questions of principle concerning theology, and the disagreement concerning the freedom of will created an irreparable rift between these scholars. Luther supported direct speech and purposeful action and considered Erasmus a selfish and godless epicurean who was capable of beautiful words but not actions. (Heininen 2006.)

Luther did not originally want to break up the Roman Catholic Church. Instead, he wanted to reform it by bringing it back to practices in keeping with the beginnings of the Church. He set teaching the absolute word of God as stated in the Bible as a pivotal goal of the Reformation. It had to be translated into the vernacular so that as many people as possible would be able to read it, and it had to be translated in a simple way so that others than highly learned theologians might also understand it. Thus, he himself began to work on a new German translation of the Bible and published several improved editions of this translation. He simultaneously revised literary German and created a foundation for the contemporary literary language.

The University of Wittenberg was established in 1502 by Frederick the Wise, Elector of Saxony, and it was still a small and relatively unknown school in 1512 when Luther graduated from there as a Doctor of Theology. Students coming from Scandinavia preferred to seek out education in the renowned Rostock nearby, but a few continued on their way to Wittenberg. For example, Olaus Petri of Sweden happened to be present when Luther nailed his *Ninety-Five Theses* to the door of All Saints' Church.

One of the first Doctoral graduates from Wittenberg was George Spalatin who became the tutor in the house of the Elector of Saxony. He later also became the Elector's archivist and librarian and also an adviser in matters concerning literature, general knowledge and the university. He was on confidential terms with Luther, and apparently, it is largely thanks to him that the Elector chose to support and protect Luther in the implementation of the Reformation. In 1521, Frederick the Wise brought Luther to his castle in Wartburg, safely away from the riots caused by the Reformation, and it was there where he got to work in isolation from the outside world and translate the New Testament into German.

Along with the Reformation, the reputation and the number of students of the University of Wittenberg began to grow. In 1518, Philipp Melanchton came to the university as a professor of Greek, and he became Luther's knowledgeable colleague and assistant. Melanchton was an almost supernaturally meticulous and systematic scholar who assisted Luther in making his message clear by presenting the key principles of the Reformation as a uniform system. Melanchton also shaped the Augsburg Confession which is still the primary confession of faith of the Lutheran Church. This confession stipulates the official stand of the Lutheran Church on all its chief articles of faith.

There were two important churches that stood next to each other in the small town of Wittenberg: the Stadtkirche, the town church, and All Saints' Church, the castle church or Schloßkirche. There was invaluable support for the Reformation available at both churches. Justus Jonas, who was well-versed in law and theology, was working as a priest at All Saints' Church, and he also worked at the university as a professor. Luther's good friend and supporter Johannes Bugenhagen worked at the Stadtkirche. He was an especially talented organiser who created a new Church Ordinance and assisted in its implementation in Northern Germany and in Denmark. Bugenhagen's Church Ordinance provided instructions on organising education and many social matters in addition to church services. Moreover, Bugenhagen, who was profoundly well-versed in Latin, lectured at the university and published ecclesiastical literature which served as a model and source material to the other Reformers.

There was a significant amount of publishing that took place in Wittenberg. A specific Gothic typeface known as Schwabacher was adopted and became a kind of trade mark of the Reformation: it could immediately be deduced from the appearance of the printed material that it was created in the spirit of the Reformation. The same typeface was adopted by other printing houses where Reformation literature was produced. One of the wealthiest and most famous people in Wittenberg was Lucas Cranach the Elder, court painter to Frederick the Wise, whose woodcuts embellished the pages of the most valued printed materials.

1.2.2 The Reformation Expands to Scandinavia

The message of the Reformation had already reached the Baltic lands and Scandinavia in the 1520s (Grell (ed.) 1995; Larson 2010). The priests and civil servants in the Baltics and Ingria used German as a common language, and so the texts from the Reformers could be read and gauged straight away. Criticism of the Catholic Church and papal dominance in Scandinavia came at a very opportune time because it could be utilised as a part of the current secular aims for power.

At the end of the Middle Ages, Denmark had successfully reigned over the Scandinavian countries while acting as the ruling country of the Kalmar Union, but at the beginning of the 16th century, Swedish nobility feverously began to rebel against and demand separation from the Union. In 1520, King Christian II of Denmark decided to have himself crowned in Stockholm as well in order to strengthen Danish power in Sweden, and once he had been crowned, he had a large part of the influential Swedish nobles executed. The aftermath of this event, known as the Stockholm Bloodbath, proved to be a catastrophe also to Christian himself: that same year, he wound up fleeing from Denmark and leaving the throne to Frederick I. Fredrick I had studied in Wittenberg and become familiar with the central ideas of the Reformation. Moreover, Lutheran preachers began to spread the new teachings in Denmark.

Denmark escapee Christian himself looked into the Reformation and decided to use it as a weapon in his own struggle for power. He had the New Testament translated into Danish by three young students in Wittenberg who followed him into exile. A picture of Christian was included with the translation and a petition asking for the Danish Lutherans to support their former king in his attempt at a return to power. The attempt failed, and the translation did not turn out satisfactory either. Regardless, King Christian's New Testament, printed in 1524, was the first version published in a Scandinavian language that was translated in the Lutheran spirit.

In 1527, young King Gustav Vasa of Sweden, who had freed his country from the Danish regime with the support of the great Hanseatic city of Lübeck and united it under his own central governing, implemented the Reformation in his kingdom, making himself the head of the Church and supreme guardian of the Church's property. He left doctrinal matters for others to tend to.

The Swedish New Testament was published in 1526, and it appears that the translation was a product of group work. The official executor of the project was Archdeacon Laurentius Andreae who worked in Stockholm as secretary to King Gustav Vasa. The Reformation in Stockholm progressed especially quickly because the city council and other leaders took to it positively. In 1529, the city council decided that church services in Stockholm were to be held in the vernacular, in other words in Swedish.

When the decision was made to adopt Swedish in both ecclesiastical procedures and church services, written aids were required. One Reformer was particularly active in his production: Olaus Petri, who had studied in Wittenberg right at the beginning of the Reformation and received his Master's degree from there. After returning to his homeland, he became the town secretary of Stockholm, a clergyman and the King's chancellor. A Swedish liturgical agenda was completed in 1529, and a printed missal, including the whole liturgy, was published in 1531. The entire Bible was available in Swedish in 1541. There were several individuals alongside Laurentius Andreae and Olaus Petri who participated in its translation. This version is known as the Gustav Vasa Bible.

The Reformation played a significant role in both Denmark and Sweden not only in terms of religious matters but also in the development of the literary language. Over the Middle Ages, along with Hanseatic trade and the merchant bourgeoisie, Low German acquired the status of an international, prestigious language, and the language spoken and written in cities was more or less a combination of Low German and the local language. However, Low German, which was considered to be vulgar, was not used in the Luther Bible. Instead, as a consequence, a new, respected literary language emerged and began to take over the dominant position of Low German. Correspondingly, both the Danish and Swedish Reformers aimed at revising and developing their own languages based upon their own needs. In comparison to Finnish, the circumstances were easier in the sense that both Danish and Swedish had already previously been written. There was thus no need to create a literary language from scratch: there was only a need to improve and develop what was already in existence.

1.2.3 The First Reformation Messengers and Strongholds in Finland

Since a large part of the bourgeoisie and intelligentsia, especially in cities, spoke Swedish, there was a possibility to use Swedish-language books as needed in Österland – that is, Finland. Swedish was, however, just as unknown to the people as Latin in the majority of the expansive country of Finland. Moreover, there were many Finns that migrated to the capital of the kingdom, Stockholm, for different reasons. Because these people were not able to speak Swedish properly, a Finnish preacher was appointed to the parish in 1533 for their spiritual needs. A few years later, using Finnish in Finland became an obligation when in 1536, the Uppsala Council ordered the vernacular to be adopted in all the cathedrals in the ecclesiastical province and also in parishes in the rural areas so far as possible.

The first strongholds of the Reformation in Finland were its largest cities, above all Turku, which was the capital of the whole diocese, and apparently to some extent also Vyborg, which was also somewhat influenced by Baltic German culture. The first Swedish-language church service was held in Turku Cathedral in 1534 by Laurentius Canuti, who was born in the former municipality of Pernå in southern Finland. The Olaus Petri Missal, which has been preserved to this day, is a sign of the progression of the Reformation. It was owned by the Archdeacon of Turku, Petrus Sild, a son of a bourgeois family from Turku who studied in Rostock before the Reformation, earned his Master's degree and became a Turku vicar. At first, he was rather sceptical about the Reformation, but he was appointed to the revered position of archdeacon in 1529 on the condition that he would teach and give sermons in the spirit of the Reformation. Hence, he went down in history as the first Finnish-speaking Finn who represented the new Evangelical Lutheran faith. When he died in 1542, he bequeathed a portion of his fortune for the printing of a Finnish-language New Testament. (Pirinen 1962; Arffman 1997.)

Apparently, the first to start translating texts required in services and ecclesiastical ceremonies into Finnish were those clergymen who needed Finnish-language aids in their work. In extreme circumstances, a linguistically skilled priest could read the text from the Swedish manual and translate it while conducting a religious rite, but not every clergyman's language skills were sufficient for this. In addition, oral, improvised translations always had the danger of turning out different at different times. The respect for and active use of literature had been a distinctive feature of the Christian Church from the very beginning. Hence, it can be presumed that written Finnish translations were composed essentially as soon as there was a need for them in practice. Mikael Agricola apparently was not amongst the first of these translators because he was studying in Wittenberg right at the time when the orders for Finnish to be adopted were carried out.

Petrus Särkilax is usually noted as the first Finnish representative of the Reformation who was taught in Wittenberg. In reality, there is no definite proof that he was even in Wittenberg, but regardless, he was on a study trip in Germany and the Netherlands, in Rostock and Leuven from 1516 to 1522. He returned to Turku with a new faith and even a wife, and was presumably the first Finnish clergyman who was joined in holy matrimony. In Catholic times, this union was not at all possible. Petrus Särkilax worked as a member of the cathedral chapter of Turku, the headmaster of Katedralskolan i Åbo and the King's most trusted representative. However, he died in 1529 and thus could not participate in the actual implementation stages of the Reformation. He is nevertheless remembered as the teacher of a young Mikael Agricola in Turku.

Beginning in 1525, Count John of Hoya and Bruchhausen was acting as the governor of Vyborg Castle. The Reformation was put into action in his home region in Germany that very same year. There is no information on whether the Royal Court of Vyborg started to hold Lutheran services straight away. Nevertheless, they began no later than in 1528 when Johannes Block arrived as the castle chaplain. He came from Tartu, Estonia, where he had joined a group of moderate Reformation supporters in 1525, and he was accompanied by both a wife and a library that included important works on the Reformation. (Heininen 2007.) The first noted Lutheran vicar of the city of Vyborg was Petrus Soroi who took office in 1536 and saw to his duties until the 1550s (Pirinen 1962).

Turku and Vyborg began to feel the impact of the Reformation roughly at the same time. In practice, what happened in Turku had greater significance because it was the capital of the diocese. However, clear, eastern linguistic elements can be seen in the earliest Reformation literature, and so there is reason to note Vyborg's role while examining the early stages of the Reformation and its oldest written sources. Apparently, there were also some Reformation communities elsewhere. For example, there were a considerable number of learned clerics that came from the Rauma region in the 16th century, as well as from the former municipality of Pernå in Uudenmaa, which was also the county where Mikael Agricola was born.

The first Finnish-speaking cleric who for certain received his education in Wittenberg was Thomas Francisci Keijoi. He left for Germany in 1531 and came back to Turku in 1533. He was the headmaster of Katedralskolan i Åbo for a few years but left again to continue his studies in Wittenberg in 1539. There is no detailed information on his second return or whether he ever earned his Master's degree, but there was no suitable position for him any longer in Turku, and so he wound up transferring to the countryside as a vicar, 160 kilometres northeast in the municipality of Hämeenkyrö. In any event, his name has often been raised when considering who could have been the translators of the first texts in Finnish.

Amongst these likely translators was Canutus Johannis Braumensis, who was awarded a Master's degree in 1536 in Wittenberg. There is no detailed account on his return to Finland, but there is definite information from 1541 that he was appointed as a vicar and member of the cathedral chapter of Turku. Even though for a long time he was a part of ecclesiastical inner circles, he was usually overshadowed by other candidates when decisions on appointed posts were made. There are vague hints in documents on the fact that in terms of his character, he was not suitable for the most important leadership roles. However, more detailed information on this is not available. In any event, he was, for many years, Mikael Agricola's closest associate and partner.

There is more information available on the achievements of Simon Henrici Wiburgensis. He left for Wittenberg in 1532, returned to Turku and then left again, earning his Master's degree in 1541. He did not, however, return immediately to his home country but stayed to work and teach in Wittenberg, sometimes travelling to Italy as well. He also met Mikael Agricola in Wittenberg, and participated in the translation of the New Testament together with Martinus Teit. Concrete proof of this translation work is a Bible index, formerly in the possession of Martinus Teit, which has been preserved. In 1544, Simon Henrici returned to Turku but did not get a seat in the cathedral chapter. He died in 1545.

Subsequently, Mikael Agricola became the best-known of all the Finnish students that left for Wittenberg during the beginnings of Reformation (Heininen 1980). He arrived in the university city with his childhood friend Martinus Teit in 1536. They were both from Pernå and apparently they had also studied together at school in Vyborg. When they left for home with their Master's degrees in 1539, Georg Norman from Germany, who was on his way to be the tutor for the princes of Stockholm, became their travel companion. This acquaintance concretely made an impact on the future of both of these Finns. As Norman made advancements in his career to become superintendent of the Church and began to reform Church administration, Martinus Teit was called to be the princes' teacher in Stockholm. As for Agricola, while working in the Bishop's office, he often benefitted from the fact that he was personally acquainted with Norman who was one of the leaders of Church administration.

Paulus Juusten, a son of a wealthy bourgeois family from Vyborg, represented the generation of students approximately ten years younger. He came to Wittenberg through Rostock in 1543. He was in the city when Luther died in 1546, and he got to witness the confusion and despair which came about at the university as a result of the passing of the great man. Juusten described these events in *Chronicon Episcoporum Finlandensium* ('Chronicle of Finnish bishops') which all in all is one of the most important historical sources from the time of the implementation of the Reformation in Finland.

1.3 The First Finnish Manuscripts

When the Reformation began to extend to Sweden, the country did not have a single, permanent printing house. If people wanted to have books printed, they had to get them done in Germany or call upon a visiting master printer who brought all of his required printing equipment with him. Printing houses were founded, for example, in connection with monasteries and cathedral chapters but their operations were usually short-lived. In early times, most of the masters were German, but amongst the printers in the early 16th century, there were also Swedes who had been trained abroad. (Perälä 2007.)

Printed books were mostly required by the Church. Since there were many congregations and priests, the most important books had to be made available in several hundreds of similar copies. Books in Latin made elsewhere in Europe could have been used in Catholic times, but when the vernacular was introduced in Church, literature printed abroad was no longer of any use. Swedish and Finnish literature was not required anywhere else than in the Kingdom of Sweden and so it had to be produced in its own country. When the King became head of the Church, the government was ultimately given the responsibility and rights to the arrangement of all matters concerning printing.

The best known of all the visiting master printers was Jürgen Richolff, from Germany, who came to Stockholm in the 1520s at the King's invitation to start up a printing operation. The first Swedish New Testament was printed in Stockholm in 1526. After being in Germany for a while, Richolff returned to Sweden, and this time travelled to Uppsala in 1539 to print the Bible in Swedish. The work was completed in 1541, and after this, Richolff printed a few other books in Swedish before finally leaving for Germany. However, he left some equipment in Sweden required for printing, such as sorts and printing plates that had been made for the Swedish Bible. These were taken into use in the new royal printing house founded in Stockholm, whose printing master from 1543 onwards was Amund Laurentsson. In the following years, Mikael Agricola became his most important patron.

Since printing books, at first, was tricky and expensive, the expansive kingdom and, in particular, the eastern part of it often had to be satisfied with manuscripts. As the Reformation required the use of the vernacular in services and ecclesiastical ceremonies, the quickest and easiest means to acquire written supporting materials was to write Finnish translations on the empty pages or in the margins of books in other languages that were already in use. Another possibility was to draft whole Finnish manuscripts by translating. There was a true need for manuscripts because the Lutheran liturgical reforms were evidently implemented in Finland in 1537, that is to say, over ten years prior to when Agricola's liturgical books (*Käsikiria* 'Agenda', *Messu* 'Missal', *Pina* 'Passion (Christ's sufferings)' – all in 1549) were printed in Stockholm.

A good example of a text that was added to an earlier printed book is the manuscript known as the Kangasala Missal. The congregation in Kangasala (a municipality located in the current Pirkanmaa region of Finland) was in possession of a copy of the *Missale Aboense* which was printed in Lübeck in 1488. During the Reformation era, the old, Catholic missal could no longer be used as such, but the congregation did not want to dispose of the handsome and valuable book either. So, a schema of church services was written in Finnish by hand on the book's bound, empty pages. There are sections in the phrasing of this schema that are clearly based on the Swedish missal used prior to 1541. In 1541, the schema of the Swedish missal was revised by removing theologically questionable sections that were a part of the missal practices of the Catholic period.

Of the lengthier Finnish manuscripts preserved, the oldest include enchiridion literature intended for priests: in practice, schemata of either worship services or ecclesiastical ceremonies, such as baptisms, marriages and burials, and instructions concerning them. It is a proven fact that some of these are older than the corresponding texts published by Agricola. The oldest of all the manuscripts is evidently an extract of the Uppsala Gospel Book (Penttilä 1931, 1942) which, on the basis of content and the analysis of watermarks, is estimated at being written in the late 1530s. It is not a free-flowing translation of biblical text but rather it consists of separate prayers and translations of epistle and gospel texts required in services. One prayer is based on a text fashioned by Olaus Petri in 1537, so the manuscript was probably composed this year at the earliest.

Other significant manuscripts include an excerpt from the Uppsala Agenda (Uppsala B 28) and a compilation of manuscripts known as the Codex Westh comprising an agenda, a Mass, a guidebook on pastoral care and also other materials concerning services and ecclesiastical ceremonies. The agenda in the Codex Westh is quite similar to the text in the Uppsala Agenda, but the liturgy included in the Uppsala Agenda is clearly different from the Mass in the Codex Westh. It is so reminiscent of Mikael Agricola's missal that it has been suspected to be a draft or a manuscript of Agricola's work. However, on the basis of graphology, it has been proven that the Mass in the Uppsala Agenda could not have been written by Agricola.

Manuscripts from Agricola's times were republished as typeset texts over 100 years ago. In 1893, Eemil Nestor Setälä, one of the most prominent figures of linguistics in Finland, began a publication series on the chronicles of the Finnish language entitled *Suomen kielen muistomerkkejä* (SKM) with his Swedish colleague K. B. Wiklund. For its first volume, texts from both the Codex Westh and the Uppsala Agenda were compiled, alongside the corresponding parts of Agricola's printed books. They were not, however, published as complete manuscripts, as, for example, all musical notions and non-Finnish parts were excluded. New critical publications on the Codex Westh have recently been released. These works comprehensively contain the whole text (Häkkinen (ed.) 2012a) and songs (Tuppurainen (ed.) 2012). Finnish and Swedish manuscripts from the Reformation era have briefly been presented in Olav D. Schalin's book *Kulthistoriska studier till belysande av reformationens genomförande i Finland I* (1946).

Song played an important role in mediaeval services, and a partially revised singing tradition continued on during the time of the Reformation as well. In its beginnings, the royal printing house in Stockholm could not yet print musical notations. There were just empty staves which, until that time, usually still only had four lines. Manuscripts with notated music could thus not be printed, even though there was a desire for it. Hence, a large portion of the oldest Finnish manuscripts are music manuscripts showing both lyrics and melodic phrases.

The majority of the literature from the Reformation times was made for the needs of the Church. Secular source materials were mostly represented by legal and official language. Only one extensive legal translation in Finnish was prepared in the 16th century. It was translated by a cleric known as Lord Martti who worked in Stockholm as a priest in the Finnish congregation right when Agricola's New Testament was being printed. There is no definite proof on whether Lord Martti translated Christopher III's Law of the Realm into Finnish right then or not until later when he returned to Stockholm to be the court preacher to John III. Many copies of the manuscript have been preserved (SKM II: 1–2) but at no point did it ever achieve the status of an official legal document nor was it printed.

In addition to Lord Martti's legal translation, some of the King's letters and announcements from the time of the Reformation as well as a few other minor documents are known. The first of these letters was sent by Gustav I to the inhabitants of the County of Nyslott (Fin. *Savonlinna*) in 1555, and it concerned the defence against the Russian threat to Eastern Finland.

The majority of preserved literature from the 16th century is spiritual or secular prose. There is less poetry, and most of it includes prayers and ecclesiastical songs. In terms of content, secular poetry is, in practice, only included in Mikael Agricola's printed works, of which a portion contains poem-formed, preface-like spiritual creations. These poems have recently been published in an anthology entitled *Mikael Agricolan runokirja* (Häkkinen (ed.) 2012c). There are 630 stanzas of Agricola's own poems as well as poems translated or adapted from sources in other languages.

International exemplars were generally followed in texts of the Reformation era, in terms of both content and form. There is a marginal amount of genuine Finnish folklore. The calendar section in Agricola's *Rucouskiria* ('Prayer book') has two samples of Finnish folklore in the form of poems and, in addition, a few proverbs. There are two hymnal texts written by hand, that have been preserved in the archives of the Finnish congregation in Stockholm, in which the old Finnish poetic metre – the so-called Kalevala metre – had been reworked. These, however, were extraordinary exceptions. Hymnal texts of the Reformation era were usually rhymes that followed the model of German and Swedish hymns.

Interesting evidence of old Finnish folk beliefs is a plague spell which was entered in the ledger of the Korsholm royal manor in 1564 by its bailiff Hannes Ingenpoika. There were no schooled doctors in Finland in the mid-16th century, and attempts to cure diseases were made with the power of words. According to Finnish folk beliefs, one was able to affect diseases and other phenomena if one knew how they originally came to be. Diseases were addressed as if they were living beings, and spells were spoken in a low, secretive voice and often so that no outsider heard the words. Skilled folk healers could perform a great number of different spells, but they usually wanted to keep the specifics of these spells for themselves and as a professional secret. The plague spell requested the disease to be satisfied with what it had already taken as its prey and to leave others in peace. The spell-caster asked Jesus and the Virgin Mary for assistance and commanded the disease to go back from where it came.

2. The Life of Mikael Agricola

Mikael Agricola, born in the rural district of Pernå on the coast of Southern Finland, was the first Finn in history to have published Finnish-written works in print. Chapter 2 describes the stages of Agricola's life and the main features of his literary life's work. At the same time, the chapter examines the reasons why and through what stages Agricola became a Protestant Reformer in Finland and the founder of printed literary Finnish. In chronological order, a description will be provided on his family background, his studies and his career as the Bishop's secretary, assistant, headmaster of the cathedral school in Turku, member of the Turku Cathedral chapter and finally Bishop of Turku.

2.1 Family Background and Early Schooling

Not a great deal is known about Mikael Agricola as a person. Furthermore, the early years of his life are indeed unknown. There are no actual pictures of him in existence or even a description of what he looked like. All portraits, statues, drawings and paintings of him created later are products of the artist's imagination. It is estimated that Agricola's year of birth is around 1510, but this estimation is in fact based on information touching upon his later stages in life.

However, there is information available on Agricola's place of birth and family home. Agricola himself used the supplementary modifier *Torsbius* in his name in certain books, signifying that his hometown was the village of Torsby in the rural district of Pernå, located in eastern Uusimaa (see map at the end of this book). Pernå is today, and has been in the Middle Ages, a Swedish-speaking district, but it turns out from the nomenclature of its homesteads and inhabitants and from historical documents that some Finnish was also spoken there. The oldest place name stratum seems to be Finnish. It is thus evident that the oldest settlement in Pernå was linguistically Finnish, but Swedish won out after the settlement of Swedish migrants on the Finnish coasts began in the 12th century. (Kepsu 2005.) The true linguistic border between Swedish- and Finnish-language settlements in Agricola's time ran approximately 20 kilometres on the northern side of Pernå (Antell 1956).

The Finnish name for Pernå, *Pernaja*, has been explained to stem from the Finnish word *perna* or *pärnä* which is an old term for an elm (*Ulmus*) or a small-leaved lime (*Tilia*). This word is unknown in contemporary, standard Finnish but it appears in certain dialects on the Karelian Isthmus and in many place names as well, also outside its contemporary dialect border (Erkamo 1983). Furthermore, small-leaved lime was an important tree in the past because there was bast fibre underneath the bark appropriate for many uses and, above all, for binding. In Finnish, the tree has two names: *metsälehmus* ('wild lime tree') and *niinipuu* ('bast fibre tree'). The tree, however, was not very common in Finnish forests. Therefore, place names could be a clue as to where the advantageous small-leaved lime grew.

Agricola's father Olav was one of the wealthiest farmers in Pernå. Nothing is known about his mother, not even a name. In old romantic, 19th century literature, Agricola was described as the son of a poor fisherman but this is not true in light of current information. The location of his childhood home is known, and archaeological excavations carried out there prove the existence of a wealthy rural homestead (Pellinen 2007). Moreover, historical documents show that there were district court sessions organised in the house in the 16th century. This thus reveals the affluence of Agricola's childhood home because usually the largest and best equipped house possible was chosen as a place for assemblies to gather.

Mikael Olavinpoika had three sisters but presumably no brothers. His surname is a patronym meaning 'son of Olav', and it would have been customary for the family's only son to inherit the farm, become a farmer and continue tending to the farm after his father. As this did not happen, there must have been serious reasons for it. Evidently, the young Mikael showed such a strong inclination towards learning and spiritual work, that he was allowed to go to school and devote himself to a career as a clergyman. His younger colleague Paulus Juusten later revealed in his chronicle of Finnish bishops that Agricola's health was never very strong. Perhaps his own family even thought that he was not physically strong enough to take on the gruelling work of a farmer. The farm, however, stayed in the family and was later named *Sigfrids* after its landowner Sigfrid Månsson, Agricola's nephew.

Researchers have debated a great deal on whether Agricola's mother tongue was Swedish or Finnish. Since Pernå was mostly a Swedish-speaking district in Agricola's times, it is likely that the language spoken in Agricola's childhood home, one of the district's preeminent homesteads, was Swedish (K. Tarkiainen 2008). On the other hand, there are linguistic elements found in Agricola's works that can be found from the Häme dialects spoken in the Pernå region – that is, in eastern Uusimaa (O. Ikola 1988). We can only assume from their existence that these features originate from the dialect found in Agricola's home region, which he learned as a child. After leaving for school, he did not return to Pernå to live, and so he hardly could later have learned the specialties of the dialect of his homeland district. We will return to these linguistic details further in chapter 4 on the language of Agricola's works.

Even if the main language in Agricola's childhood home were Swedish, it is still certainly possible that Finnish was also spoken at the homestead. One possibility that has been considered is that Agricola's mother, on whom there is no actual information, may have spoken Finnish (O. Ikola 1988). On the other hand, it has also been speculated that there may have been Finnish-speaking servants at the homestead (K. Tarkiainen 2008). Regardless, we do know that Agricola's childhood friend and fellow student Martinus Teit spoke Finnish so well that he later got to teach it to the royal princes in the Stockholm court. It is quite evident that both Agricola and Teit were bilingual from childhood.

Today, Pernå is a small, secluded rural locality on the southern coast of Finland. However, in many respects, it was a significant region in Agricola's time. In the 16th century, the area of the rural district was approximately two times as large as it is nowadays. There were around 300 tax-paying homesteads in the area of the current district alone. In addition to ordinary farmhouses, there were eight manors of nobility in the district. For example, the nobility lines of Creutz and Teit come from Pernå. It was also located on the country's most significant route: the coastal road Suuri rantatie (today known as *Kuninkaantie* 'king's road'), built in the Middle Ages, ran though Pernå and served as a link between the two most important castles and cities, Turku and Vyborg. (Pellinen 2007.)

There is no information available on the early stages of the Pernå parish. In the beginning, Pernå was possibly part of the parish of Porvoo, but no later than 1363 it was noted in documents as an independent parish. In the early 15th century, the construction of a grey stone church in Pernå began, and Archangel Michael was chosen for its patron saint. (Hiekkanen 2007.) In the beginning of the 16th century, Mikael Olavinpoika was baptised in the church's great stone baptismal font, taking the church's patron saint as his namesake.

A cleric by the name of Bertil worked as vicar of Pernå at the time of Mikael Olavinpoika's birth. He became Mikael's first teacher. (Heininen 2007.) He was not just any rural priest. He was a nationally noteworthy and respected clergyman judging from the fact that he was assigned with the task of participating in a mission for Sweden to Novgorod in 1513 to sign a peace treaty between Moscow and Sweden. Evidently, it was largely thanks to Vicar Bertil that many boys from Pernå left to study in Vyborg and then abroad to university (Heininen 1980).

Vicar Bertil took a positive stance on the Reformation. When the rules of clerical celibacy prevailing over Catholic times were abolished, he was amongst the first Finnish clergymen who got married. He already had a son by the name of Eskil. It was not at all unusual because many priests in Catholic times lived in a relationship much like a marriage, begetting a whole brood of children with their housekeeper. Eskil became the vicar of Pernå in 1537 after his father, and so it happened for the first time in Finland that the position of priest was in a sense passed down from father to son. It later became quite common for the sons of priests to become priests, and thus long, significant lineages of priests were born.

2.2 A Schoolboy in Vyborg

There were schools in only a few sporadic cities in 16th century Finland. Long before the Christianisation of Finland, the Roman Catholic Church of Western Europe had already upheld the general principle stating that all cathedrals and other parishes had to have a headmaster employed for the education of youth and above all future clergymen where possible. There were evidently aims to follow the same principle in Finland as well, but not many cities were home to actual schools. In addition to cathedral and city schools, there were also monastic schools during the Middle Ages where studies for novices were at the hand of a specially appointed lector.

The most distinguished school in Finland was Katedralskolan i Åbo, the cathedral school of Turku. In addition, there were schools in Vyborg and Rauma. Pernå belonged to the school district of Vyborg, so after he was provided with a sufficient amount of primary education from Vicar Bertil, Mikael Olavinpoika got to leave, possibly together with Martinus Teit from the same rural district, to continue his studies in Vyborg. There is no detailed information on when this happened but the boys were apparently sent to Vyborg around 1520 when Mikael was about 10 years old.

The headmaster in Vyborg was Johannes Erasmi, who, according to Juusten's chronicle of bishops, was "an industrious and loyal educator of schoolchildren". Evidently under his mentoring, Mikael Olavinpoika took a new Latin byname meaning 'farmer', *Agricola*. It was a popular humanist name in Germany, for example, but it also appropriately referred to Mikael's agricultural upbringing and his father's profession. The first preserved document with this name, however, is nothing more than a cover page with owner's details which Mikael Olavinpoika Agricola (*Michael Olaui Agricola*) wrote in his personal copy of a Lutheran postil in 1531 (Heininen 2007).

Information on the school in Vyborg and the education given there is quite scarce. It appears that the foundation of the educational programme there, much like at the cathedral school in Turku, was a *trivium* stemming from the Middle Ages: this comprised Latin grammar, rhetoric and dialectic. Latin skills were crucial for learned men because, in addition to reading the Bible and other religious literature, they also had to have conversational skills as well as the ability to write letters and documents in Latin, following generally known and accepted schemata. Moreover, song played an important role in schooling because the future priests had to teach liturgical songs and melodic phrases included in them. The most common method of teaching was rote learning. By the time Agricola arrived at school to study, the influence of the humanists began to show in its educational programme.

Vyborg was a lively and multilingual merchant city which had close relations with the Baltics. Social life in Vyborg was quite different from that of a rural district such as Pernå. In addition to Finnish and Swedish, there was an opportunity to hear and learn to speak German and Russian and sporadically many other languages as well. The merchant bourgeoisie of Livonia in the Middle Ages were also inclined to send their boys to study languages in Vyborg (Taavitsainen 2007).

Right at the end of the 13th century, a castle was erected as the city's administrative centre and protection. Eventually, it also had a significant role in the progression of the Reformation. In 1525, King Gustav Vasa appointed his former ally and brother-in-law, Count John of Hoya and Bruchhausen, as the governor of Vyborg Castle, at the same time when the Reformation was put into action in his home region in Germany. In 1528, German-born Johannes Block became the castle chaplain. He had previously worked in Tartu where he converted, becoming a moderate supporter of Lutheranism. He also brought over an extensive library which included works by, for example, Martin Luther and Erasmus of Rotterdam. (Heininen 2007.)

There is no definite information as to the extent to which Agricola was able to get acquainted with Johannes Block and his library. At the beginning of 1528, Turku was appointed with a new bishop, Martinus Skytte. Before becoming bishop, Skytte had worked, among others, as Prior of the Dominican monastery of Sigtuna, which was one of Sweden's oldest ecclesiastical centres, and as inspector of the Dominican monasteries in the Kingdom of Sweden. Lord Martinus called Vyborg headmaster Johannes Erasmi to be his secretary, and he took his student, Mikael Agricola, along as a scribe. However, Johannes Erasmi died the very next year from an epidemic much like the plague – the so-called English sweate – and his duties in the Bishop's office were passed on to Agricola in 1529.

2.3 Work as Secretary to the Bishop

Upon Agricola's arrival in Turku, the changes brought about by the Reformation were already clearly felt there. In 1516, Petrus Särkilax, the son of the mayor of Turku, left to study in Central Europe, first in Rostock and then in Leuven, where the impact of Erasmus of Rotterdam and humanism and were felt particularly strongly. Before he returned to Turku in 1523 or 1524, he had converted as a supporter of the Reformation and taken a legally wedded wife for himself. In Juusten's chronicle of bishops, he is noted as the first Finn who may have studied at the University of Wittenberg, but there is no record of him found in the university's register (Heininen 2007). Nevertheless, after returning to Finland, he worked as headmaster of the cathedral school in Turku, gave sermons at Turku Cathedral on new Evangelical teachings and encouraged cleansing the church of papal idolatry. Moreover, Agricola took some time to listen to Särkilax's teachings before he died in April 1529 from the same epidemic that took Johannes Erasmi, Agricola's teacher from Vyborg.

At no stage in his life did Bishop Skytte directly convert to Lutheranism, but he made no attempts to hinder the Reformation from progressing in Finland. On the contrary, upon becoming bishop, he was committed to promoting Evangelical teachings, giving sermons under these teachings and being faithful to the King. In his chronicle of bishops, Juusten describes Skytte as an exceptionally pious, fair and lenient cleric who lived an irreproachable life, gave help to beggars and other poor people, loved Christianity and promoted the proper conduct of church services. Skytte was of an old and wealthy line of nobility from Häme whose members had worked in noteworthy positions in the judicial system, but he was nevertheless humble and modest in character. Upon becoming bishop, he was already quite an elderly man, evidently about 68 years old. (Tarkiainen & Tarkiainen 1985.)

It is impossible to know the true impact of Skytte on Agricola's religious ideology because no actual documents on this have been preserved. Nevertheless, there are materials in Agricola's Finnish-language works which are in accordance with the Turku diocese and, at the same time, Dominican liturgical tradition. For example, many prayers in *Rucouskiria* are originally from *Missale Aboense*, the mediaeval Dominican missal of Turku. Skytte's reconciliatory influence can also possibly be seen in that Agricola, his secretary and successor, did not immediately aim at breaking away from everything to do with Catholic times and its faith with rigid words and actions in the ways of many foreign Protestant Reformers. He instead implemented the reforms gradually. In Finland, there were no religious wars associated with the Reformation.

Agricola continued his work in the Bishop's office, and around 1530, he had reached an age and accumulated enough experience so that he could be inaugurated as priest. In order to thoroughly prepare himself for his new position, he purchased a Latin Lutheran postil in 1531, and the hundreds of handwritten margin notes are evidence of its use (Heininen 1976). A great amount of these notes can be found in sermon texts concerning the liturgical year followed in the Turku diocese and which Agricola had most certainly made use of in his own sermons.

The margin notes are mostly in Latin and Swedish throughout. Most of them are references to different sections of the Bible, but many of them explain the meanings of words found in the text. Moreover, there are proverbs and comments on Luther's text. Only one explanation seems to be in Finnish. In the section where Luther compares sanctimonious people to fat cats begging for affection, Agricola wrote the word *catti* in the margin. In addition to the word *kissa*, the Swedish loanword *katti*, also meaning 'cat', indeed exists in Finnish, which is what Agricola may have meant with his note. However, it also could very well be the plural form of the Late Latin word for cat *cattus*. The language of services in Turku in the beginning of the 1530s was still Latin, hence explanations and synonyms in Latin could have been useful in a sermon.

Good exemplars for a preacher starting out were needed because through the Reformation, the meaning of the sermon as a part of church services had grown, and giving sermons on Evangelical teachings was one of the most important tasks of the priest. When Agricola later wrote preface poems for his own published works, he highlighted repeatedly the value of sermon. According to Juusten's chronicle of bishops, Agricola followed Bishop Skytte on missions and meticulously gave sermons in different localities in Finland in the same way he did at Turku Cathedral.

2.4 A Student in Wittenberg

In addition to the poor and disabled, Bishop Skytte gave support and financial assistance to students planning on an ecclesiastical career. He arranged the opportunity for eight talented young men in his diocese to continue their studies abroad, specifically at the University of Wittenberg which was the heart of the Reformation. Out of these eight students, there were six who, like Agricola, came from the Vyborg school district (Schalin 1946–1947).

The University of Wittenberg was founded in 1502. Its founder and patron was Frederick III, Elector of Saxony – also known as Frederick the Wise. At first, the University of Wittenberg was small and insignificant alongside the older and more reputable universities in Germany, such as those in Rostock, Leipzig and Greifswald. At the end of the Middle Ages, students from Scandinavia left gladly for universities located specifically on the Baltic coast or near it because thanks to good commercial ties, it was possible to travel there more easily and inexpensively than, for example, to famous Paris. Furthermore, it was relatively easy to learn to get by with Swedish because the language spoken in Germany was rather closely related to it. Even though the academic language of the universities was Latin, it was also useful to know the local language in everyday life. Moreover, universities were founded in Uppsala and Copenhagen in the 1470s, but they could not compete with the appeal of the German universities. (Nuorteva 1999.)

Approximately ten years after its establishment, the University of Wittenberg began gaining significance when its former student, Augustine monk Martin Luther became professor of theology. He, together with his colleague Andreas Karlstadt, began to oppose the predominant Aristotelian Scholasticism with determination. The humanistic reform was seen thorough in the university's programme, and George Spalatin, chaplain, tutor and adviser to the court of Frederick the Wise, gave valuable support in its implementation.

In 1517, Luther nailed his famous *Ninety-Five Theses* to the door of All Saints' Church in Wittenberg. It is this event that is considered to be the start of the Protestant Reformation. In 1518, the young and diversely talented Philipp Melanchton was hired as professor of Greek. He was almost supernaturally meticulous in his dedication to research and teaching. In addition to theology and sacred languages, he was an expert in many other fields, such as history, psychology, mathematics and the natural sciences. With the orderliness of scholars, he supported Luther in defining the key principles of the Reformation and presenting them in a literary form. At the hands of these men, the *Academia Leucorea* in Wittenberg became so famous in a short time that the lectures could draw in over 500 attendees. (Heininen1980.)

Students from all of Scandinavia came to Wittenberg, and from there, the Reformation began to spread to Northern Europe along with university alumni and other supporters of Luther. Luther himself found it important that the word of God be translated into the languages of the people in such a simple way that it could be understood by everyone. He wrote a short guide for translators and used his own translation work as a model for it.

Many translation tasks in Wittenberg were initiated by the inspiration of Luther and his colleagues.

The Danish New Testament was the first Lutheran Bible translation done in a Scandinavian language. It was commissioned by former king of Denmark Christian II after he ended up ceding the crown in a struggle for power and fled into exile. He converted to Lutheranism and assigned the translation of the New Testament to Christiern Vinter, Hans Mikkelsen and Henrik Smith, three students who had followed him to Wittenberg. Luther's German Bible and Erasmus of Rotterdam's Latin translation were both used as sources. The book was printed in 1524, probably in Wittenberg, although for political reasons, Leipzig was noted as the place of printing. One of the translators appended a preface to the book embellished with numerous images. The preface praised Christian and urged the people to support his return to power. This attempt failed, and the book, which was otherwise viewed as suspicious, began to sell just as soon as the image of the former king and the politically tinged preface were removed. (Santesson 2002.) The Reformation nevertheless progressed in Denmark because the new king, Fredrick I, studied in Wittenberg and took a positive stand on the reforms.

The Swedish-language New Testament was printed in 1526, a year before King Gustav Vasa officially put the Reformation into effect in his kingdom. The translation appears to have been a product of group work in which the central authors were Archdeacon Laurentius Andreae, secretary to King Gustav Vasa, as well as vicar of Stockholm Olaus Petri, who had studied in Wittenberg right at the beginning of the Reformation. (Santesson 2002.) Renowned German printer Jürgen Richolff was invited to Stockholm to take on the task of printing of the book. It was printed there under protection of the King, whereupon the Stockholm royal printing house was also established. It was this printing house that later printed all of Agricola's works. (Perälä 2007.)

According to Juusten's chronicle of bishops, Petrus Särkilax was the first Finnish student who may have studied in Wittenberg. However, there is no conclusive evidence of this. At any rate, Särkilax studied over six years in Rostock and Louvain, and after returning home in 1523 or 1524, he taught the new Evangelical faith as Turku cathedral school headmaster. (Nuorteva 2012.) Prior to Särkilax, Petrus Sild studied in Rostock, and he worked in his hometown of Turku as one of King Gustav Vasa's trusted representatives alongside Särkilax (Pirinen 1962). Sild earned his Master's degree in 1513 in Rostock, and there he became familiar with humanistic ideological trends. In 1515, he became vicar of Turku and canon of the cathedral chapter. When he was selected as archdeacon in 1529, he committed to preaching the gospel in the spirit of the Reformation. He took a positive stand on the translation of the Bible into the language of the people and bequeathed a portion of his fortune for the printing of a Finnish-language New Testament. (Palola 2002.)

In the late 1520s, it was not possible to send students abroad due to political turmoil. However, when the situation stabilised at the beginning of the 1530s, travels could begin again. The first to leave for Wittenberg in 1531 were Thomas Francisci Keijoi and Canutus Johannis, both of whom begun their schooling in Rauma. After returning home, Keijoi worked for a while as Turku cathedral school headmaster but left in 1539 to Wittenberg once more to continue his studies. When he came back again, probably in 1543, there was no longer any suitable position for him in Turku. He wound up transferring to the countryside as a vicar, 160 kilometres northeast in the municipality of Hämeenkyrö and he died a few years later. His name has often been raised when considering who else, in addition to Agricola, could have translated the required ecclesiastical literature into Finnish during the Reformation. Canutus Johannis, who was awarded a Master's degree in 1536, had taken the post of vicar of Turku upon his return home, and later he became a close associate of Agricola. In his later years, he was appointed as Bishop of Vyborg after Juusten. (Pirinen 1962.)

The next one to leave for abroad was Simon Henrici Wiburgensis in 1532. He was successful in Wittenberg as both a student and a teacher. In 1538, he returned to Finland but left again to Wittenberg where he earned his Master's degree in 1541. He joined the university's collegial body of teachers in 1543 but died within two years. For a while, Simon Henrici was in Wittenberg at the same time as Agricola, and he was one of those friends and associates who we are quite sure took part in the Finnish translation of the New Testament. (Heininen 2007.)

In 1533, Sweden ended up in a state of war with Gustav Vasa's former ally Lübeck, and because of political turmoil, going abroad was out of the question. In 1534 and 1535, no student from Sweden left for Wittenberg. A peace treaty was signed in spring of 1536 and soon afterwards, it was Mikael Agricola and Martinus Teit's turn to leave. They evidently traveled by boat to Lübeck in early autumn and from there to Wittenberg. (Tarkiainen & Tarkiainen 1985.)

When Agricola was studying, Wittenberg was a small city, roughly the size of Turku of that time. It had approximately 2,300 residents and roughly 450 houses. The university was seen and felt strongly in the life of the whole city because there were approximately 700 students. In winter term 1536, there were 251 first year students entered in the register, amongst them "Michael Agricola de Villand Suetiae". Agricola's arrival in a strange city was greatly alleviated by the fact that Simon Henrici from Vyborg was there and he was able to advise and assist in him practical matters concerning studies and living. (Heininen 2007.)

Nicolaus Magni – or Nils Månsson – was also a helpful acquaintance for Agricola. He was a scholar who had studied in Wittenberg under the patronage of King Gustav Vasa. At the same time, he worked as the King's advocate in Germany, and there, his task was to seek out qualified officers for the King's office. With Luther's help, he found an appropriate tutor for four-year-old Prince Eric. This was German nobleman Georg Norman who was called to Stockholm in spring of 1539. (Tarkiainen & Tarkiainen 1985.)

Studies in Wittenberg traditionally began at the faculty of philosophy, and from there, there was a gradual progression towards the highest objective, theology. How quickly the studies progressed depended on the student's talent and previous schooling. Since the Finnish students usually acquired a good foundation of knowledge at home, it was possible for them to also attend lectures on theology at the very start of university.

There were a total of four professors of theology in Wittenberg: in addition to Martin Luther, there were vicar of Wittenberg Johannes Bugenhagen, All Saints' Church preacher Justus Jonas and specialist of Hebrew and Arabic Caspar Cruciger. Cruciger also distinguished himself as a specialist in the natural sciences and the founder of the university's botanical gardens. Two of these professors lectured on the Old Testament and two on the New Testament, and the Latin Bible was used as the textbook. Teaching primarily comprised interpreting the Bible, taking care to cover all doctrinally important points. The Books of Genesis, Psalms and Isaiah were considered the most important parts of the Old Testament. The Gospel of John and the Epistle to the Romans were the central parts taken from the New Testament. (Heininen 2007.)

Agricola himself did not describe his studies or stay in Witteburg, but there is information available, to some extent, in the letters which he sent to King Gustav Vasa in 1537 and 1538. He mentioned that he was studying the humanities and theology but bemoaned how expensive his studies and how meagre his livelihood were, beseeching the King for help. He stressed that his studies would be beneficial to his homeland and the Church, which was why it would be quite reasonable for the King to provide him support with a prebend, that is, income from the earnings of specific farms owned by the Church. This support would also ensure that the translation of the New Testament into Finnish that was already started would eventually be completed.

Agricola did not directly say in his letter who or how many people were doing the translation. Apparently, he did it together with his fellow Finnish students because many similar translations were done as a product of group work. The theologians in Wittenberg are also an example of this. Together they participated in improving Luther's translation of the Bible. There is a preserved Bible concordance which is proof of translation work carried out by the Finnish students. It was formerly in the possession of Teit, and because of the notes in it, we know that it had been in use. (Heininen 2007.)

According to his letter, Agricola sent Crown Prince Eric, who was a beginner reader, a small booklet as a gift. It has sometimes been speculated that this booklet could have been Agricola's own Finnish-language primer *Abckiria* ('ABC book') which would have been printed in Germany, but there is no proof of any of this. On the contrary, the preserved fragments of the first printing of *Abckiria* refer to the fact that all editions were printed in the Stockholm royal printing house, not in Wittenberg or anywhere else in Germany. Today, it is considered more likely that the small gift was Philipp Melanchton's Latin catechism which was released in 1536.

Agricola's request in Latin for financial support produced no results, but thanks to his second letter in Swedish, he received a sizable amount of aid. This support was taken from funds that the Bishop and cathedral chapter of Turku had available, and it enabled him to bring his studies to honourable completion. He used a portion of the funds for purchasing useful books. It seemed that he was interested in, for example, the philosophy of Aristotle, the comedies of Plautus, the works of Church Father Augustine and the geography of Strabo. He probably also acquired religious literature as source material for his own translation work because an adequate selection of new German literature would otherwise hardly have been available in Finland. (Tarkiainen & Tarkiainen 1985.)

Agricola and Teit earned their Master's degrees in spring 1539 after three years of study. The two friends left for home with Georg Norman: first they went to Hamburg via Lüneburg, and from there to Lübeck and over the sea to Stockholm where Norman was headed to be the prince's tutor. Nicolaus Magni arranged to have Melanchton write a joint recommendation for Agricola and Norman, which was addressed to King Gustav Vasa. Nicolaus himself wrote the King a letter in which he explained that Agricola served Christianity with proper and earnest knowledge. He also stated his sincere hope that Agricola would be given an opportunity to introduce himself to the King and that an appropriate spiritual post or some source of livelihood could be found for him after he returned home. (Tarkiainen & Tarkiainen 1985.)

2.5 A Cathedral School Headmaster

There was a practice in the Turku diocese that the last Master of Arts graduate returning from abroad worked as a Katedralskolan i Åbo schoolmaster – that is, the cathedral school headmaster. When Agricola returned to Turku in the summer of 1539, the previous headmaster Thomas Francisci Keijoi got to continue his studies in Wittenberg, and Agricola assumed his position in the cathedral school. His schoolmate Teit became a Turku Cathedral chapter member and vicar of Maaria, Turku's neighbouring rural district. In 1542, Teit was called to be tutor to Stockholm's younger princes John and Carl because Norman, who was earlier called from Germany, went on to other, more important duties in the administration of the Swedish Church. In 1539, Norman had already become a superintendent, a high-ranking official who, by the King's proxy, was on a secular scale appointed above all the bishops, prelates – that is, the holders of the most valued posts of the cathedral chapter – and other men of the cloth. In his post, Norman renewed the Church Order, reinforced the crown's taxation of the Church and organised the seizure of the Church's priceless artefacts for the needs of the kingdom, in other words, for the King. Moreover, Agricola was given tasks as assigned by Norman, as the following section shows in more detail.

Paulus Juusten from Vyborg, an orphaned son of a bourgeois family, became a teaching assistant for the cathedral school in Turku during Keijoi's time. Wittenberg alumnus Simon Henrici Wiburgensis, who was visiting his home country in 1538, had recommended Juusten to Bishop Skytte, who took the boy into his house as a reader and teaching assistant for the school. (Heininen 2012.) When Agricola became the school's new headmaster, the roughly 20-year-old Juusten got to continue in his teaching assistant duties for two years. He then, despite his young age, ended up moving on to the responsible position of headmaster in his home city of Vyborg.

Working as a headmaster during the time of the Reformation was not that easy. The appeal of posts in the Swedish Church and education for these posts had decreased when the Church had impoverished and little by little was forced to give up its mediaeval wealth and splendour. In addition to the Church's assets, the King deployed school pupils who were called to work in his office as necessary. Attempts were made to save the best pupils for serving the Church by ordaining them as priests as soon as it was possible.

Many schools were in such a bad state during the Reformation era that at the Diet of Arboga of 1546, the bishops of Sweden bemoaned the decline of schools: the number of schoolchildren had decreased and many dropped out. The supply of information was limited and teaching methods comprised dry rote exercises and harsh discipline, sometimes outright abuse. The schooling of stubborn pupils could last up to 20 years, and yet there was a poor amount of information and skills that accumulated over the school years. (Tarkiainen & Tarkiainen 1985.)

Even Agricola talks about the weak level of seminary education in the preface of his New Testament in 1548: many of the priests were fools who did not understand any Latin and could not even speak Swedish. They were pitiful and lazy when it came to teaching the people, and they could not be bothered to prepare their sermons nor could they even teach the people the most important prayers. Furthermore, teaching duties were included in their posts, and even though the priests themselves did not tend to them, a few of them were so malevolent that they did not allow others to teach.

Even though the Church was impoverished and an increasingly greater part of its tax revenue was being transferred to the King's bottomless treasury, there was no complaining when it came to Agricola's own livelihood. Upon becoming headmaster, he was also appointed a seat in the cathedral chapter and entitled to benefit from the revenue of the Laurentius prebend. The prebend system goes back to the Middle Ages. According to this system, a portion of the Church's assets, for example from farms located in different parts of the country, were sorted out in groups, and the cathedral chapter members utilised the earnings of these groups as their revenue. In addition to the earnings of certain farms, Agricola's emoluments also included a townhouse which was quite close to the cathedral. This so-called Laurentius House became Agricola's home. He only had a few dozen metres to travel to work because the school operated in nearby a building that was a part of the wall surrounding the cathedral.

There is no direct information available on how Agricola himself schooled his own pupils nor had any of his pupils reportedly written about their teacher and their time at the Turku cathedral school. The only pupils who were definitely known to have studied at the hand of Agricola at the cathedral school were two Swedish boys of nobility: Hogenskild Bielke and his cousin Nils Axelsson Banér. These boys arrived in Turku in 1547. Bielke's mother Anna, whose mother Anna Tott was of a wealthy Finnish nobility line, considered Agricola her good friend and confidante. This was perhaps partly the reason why the boys were sent to school in Turku and specifically under the care of Agricola. Moreover, Bielke's father Nils, who had a significant position in the King's counting house, was Agricola's friend and supporter. In any case, the boys continued studying in Turku even after Agricola left his headmaster duties. This can be seen in a letter of an otherwise unknown individual named Laurentius Agricola. The letter tells the parents of the progression of the boys' studies. Judging from its style and wording, Mikael Agricola did not write the letter. Instead, it was some other cleric working in Turku who used the same byname. Laurentius Agricola is not known in any other historical sources. (Lahtinen 2007.)

Studying in a Finnish school was not at all difficult for the two cousins because the Bielke family had land assets, among others several manors, and relatives also in Finland. The mother tongue of the other students in school could have been Swedish or Finnish. Later on, Bielke continued his studies in Wittenberg, and he became a very influential man in Sweden, a lawspeaker and a member of the Privy Council of Sweden. (Tarkiainen & Tarkiainen 1985.) However, Banér, who seemed to be more talented in school, grew tired of studying and his life went downhill. In the end, he was killed in a student fight in Rostock. (Heininen 2007.)

Agricola briefly wrote about matters of principle concerning education in the Latin beginning section of his *Rucouskiria*. In this section, he suggests that in addition to traditional education in Latin to prepare a boy for clerical work, schools for scribes and girls' schools should be established in cities, and these schools should be taught in the vernacular. If secular officials were educated in their own schools, trivium schools could focus better on teaching the knowledge and skills required in clerical duties. Agricola does not provide any reasoning whatsoever for supporting the education of women, but the issue was not unheard of per se. Monasteries had already been organising education for girls in the Middle Ages, but when monasticism ended with the realisation of the Reformation, girls were excluded from the traditional educational system. At any rate, these reflections concerning the development of education were not Agricola's, they were borrowed from Luther. Only the slightly ambiguous position concerning the use of the vernacular is Agricola's own addition.

In his chronicle of bishops, Juusten states that Agricola diligently and carefully taught school youth, but also worked for the benefit of the parish by publishing his prayer book *Rucouskiria* and the New Testament. Strangely enough, Juusten does not say anything about the primer, even though specifically commenting on it would have been expected in connection with schoolwork because out of all of Agricola's works, *Abckiria* was the one most certainly meant to be a schoolbook for beginners.

The fundamentals of education in the cathedral school were evidently arranged in a way that was typical at the trivium schools of the time. Agricola undoubtedly paid especially close attention to Latin teaching because he stressed its significance to priests in the prefaces of his own publications. In addition to Latin grammar, students learned dialectics, that is, the ability to define matters clearly, explain unclear and ambiguous matters, give grounds to arguments and prove incorrect claims to be unfounded. The third essential subject was rhetoric which was practised by following good examples. Priests had to be able to speak clearly, with style and with ease.

Song was also practised in school, starting right at the lower grades. In the Middle Ages, there was a strong tradition of composing and singing especially devout school songs (*Piae cantiones*) in Latin, and these songs were also showcased by the pupils publicly while travelling around the countryside on their holidays with beggar's bags on their backs. If the schoolchildren did not have a wealthy family or some other sponsor to support them, their livelihood largely depended on the financial support given by charitable people as a wage for singing.

Schoolchildren in the upper grades also participated in church services, singing liturgical songs in the choir alternating with the priests conducting the services. A new form of ecclesiastical song emerged during the Reformation era, as hymns written in verse begun to be composed for the congregation to sing. This reform, however, was not yet realised in Finland during Agricola's time, so singing was still the responsibility of the priests and the choir.

Of all the textbooks, the Bible was the most crucial, and when the art of printing had become more common, reasonably priced books were available for students to use. In 1529, the Örebro Church Assembly in Sweden had decreed that every schoolchild must have a copy of the New Testament in Latin. Lessons included reading it and its interpretation, and the Finnish pupils most likely also got to practice translating the texts into their mother tongue. The Swedish-language New Testament had already come out in 1526, but in Finnish, there were at most manuscript excerpts in existence. Of these, the oldest collection of texts preserved to this day is a fragment of a gospel that has been conserved at the Uppsala University Library. Based on its content and watermark, it appears that the fragment is from 1537.

In addition to the compulsory trivium subjects, dogmatic theology and song, Agricola had probably made use of the various subjects he learned during his university days in his teaching. Judging from book acquisitions, margin notes and choices made in publishing, he himself was interested in quite a diverse range of subjects, for example geography, history, chronology, astrology, plants and medicine, and it was this knowledge that he probably utilised when interpreting biblical texts and overseeing translation exercises.

A majority of pupils aimed at a career in the clergy, and for them, teaching and practice for conducting worship services took place after proper schooling. To some extent, there were also pupils from the lower grades who were going to be officials and clerical officers. They were in school mostly to attain writing and counting skills and to become familiar with writing documents. The teaching assistant was usually an advanced pupil in the school.

In his letter to Georg Norman in Stockholm in 1543, Agricola bemoaned how burdensome his work was. He explained how difficult a job it was to lead boys who behaved like untamed animals. There was a commotion stemming from the rumour going around the city that the priests' wages were undergoing a change. This meant that with the lowering of wages, the appreciation of science and teaching plummeted. The schoolboys were no angels either. They fought with the castle servants and caused havoc in the city.

In addition to problems concerning management of the school, Agricola and all of Turku met with misfortune as a large part of the city burned down in March 1546. The roof of the cathedral and the Bishop's house were completely destroyed, as was the schoolhouse in the church's surrounding wall. Moreover, the Laurentius House – that is, the building Agricola used as his home – nearly burned to the ground. The books and manuscripts were saved, however. Agricola had to move somewhere else and so he got to use the Dean's house which was located a bit further from the cathedral and thus spared from the fire. Agricola got to use it on the condition that he would see to renovating the dilapidated building. Agricola made an appeal to the King for the Dean's post and emoluments as well, but he was not granted these requests. Instead, this bounty was kept under the crown's possession.

Acquiring the house proved to be a bad move. The building was in terrible shape and repairing it became more expensive than expected. Furthermore, there were many guests who came to the house in need of lodging and hospitality because there was not a great deal of buildings in livable condition in the almost completely destroyed city. So, Agricola thought it wiser to begin renovating the Laurentius House at his own expense so that he could move back there. At the King's behest, all other owners of prebend houses also had to be responsible for the building and renovation expenses so far as they were able to do so.

At the same time along with the fire, there were many deaths amongst Agricola's closest associates. The number of Wittenberg alumni thinned out when Simon Henrici died in 1545 and soon thereafter the following year Teit and Keijoi. Moreover, the founder of Lutheranism, Martin Luther died in 1546 in Eisleben, Germany. Dean of Turku Johannes Petri, who was the oldest member of the cathedral chapter and once studied in Rome, died in 1547. Due to the King's strained economic policy, no new members were appointed to the cathedral chapter. Instead, as each member died, thus each seat remained empty, and in these new circumstances, the prebendry income they had during their lifetime was administered to the crown treasury.

Although Agricola on many occasions expressed dissatisfaction with how burdensome schoolwork was, he parted with it rather reluctantly. In early 1548, however, he had to leave his post when his former teaching assistant Juusten came back from his study trip in Wittenberg, Rostock and Königsberg along with excellent recommendations from Philipp Melanchton. By the King's authoritative decree, he was given the duties of Turku cathedral school headmaster, and Agricola was ordered to resign.

Agricola tried to salvage his position by appealing to the King by letter though his friend Nils Bielke and the King's secretary. Even though he had previously delayed in and rebelled against sending schoolchildren to work in the Kings' office, he now promised to train a few young men every year for the King to employ. He suggested that Juusten be sent to Vyborg as headmaster as it too needed a fine man to run the school. However, his appeals were in vain. Juusten did become the headmaster of the Turku cathedral school, and Agricola got to continue in his other duties as assistant to the Bishop and as member of the cathedral chapter. It was a great consolation to Agricola that he got to keep his home as well as his former tithes and the earnings from them. Only the headmaster's low salary, which was paid in grain, was now no longer available to him.

2.6 From a Bishop's Assistant to Bishop

Alongside his work as headmaster, Agricola also carried out other tasks. Right from the beginning of his career, he had worked in the Bishop's office amongst administration and attained the position of the Bishop's close assistant. After becoming headmaster, he had achieved the position of canon in the cathedral chapter – that is, an inferior member of administrative authority. He thus knew exactly what was happening in the administration of the diocese. Being the youngest member of the cathedral chapter, he had many duties. He conducted masses and prayers at the cathedral, participated in chapter meetings and took care of day-to-day business. He also worked as the chapter's scribe. (Knuutila 2007.)

Being the scribe of the cathedral chapter of Turku, Agricola had to write a report to the King and his Stockholm treasury in 1542 on the assets and earnings of the cathedral chapter and the cathedral clergy from 1541 to 1542. As far as is known, this was his first administrative task of great magnitude. The report has been preserved to this day in two manuscripts, each slightly differing from each other and both in Agricola's handwriting. The composition of the cathedral chapter and all the prebandry earnings to the cathedral, prelates and canons, which have been accounted to the Church from different parishes, are shown in detail in the Swedish-language report. It appears that a total of twelve farms were in the Laurentius preband allotted to Agricola. In addition to that, right before finishing the report, Agricola was also entitled to have the earnings of three farms included in the Bartholomeus preband. (Tarkiainen & Tarkiainen 1985; Knuutila 2007.) It was especially well-grounded in this part of the report that the Bishop confirmed that the earnings of the Bartholomeus preband would go to Agricola as a small compensation after his return from Germany.

Since Agricola held no authoritative position when he was writing the report, it can be presumed that the actual reporting was done at the hand of the Dean and the cathedral chapter and that Agricola worked only as a scribe and a scrivener in keeping with his basic duties. (Knuutila 2007.) Nevertheless, the report is an interesting document on how much income the Church collected from different parishes, the names of the farms owned by the Church in each parish, and also what kinds of products they provided. At the same time, the report explains the change in the country's administrative system. In the Middle Ages, Finland was divided into administrative divisions called *slottslän* (Fin. *linnalääni*) – districts which had a castle as their administrative centre. The management of the castles was given to nobility or other trusted representatives, and they got to collect tax earnings from the area of their own district just as the Church itself got to take care of its taxes. King Gustav Vasa put an end to the slottslän system and divided the country into bailiwicks where bailiffs collected earnings directly for the King. The first bailiff records have been preserved right from the period when Agricola wrote his report on the earnings of the Church. (Mäkelä-Alitalo 2007.) The pages of many mediaeval parchment manuscripts have been preserved to this day as cover pages of the bailiff records, as they lost their ecclesiastical importance due to their Catholic content.

Martinus Skytte was already an old man upon becoming bishop in 1528, and over time, the practical responsibility of taking care of the Bishop's official duties increasingly went to Agricola and his close colleague and Wittenberg alumnus, vicar of Turku Canutus Johannis. At no stage was Agricola officially designated as the Bishop's stand-in, but in practice, he ended up taking the responsibility of many of the official duties of the Bishop's post.

After being dismissed from his duties as headmaster in the beginning of 1548, Agricola could also delve into his literary work more freely than before. The long-awaited translation of the New Testament came from the printer the same year, and the following year, he published three liturgical books: *Käsikiria* 'Agenda', *Messu* 'Missal' and *Pina* 'Passion'. These books became indispensable literature for priests in all Finnish-language parishes. The release of these books without a doubt significantly furthered the standardisation of Evangelical Lutheran services and ecclesiastical procedures carried out in the vernacular. With these books, a priest who was lacking in Finnish-language skills could convincingly and ceremonially see to his official duties.

At the end of 1549, Agricola translated the Visby admiralty law from Low German into Swedish. His original translation was lost, but six copies of the text from the late 16th century have been preserved. The copies show Agricola's name as well as an introduction he added on his own accord. (Heininen 2007.)

Translating the admiralty law was evidently commissioned on the initiative of a powerful individual in the kingdom. However, Agricola himself was apparently interested in legal texts in addition to his many other assets. This can be seen from the fact that he added a collection of regulations concerning engagement and matrimony at the beginning of the section concerning marriage in his *Käsikiria*. These rules and regulations were not in the original Swedish agenda. Agricola had at least temporarily got a hold of a few valuable juridical texts, such as the illuminated manuscript known as the *Codex Kalmar* which contained the mediaeval Law of the Realm (Fin. *Maanlaki*, Swe. *Landslag*), and he took notes in them. The *Codex Kalmar* was also previously known as the *Codex Aboensis* because the manuscript included a mediaeval calendar of the Turku diocese.

Moreover, Agricola was still employed by diocesan administration. When old Bishop Skytte could no longer go on missions, Agricola and his closest associate Vicar Johannis got to tend to the task. There is no detailed information on all the routes, but they were in Savo in 1549. This is known because they sent a letter from the rectory in the former municipality of Sääminki to the head of Savonlinna (Olavinlinna, the castle of St Olaf) Gustaf Fincke in which they gave observations and recommendations. They were absolutely mortified by the spiritual state of the people. Hardly anyone could recite the most rudimentary prayers by heart, not to mention that they could have taught them to others. They requested that the head of the castle would assign chaplains and lensmanns and other able authorities to teach the people. They advised on erecting a chapel in Kuopionniemi, in eastern Finland, where the city of Kuopio was later built.

In addition to his official duties, Agricola also took care of tasks of a more personal nature entrusted to him. When his former pupil Hogenskild Bielke's grandmother, Finnish-born noblewoman Anna Tott died in 1549, Agricola was called to complete the estate inventory at the Finnish manors she owned in Nousiainen, Sääksmäki and Kemiö. Even later on, as a trusted representative, he got to sort out the border disputes concerning the landholdings of the same line of nobility. (Tarkiainen & Tarkiainen 1985.)

There is not much known about Agricola's personal life, but he evidently got married to a woman named Birgitta right at the end of the 1540s. There is no information on her family background other than that her father's name was Olav, but it is usually presumed that Birgitta was the daughter of a bourgeoisie family from Turku. In December 1550, the Agricola family had a baby boy named Christian, and the proud father wrote about the birth of his son in the preface poem of his *Psaltari* ('Psalter') – that is, his Book of Psalms – published in 1551. Christian was evidently an only child: at least no information has been preserved on any other offspring.

Old Bishop Skytte died at the end of 1550, and the episcopal see remained empty for a few years. These were also extremely difficult times in other aspects. In 1551, winter lasted longer than usual, and there was no food to be found in the whole country. Agricola published a book (*Weisut ia ennustoxet* 'canticles and prophecies') containing parts of the Book of Prophets from the Old Testament to which he added a long margin note on the on-going famine. He reported on the same misfortune by letter to his friend and printer Amund Laurentsson also hoping for aide from the motherland.

It seems that Agricola's family survived these hard times without any problems because in January 1551, it is known that he acquired a part of his home farm located in Torsby in Pernå. His sister inherited this property and he purchased the farm from his brother-in-law Klemet Krook. After this purchase, he owned half of the entire property. The following year, Agricola purchased the building next to the Laurentius prebendry house – that is, his city home – as new living quarters for his family. This was the St Katariina house, which was previously one of the church prebandry houses but was taken over by the crown. The cathedral chapter accounts between 1553 and 1554 have been preserved, and they show that Agricola received income from the earnings of 15 farms altogether. (Tarkiainen & Tarkiainen 1985.) On top of this were his personal assets.

In addition to property sales, Agricola continued his literary work for some time. In 1552, his Finnish translation of the last three books of the Minor Prophets – Haggai, Zechariah and Malachi – was published, and this was his last printed work. After this, he is known to have prepared at least one piece for publication, but only an extract from a preface of a few pages covering proverbs and adages has been preserved. At the end of the manuscript, Agricola states that when recited in moderation, the effect of proverbs can be compared to stars that make the heavens shine or flowers and herbs that make the earth beautiful to look at. The date included in the manuscript indicates that the work was completed in 1553 but for some reason it was not printed. A majority of the manuscript disappeared without a trace. (Sarajas 1956.)

Agricola took an interest in the proverbs of multiple languages because the languages used in the preserved sections were Latin and Swedish, but in the preface, reference is also made to Finnish as well as Swedish proverbs. In Agricola's time, many learned people took an interest in and published proverbs. The best-known enthusiast was Erasmus of Rotterdam whose collection entitled *Adagia* was an absolute bestseller. Agricola used it as his exemplar as he borrowed some of the materials from Erasmus. (Sarajas 1956; Heininen 2006.) Agricola's interest in proverbs can also be seen in his own works, in which a few Finnish-language proverbs can be found. There are verses in the preface poems of his *Rucouskiria* adapted from proverbs, and there is an example of weather forecasting in the form of a proverb in its calendar section (Häkkinen 2013). However, there is no actual information on the subject of the piece that was supposed to be published. It is possible that the reflections and examples concerning proverbs had been composed just for the preface and that the actual text of the manuscript covered something completely different. (Heininen 2007.)

Agricola's Finnish translations ended with the Prophetic Books of the Bible. There were difficult times ahead, and it did not help matters at all that the King took his time in appointing a new bishop. It was previously the cathedral chapter's task to select a new bishop, but now, at most, it could recommend candidates to the King. Furthermore, the cathedral chapter had shrunk down, as no new members were appointed to take the place of those who had died. For three years, the Turku diocese had to get by with temporary arrangements, and in those times, no new priests could be ordained in Finland. Instead, they had to travel across the sea to Stockholm.

In May 1554, the King finally called the four remaining members of the cathedral chapter of Turku to Stockholm, amongst them Agricola and Juusten. When it was time to discuss selecting a new bishop after other business was negotiated, the King had a surprise in store which was quite unpleasant in Agricola's eyes: instead of the one diocese, the region of Finland would be divided into two. Thus as Agricola became bishop of the larger and more significant Turku diocese, his younger colleague Juusten was entrusted with running the Vyborg diocese. The Vyborg diocese included the eastern parts of Finland: Karelia, Savo, the province of Porvoo and the Hollola hundred located in Eastern Häme. In the entire region of Finland, there were a total of 102 parishes, and out of these, 24 were in the Vyborg diocese. (Tarkiainen & Tarkiainen 1985.) Of the two, the Vyborg diocese was clearly more underpopulated, but in his chronicle of Finnish bishops, Juusten nevertheless noted with seeming malicious glee that this division did not particularly please Mikael. This is understandable because undermining the influence of individual bishops was the goal of this division. The dioceses in Sweden were divided in the same way not much later.

Agricola and Juusten were ordained as bishops under the Lutheran tradition. Archbishop of Sweden Laurentius Petri was not even called to ordain them. Laurentius Petri was not popular with the King at this time. The reason evidently was that he objected to the monarch's third marriage with his previous wife's young niece. Consequently, the ceremony was conducted by Bishop Botvid Suneson at the nearby Strängnäs Cathedral.

Suneson earned his Master's degree in Wittenberg and was a fellow student of Turku vicar and cathedral chapter member Canutus Johannis.

The decline in the bishop's post can also be seen in its terminology. In place of the former title *episcopus*, the King used the term *ordinarius* ('ordinary') for the new bishops. The old term was temporarily used only in special circumstances in which the bishop's honour of rank had to be emphasised to outside parties.

Upon his return to Finland, Agricola had to quickly demonstrate his loyalty to the King. He had to leave for a mission immediately in July to the municipalities in the Turku archipelago and catalogue all the valuables of the churches. All of the valuable assets were entered in the books, from communion vessels to altar clothes. Within a few years, after Agricola's death, a majority of these valuable items were taken over by the crown. The Birgittine Monastery of Naantali was at the end of Agricola's journey. The abbey, which in the distant past had been so great and reputable, was now fading to make way for the Reformation. There was no need to record any valuables there because the Turku Castle bailiff had already been there, taking possession of them a month earlier. However, the monks and nuns that remained, who had still continued practicing their faith as Catholics until that time, wound up giving their word that they would stop worshipping saints, give up Latin mass, cease reading the visions and apparitions of Saint Birgit, and become Evangelicals.

The bishop ordination ceremony was modest, but back home in Turku, Agricola got to have what he did not get in Strängnäs. On the birthday of the Blessed Virgin Mary – 8 September 1554 – both the diocesan synod and the traditional autumn market fair were simultaneously organised. At this time, there was an exceptionally large number of people in Turku. Agricola used the occasion to his advantage and organised a magnificent, mediaeval-style bishop's mass in which he introduced himself to his diocese and gave a blessing to the people with the bishop's mitra on his head. In his chronicle of Finnish bishops, Juusten talks about this occasion, stating that the King could not tolerate such papality very lightly.

As bishop, Agricola got to participate in taking care of business and making decisions on a new, more prestigious level. The mediaeval custom was that the Bishop of Turku represented Österland – in other words, Finland – in the Privy Council of Sweden. Gustav Vasa no longer wanted men of the cloth in his Privy Council. However, part of the secular authority of the Bishop of Turku included in this task was preserved. He also had other social duties. He was responsible for the administration of the Church and was the highest teacher of the members of the clergy and the Church in his diocese as well as the overseer of education. He presided as a judge in marital issues and gave certification in matters concerning wills and inheritance. The Bishop arranged ministerial conventions, sent circulars to the priests and called on information on their annual earnings. It is unclear as to what extent Agricola had the opportunity to appoint new priests in his episcopal term because only one case is known. In keeping with the old custom, a part of the rural districts were so-called "regalia parishes" which were appointed with priests by the King. (Paarma 1980; Tarkiainen & Tarkiainen 1985.)

While he was bishop, Agricola went on numerous missions to various parts of his expansive diocese. He got to consecrate a stone church in the parish of Närpes in 1555. The Närpes stone church was, in a sense, a historic building in that it was the last of those many mediaeval stone churches which were erected in Finland in the glory days of the Catholic Church, especially since the 15th century. The church was small and evidently still slightly incomplete when it was dedicated, but later, the building was expanded whereupon its old sections were taken down to make way for new ones. Today, only a few wall sections of the church remain. (Hiekkanen 2007.)

Agricola got to mediate many kinds of problems on his journeys alongside his missionary duties. Border disputes, ignorance and poverty were the common occurrences in the countryside. A continual dispute with the Russians prevailed on the eastern border of the kingdom because the borderline was nonspecific in the mainland and disputed in many places since the signing of the Treaty of Nöteborg in 1323. In 1554, a full war broke out. Moreover, there was unrest amongst the people in the homeland. Agricola arranged for an especially strong student from the cathedral school to be the priest of a certain rural district in Ostrobothnia because the former vicar was killed and no one wanted to voluntarily be his successor. To guarantee his safety, the new priest got to take four farmhands and three German shepherds with him. (Virrankoski 1956.)

In August 1555, Agricola got to host King Gustav Vasa in the Bishop's house in Turku. The King was on a long journey in Finland, acquainting himself with the conditions and, at the same time, the tax revenues which the Church still had the right to collect for the time being. From 1556 onwards, all the taxes were directed to the crown treasury. Because of the state of war, the King travelled to Vyborg in 1555 with his army. Battles continued but neither party could strike down the other for good. The following year, Vicar Canutus Johannis was sent to Moscow to make preparations for the Swedish ambassadors' journey for the upcoming Russo-Swedish peace negotiations.

At the end of 1556, a prestigious peace delegation left on a journey, including among others the King's brother-in-law, Councillor Sten Leijonhufvud, Archbishop of Uppsala Laurentius Petri and Agricola. There were altogether approximately one hundred men and around forty horses in the delegation. Through Shlisselburg, the journey proceeded to Novgorod and from there to Moscow. The ambassadors were ceremoniously received but soon afterwards, their treatment was dependent on the whims of the sovereign tsar, Ivan the Terrible. The ambassadors did not get to move about freely, and the negotiations proceeded slowly by the mediation of the interpreters. The Tsar wanted to humiliate the King by demanding that peace had to be confirmed in Novgorod with the stadtholder. He wanted it to make it clear that he was too prestigious to work on the same level as a king not of noble origin.

When a unanimous agreement on the borders, prisoner exchange and the time frames within the peace treaty was finally reached, the delegation returned to Novgorod where the treaty was fortified under instructions from Moscow. After that, they promptly left for home by sleigh in the severe cold. This was all too much for Agricola. Although he was presumably in good shape before travelling, he became ill and died due to the stress of the journey on 9 April right after the delegation had crossed the icy sea and reached Finland on the Karelian Isthmus in the rural district of Kuolemajärvi. The accounts on the exact place of death went in two directions in the reports given by his contemporaries. It was either the village of Seivästö or Kyrönniemi. (K. Tarkiainen 2004.)

Agricola's body was brought to Vyborg where a quick funeral was arranged. Archbishop Laurentius Petri and other members of the peace delegation were present, and the funeral service was most likely conducted by Bishop Juusten. Agricola was evidently buried at Vyborg Cathedral, but the burial site is unknown, and despite investigations and searches, its location has not been discovered. So much renovation and construction work has been done at the cathedral afterwards that finding and identifying the grave many centuries later is extremely improbable. The grave was probably modest in his time because due to the sudden death and quick burial, preparing a grand memorial was impossible, even though he was a dignitary. (Hiekkanen 2004; Taavitsainen 2007.)

After the death of her husband, Agricola's wife Birgitta was allotted a pension as compensation for the fact that her dead husband had suffered much difficulty for the good of the delegation. Two poems were composed in Latin in memory of Agricola. One was a short epitaph meant to be carved on the headstone, but there is no proof that the stone was entirely completed and poised for his grave. The other was a 48-verse funeral poem which describes Agricola's life in a praising tone and thanks him for his life's work. The poem offers no new information on Agricola's life and death. Nor is there any knowledge on who wrote the poems. Simo Heininen (2007), who has thoroughly researched Agricola's life and his undertakings, has speculated that the longer poem was possibly composed by Agricola's closest associate Canutus Johannis.

A far more informative description of Agricola was written by his younger colleague Juusten as part of the chronicle of Finnish bishops. This is an extensive manuscript which introduces all the figures who have been Finnish bishops, starting from the Middle Ages and continuing all the way up to Juusten himself. This chronicle is furthermore a central source when studying both the earliest history of Finland and Agricola's life and his undertakings. There have already been several references to it in this chapter. Finnish historical study is usually seen to have started when Henrik Gabriel Porthan published a commentated version of Juusten's Latin chronicle at the end of the 18th century. Later, the chronicle was researched by Simo Heininen, who also published it in Finnish.

3. The Finnish Works of Mikael Agricola

Mikael Agricola was not the first to translate spiritual texts into Finnish. The fundamentals of Christianity and some of the most important prayers were already being taught to the people in their own language in the Middle Ages. The monks that were circulating amongst the people gave sermons and taught in Finland in Finnish. However, there were no notes in Finnish preserved in the Middle Ages. Manuscripts in Finnish are only known from the Reformation, and a few of them are slightly older than the similar works by Agricola. Agricola, however, was the first one who got Finnish-language works to print.

Only the printing of books could make the creation of a cohesive literary language possible. There were only individual manuscripts, and they were only used by a small circle of people. When printed books were introduced to different parishes in hundreds of identical copies, a general conception began to be formed on how topics were supposed to be expressed in a literary language. Printed works were also used as a concrete model for later translators and writers. Many text excerpts and manners of speech were copied untouched from one book to another.

This chapter introduces all nine Finnish-language works written by Agricola in chronological order of publication. These works fulfilled the need for Finnish-language literature for a long time: it took over 20 years before the next printed works in Finnish were published.

3.1 Agricola's Primer / Abckiria

Mikael Agricola's first published work was his primer catechism *Abckiria* ('ABC book'). The word *kiria* ('book') in this title and in his other works in this chapter is Agricola's written form in comparison to its contemporary standard form *kirja*. These orthographic differences will be covered in chapter four. *Abckiria* was printed at the Stockholm royal printing house, most likely in 1543. The printing house had just been taken over by printing master Amund Laurentsson who had been taught by Jürgen Richolff of Germany. In later contexts, Agricola noted Laurentsson as a good and dear friend. There was not a great need at this time for printed Swedish works because the first whole Bible – the Gustav Vasa Bible (*Biblia, Thet är: All then Helgha Scrifft, På Swensko*) – had already been published in 1541. Moreover, the Swedish-language liturgical agenda and missal had been revised that same year. Consequently, Agricola became the most noted client of the Stockholm royal printing house for some time.

Agricola's primer was not a Finnish translation from any one exemplary work. Instead, elements from different sources were compiled for it. The central exemplars were Martin Luther's *Enchiridion; Der kleine Katekismus*, Philipp Melanchthon's *Catechismus puerilis* and Andreas Osiander's catechism which was originally in German and also published in Latin under the translated title *Catechismus pro puerilis et iuventute*. There is a poem adapted from Melanchton on the cover page of *Abckiria* for encouraging the readers. As for the other subjects in Agricola's primer, the Ten Commandments, the Apostles' Creed, the Lord's Prayer as well as sacraments of Holy Baptism and the Eucharist are all common to each one of the aforementioned exemplary works. In keeping with Luther and Osiander, the primer also contains the sacrament of Holy Absolution. Furthermore, in the style of Luther, Agricola included grace before and after meals as well as morning and evening prayers.

There are also parts of *Abckiria* which are not found in the central exemplars. These include lists of letters and letter combinations which come right after the introductory poem. These lists were for teaching reading skills. Two gothic typefaces were used in the primer: an early, embellished form of Fraktura known as Theuerdank and the slightly smaller and simpler Schwabacher. Capital and lowercase letters in both typefaces are shown on the second page, listing the alphabet four times (see Plate 1 on page 55).

There are calls to prayer from the Middle Ages at the end of *Abckiria*, and these prayers were recited at the infrequent ringing of the church bell with the striking of the clapper against the bell's edge. The end of the primer also contains the most important numerals in Finnish, both in numeric form and spelled out. Roman numerals were quite commonly used in Agricola's time, and they are listed first in addition to the Arabic numerals alongside them.

As somewhat of a reminder of the Middle Ages, Agricola's *Abckiria* also includes the Angelic Salutation (Hail Mary or Ave Maria). In 1492, the Turku Diocesan Assembly had already made the Angelic Salutation obligatory to be read in Finnish in connection with church services and always in the same way, so that the people could have learnt it by heart. The decision was revised on the threshold of the Reformation at the Örebro Church Assembly in 1529. The Angelic Salutation is also included in Agricola's prayer book *Rucouskiria Bibliasta* and his New Testament, but their Finnish translations are not identical. The differences demonstrate that there were no exact established forms in Finnish at the beginning of the Reformation, even for the most significant prayers. The reason for the differences may be that the translations were done separately by different parties, and that in addition to preservation, efforts were made to also correct and update sacred texts according to new doctrinal principles.

The Lutheran Church began to be critical of prayer to the Virgin Mary, as the Reformation forbade worshiping her and the saints. Agricola's primer,

Plate 1: Alphabet styles in Abckiria.

however, shows that there was no desire quite yet to give up the well-known and beloved Angelic Salutation. It was printed in the same kind of large and embellished Theuerdank typeface as those texts that, according to the Örebro decision, had to be read to the people always in the same manner. The size and attractiveness of the letters emphasise the special significance of the texts.

Not one complete copy of Agricola's *Abckiria* has been preserved. Its later produced facsimiles were compiled from preserved fragments found in the pasteboard covers of other books. Moreover, there have been a few loose pages preserved. The first discovery of the primer was in 1851, in Uppsala,

Plate 2: Two different front page borders of Abckiria. *Note the fragment above (probably from 1543) has commas, whereas the later version below (probably 1551) has slashes.*

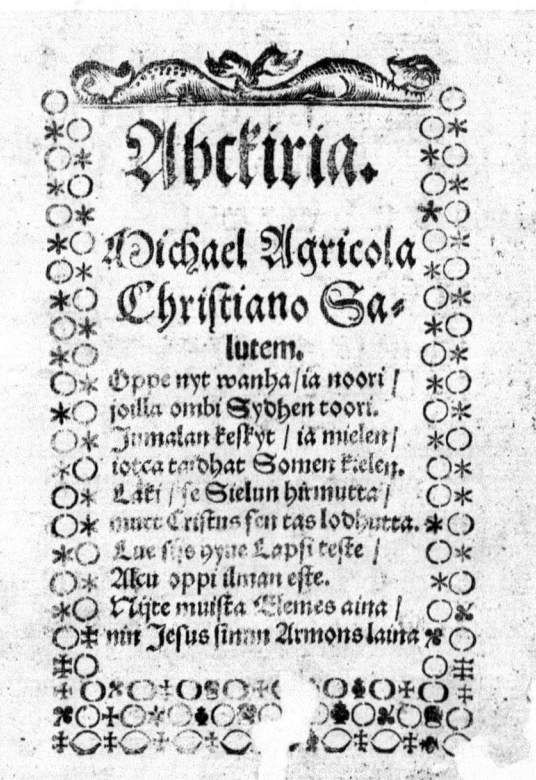

Sweden, when Doctor of Medical Science and bibliophile P. J. Hyckerström found three copies of the first press sheet. This press sheet was marked with the letter A and it included the first 16 pages of the book. It had no information on the year of printing and the text seemed to stop midway. On the basis of this, it could be suspected that the discovery only represented the beginning of a more extensive publication. Regardless, it was understood as a part of the first book printed by Agricola, because Agricola himself had listed his publications in the preface poem of his 1551 Psalter and explained that *Abckiria* was his first book.

In 1904, lector E. Granit-Ilmoniemi found copies of a press sheet in the National Archives of Sweden, which included parts of the primer's first and fourth leaves. However, they were not identical to those found earlier. Instead, the text was smaller and was placed on the pages in a different way than on the press sheets found in Uppsala. The new discoveries must have thus been a part of a different printing of the same book.

Judging from the basis of typographic details, it can be presumed that the fragments from 1904 represent the first, 16-page printing of the primer and the sheets from Uppsala another printing, most probably done in 1551. According to Anna Perälä (2007), who has studied the typography and other features of Agricola's works, the development of the opening poem on the cover page of both printings can be considered the determining piece of evidence. The border in the first printing is formed from old woodcut blocks from Richolff's printing house, but the second printing has a new kind of bordering made up of asterisks, parentheses in circular shapes and other special symbols.

When the facsimile of Agricola's works was published for the first time in 1931, the section with his primer was eight leaves or sixteen pages long. However, the 1987 facsimile of *Abckiria* is made up of 24 pages. The closing section of the primer, the half with the B press sheet, was discovered in 1966 by librarian Åke Åberg in the Västerås diocesan library in Sweden. There was a colophon – an inscription placed at the end of a book – according to which the book was translated in Turku and printed in Stockholm in 1559 at Laurentsson's printing house. Agricola had already died in 1557, and so the newest discovery represented a posthumous edition, which was evidently the third printing of the primer. As regards its content, it was seamlessly united with the earlier discovered A press sheet, and judging from this, the second and third printings were virtually the same. To this day, there is still no trace of the second half of the press sheet of the second printing. Consequently, the final section of the primer is only known on the basis of the third printing.

It has been deemed plausible in older research literature that in addition to the primer, Agricola could have separately published a Finnish translation of Luther's catechism. However, there is no conclusive evidence on any separate catechism. As the primer nevertheless seems to include the core sections of the catechism, it is evident that in some contexts it may have been also called a catechism.

3.2 Agricola's Prayer Book / Rucouskiria Bibliasta

Immediately after *Abckiria*, Agricola took his true great work to print: *Rucouskiria Bibliasta* ('Prayer book from the Bible') which was published in 1544. *Rucouskiria Bibliasta* is often referred to as just *Rucouskiria* ('prayer book'). Today's Finnish prayer book in its standard contemporary form is simply entitled *Rukouskirja*: the velar stops in the name *Rucouskiria* are represented both by a *c* and a *k*. We should also note that Agricola's word for the Bible *Biblia* is *Raamattu* in contemporary Finnish. The book had 877 pages though they were small in size. There were usually only a few hundred pages in Reformation prayer books (Heininen 2007), and so it was a question of an exceptionally expansive work along the lines of international standards. The book was embellished with woodcuts, and in addition to black, the beginning section was also printed in red.

As its name suggests, Agricola's prayer book mostly includes prayers. There are three types. For its first part, prayers from the Bible were compiled, 40 psalms for example. This followed the model of the prayer book by Otto Brunfels of Germany. Agricola, however, did not translate the psalms from Brunfels' book. Instead, they were translated directly from the Bible. It is possible that the translations were in existence prior to this because the psalms were already recited and sung meticulously in the Middle Ages. There was hardly any desire to break from this tradition at the stage of the Reformation when it obligated the use of the vernacular in church services and devotions.

The second section of *Rucouskiria* comprises prayers required in services at different times during the liturgical year. Agricola's most important exemplar used in their selection was the 1488 Turku mediaeval missal *Missale Aboense*, which was historically the first printed book for Finland. There are also texts in *Rucouskiria* which were traditionally sung, and in some cases, the type of text is noted in the book, such as a sequence. However, there are no musical notations in *Rucouskiria* or any reference made to any melody used.

The prayers in the third section are for personal devotions, and for this, Agricola took in elements from both mediaeval tradition and from the new prayer literature of the Reformation, altogether from at least 15 different works. The sources used for *Rucouskiria* have especially been studied by Jaakko Gummerus (1941–1955). New additional exemplars have been presented by Juhani Holma (2008).

There is a separate calendar section at the beginning of *Rucouskiria* whose text is mostly Latin. It has been said to be the first Finnish encyclopaedia because it provides many kinds of useful information on chronology, astronomy and astrology, medicine, anatomy, psychology, history and theology. There is a perpetual calendar right at the beginning in which the days of each month have been listed with special identifying letters. With complicated calculations, these letters could be converted into days of the week of any given year.

There is also a column in the calendar which gives the commemorative days of different saints and other important events, such as the sun's movement to a specific zodiac sign, spring or autumn equinox and the start of dog days. Some of the days are marked with an asterisk. These included "dismal days", particularly bad days for one to begin any important venture.

A short poem was translated from a Swedish hymnal for each month. The poems are about the normal weather and topical work for the different months, but as their content shows, the verses were originally written for Central European conditions. For example, the time for spring sowing is noted as happening as soon as April, and October is recommended as the month for picking grapes. Sowing in Finland usually does not occur until May or the beginning of June, and harvesting grapes is not possible at all because of the short summer and harsh winter. Following the poems are instructions for health which recommend eating healthy foods and herbs, bloodletting and consuming beverages appropriate for that season. The instructions are based on mediaeval herbalism which was practised especially at monasteries.

The most original part of *Rucouskiria* is represented by the preface poems found in the beginning of the book. A few of them are adaptations of biblical text or international exemplars, but some were composed by Agricola himself. The poetic metre is in Knittelvers which, in Agricola's time, was the favoured metre especially in the Germanic linguistic area.

In the most basic case, there are four stressed syllables in a Knittelvers metrical line, and each one is followed by one or more unstressed syllables. However, the number of stressed syllables can, in practice, waver between three and five, and the unstressed syllable can sometimes be left out. The metre is thus somewhat irregular. The lines are rhyming couplets. A poem in the Knittelvers metre is structurally simple, whereupon it is has been used, for example, in didactic poems for the common people. On the other hand, it is rhythmically choppy and awkward, as a result of which it was not usually suitable as a metre for more demanding lyrical poetry.

Agricola is the first person known by name who had attempted to write poetry in Finnish in the modern European poetic metre of the time, but he was no master poet by any means. He had great difficulties in working out rhymes because they were quite unknown in the old Finnish poetic metre.

Nevertheless, Agricola's own poetry is contextually colourful and interesting. The poems reveal what kinds of thoughts were running through Agricola's mind when he translated and had books printed for the Finnish reader. He criticised lazy priests who could not be bothered to teach the people. He defended himself against those who ridiculed and looked down upon his books. He spoke of the great change that the Reformation had brought about in the Finnish Church. The voice of Agricola is thus a part of the preface poems.

3.3 Agricola's New Testament / Se Wsi Testamenti

Agricola's main work is his *Se Wsi Testamenti* – the New Testament. It can be noted that the contemporary form of its name is *Uusi testamentti* ('New Testament') without the pronoun *se* ('it') which Agricola used as an article:

Finnish actually has no articles specifically corresponding to English *a/an* or *the*. Agricola evidently already started to translate the New Testament into Finnish before leaving for Wittenberg in 1536. However, the first definite acknowledgment of this translation was in the letter he wrote in Latin to King Gustav Vasa in 1537, sent from the University of Wittenberg. Agricola bemoaned how meagre his assets were and how difficult his situation was and beseeched the king for some kind of assistance so that he could continue his studies and proceed with the translation of the New Testament. This time around, he did not get the support but Agricola nevertheless continued studying and stayed in Wittenberg until 1539 when he graduated with a Master's degree. In 1538, he approached the King again, this time with a letter written in Swedish in which he stressed that his studies would be for the common good of the King's subjects. In addition, he made reference to the Finnish translation of the New Testament that was underway. This time, the King was more favourable and Agricola was granted a sizable amount of aid from the resources of Turku Cathedral.

There were two other Finns during Agricola's time in Wittenberg: his travel companion and childhood friend Martinus Teit and also Simon Henrici Wiburgensis who had already been in Wittenberg since 1532. It is clear that they participated, at least to some extent, in translating the New Testament. Teit's Bible concordance – a list of all the words appearing in the Bible – is a direct indication of this: as the owner, he entered his initials and the year 1538 in it. Teit's concordance has been preserved to this day. This kind of list was an excellent aid for a translator who had to check how words were used in different contexts. In his letter to the King, Agricola spoke of translation work that had previously been started, but he did not give any detailed information as to who were working on it, nor did he present it in such a way that it would have specifically been his own personal project. Since we know that many other translations at that time were carried out as a product of group work, it seems natural to presume the same in regard to the Finnish translation of the New Testament. In his translation guide and at his table talks, Luther had stressed that a translator will not come up with appropriate words if he works alone. This is why it was good for a translator to have help.

Translating the New Testament and refining it lasted a total of over ten years. Evidently, it was a very lonely toil to move forward with the endeavour after returning from Wittenberg. In 1543, the work was at that stage when Agricola saw that it was crucial to beseech the king through Georg Norman for permission and assistance to get his work printed. In this letter to Norman, Agricola compared himself to Sisyphus who in vain tried to roll an immense boulder up a hill. At the same time, he made it understood that the work was still unfinished. The king did not grant the additional monetary support Agricola had hoped for and so the New Testament had to be put on hold for the time being. Instead, Agricola brought his *Rucouskiria* to print and got it published in 1544.

In November of 1547, Agricola could finally write to his friend Nils Bielke, saying that the printing of the New Testament was in the works in Stockholm. He reported that he had wound up having large debts due to the book's printing costs. In addition to this, he explained that Turku chaplain Mikael Stefani had been sent to help with the printing. There certainly was a need for a Finnish proofreader because the workers at the Stockholm royal printing house did not know Finnish.

Several researchers have speculated that Agricola's New Testament was released in two parts (N. Ikola 1966): the first part having the Gospels and the Acts of the Apostles and the latter comprising the other books of the New Testament. In fact, there are two title pages in the book, the first at the beginning of the book and the second before the Epistle to the Romans. This, however, does not prove anything, because various parts of one cohesive work, the Old and New Testaments of the Bible for example, have traditionally had their own title pages. There is no indication known that the first and latter parts of Agricola's New Testament would be separate volumes. Furthermore, the title page at the beginning of the whole book notes the year 1548, the same year that appears in the colophon. Perälä (2007) has affirmed that the New Testament printed in Swedish a few years after Agricola's New Testament has a second title page at the beginning of Romans, in exactly the same fashion.

Evidently, having an extra title page helped in drawing attention to a text considered particularly significant. Right in the introduction preceding Romans, Agricola explains the core notion of the Reformation according to Luther. According to this notion, a person will become righteous solely through faith and not by the works of the law. Immediately at the beginning, he states that the Epistle to the Romans is the clearest gospel and the true main section of the entire New Testament. He interprets what the Pauline Epistles mean by the words *law, sin, mercy, faith* and other key concepts and states that there is no point to reading the epistles if they cannot be understood.

Agricola's New Testament is a fine-looking tome, large and hefty and with plenty of illustrations. Agricola did not begin his New Testament with any poems as he did for *Abckiria* and *Rucouskiria*. Instead, it has two long, non-verse introductions at the beginning and between them is the table of contents listing all its books. Furthermore, each book in his New Testament has its own introduction, with the exception of the Book of Revelation. Instead, Revelation has a number of large images which depict horrifying beings and events of the apocalypse.

Of the two introductions at the beginning of his New Testament, the second is especially interesting because in it, Agricola gives information on the sources he used: *Se Wsi Testamenti* was translated "half from Greek books, half from Latin, German and Swedish books" (*politain Grecain/politain Latinan/Saxain ia Rotzin kirioista*). Researchers have later expounded on this description Agricola gives and have stated that there were in fact several key sources (Itkonen-Kaila 1997). These included the original Greek published by Erasmus of Rotterdam and his Latin translation, the traditional Vulgate of the Catholic Church, Luther's German translations and finally the Swedish translations of the New Testament and the whole Bible.

Using several exemplar texts alongside each other is understandable in many ways. A Finnish translator did not have any tools to help with Finnish and the text in the New Testament could not entirely be deciphered.

Comparing many other translations helped a translator better understand the text and see how the same idea could be expressed in different ways.

In the last part of his introduction, Agricola speaks of the conversion of the Finns to Christianity according to the Swedish chronicle of Olaus Petri. At the end of his preface, Agricola gives details on his own translation work and language choice. He states that there are various dialects spoken in the different regions in Finland, but he himself uses the language of "Finland" – that is, Finland Proper – because "the bishop's cathedra and the Episcopal see" are in Turku and the entire region is like the mother of the other regions. He finally states that literary Finnish might sound horrible and odd at first, but assures that it will get more attractive over time. Of course, any newly begun endeavour cannot be completely perfect!

Upon closer examination of Agricola's translation, it has turned out to be a real puzzle made up of many pieces (Schmeidler 1969). It is possible that there are excerpts translated from different sources even within the same sentence. The clearest influence is from German and Swedish. In many places, it is impossible to differentiate them from one other because the Swedish translation also followed the German model. The Latin and Greek model can especially be detected in sentence structures and word order that include the infinitive forms of verbs.

No one knows exactly how many copies of Agricola's New Testament were printed, but it is speculated that the number was around 500. This was enough for the approximately 125 churches in Finland at the time. There were also enough copies for the small number of schools, wealthy clergymen and other members of the upper class. The ordinary people did not yet need books because they were illiterate. In addition, there are more copies of *Se Wsi Testamenti* that have been preserved to this day than Agricola's other works. There are 59 copies of the book in public libraries in Finland, and in addition to this, there are some in private collections. The copy of *Se Wsi Testamenti* in the Skokloster Castle Library in Sweden is especially interesting: corrections were made in it by vicar Henrik Hoffman of Masku, a municipality 18 kilometres north of Turku in the 17th century (Rapola 1963). Hoffman was a member of the committee that prepared the first complete Finnish translation of the Bible and played his part by correcting Agricola's language. The first Finnish-language Bible was printed in Stockholm in 1642.

3.4 *Agricola's Agenda* / Käsikiria Castesta ia muista Christikunnan Menoista

Agricola's following work was his liturgical agenda *Käsikiria Castesta ia muista Christikunnan Menoista* ('Agenda on baptism and other Christian ceremonies'), often shortened to *Käsikiria* ('Agenda'; lit. 'handbook, manual', stemming from the Latin *manuale*). In addition to Agricola's prayer book and his New Testament, a liturgical agenda for ecclesiastical life was also required for carrying out ecclesiastical ceremonies. There were already some complete elements that were passed down from the Middle

Ages. Although Latin prevailed in the church at that time, the vernacular to some extent was also used. The literary tradition of the vernacular in Sweden was already quite a strong, thanks to the Birgittine Abbey of Vadstena for example, but there were still no signs of a Finnish literary culture in mediaeval Finland. Regardless, the fundamentals of Christianity, the most important prayers for example, had to be taught to the Finnish-speaking Finns in Finnish. Moreover, certain parts of ecclesiastical undertakings, such as issues involving baptism and wedding ceremonies, banns of marriage, impediment to marriage and confession, required the active participation of congregation members and, accordingly, the use of the vernacular. However, it was restricted to only a few parts of these ceremonies. Consequently, the change brought about by the Reformation was immense as there was a complete transformation and all the important ecclesiastical ceremonies were then held in the vernacular.

The first agenda written in the vernacular during the Reformation was the Swedish translation *Een Handbook, ther uthi Döpelsen och annat meer Christeliga förhandlas* by Wittenberg alumnus Olaus Petri, printed in 1529. Its later editions were printed in 1533, 1537, 1541 and 1548, and the book was simultaneously revised according to what was required each year.

The Lutheran liturgical reform was implemented both in Finland and the rest of Sweden during the 1530s. Translating an agenda into Finnish had begun by 1537, but neither a printed nor a manuscript of a Finnish-language version is known to have been completed this early. However, a few of the preserved later manuscripts have elements which show that they originated from the Swedish agendas of the 1530s (Pirinen 1962). There are sections in both the Codex Westh and the Uppsala Codex B 28 which have been removed from the Swedish agenda in 1541. Therefore, the Finnish translation of the texts had clearly begun on the basis of agendas published in the 1530s, albeit they were corrected and supplemented in the 1540s.

The foundation for Agricola's agenda was the 1548 revised Swedish agenda, but it did not completely follow it. Agricola had two chapters which were not in the Swedish agenda: chapter nine, which discusses comforting the ill and grieving, and chapter ten, which describes the life of Jesus. Chapter nine is based on Caspar Huberinus' devotional book *Vom Zorn und der Güte Gottes* (On the Wrath and Mercy of God), first printed in 1529. Agricola translated the whole section at the end of the book into Finnish which provides instructions on comforting the dying and their close relations and on the validation of faith.

Chapter ten is based on the book *Panarion* by Greek Church Father and Bishop Epiphanius of Salamis. *Panarion* provides instructions on proper faith and opposing heresy. The section chosen for Agricola's agenda, however, primarily discusses the life of Jesus in light of historical information. This chapter differs stylistically and linguistically from other parts of the book and also has a great number of noticeable typographical errors. It is possible that it was originally the work of some other translator than Agricola.

According to the table of contents, there should be a litany in Agricola's agenda but he included it in his missal which was also published in 1549. On the other hand, there was already a slightly shorter litany in his *Rucouskiria* which was practically the same as the one found in the Codex Westh. There was no litany in the Swedish agenda compiled by Olaus Petri, but it was added to Laurentius Petri's revised version in 1541. However, taking into account that the litany represented a long, mediaeval tradition beloved by the people, it is evident that, in practice, it was not forsaken between these two works. The content, however, had to be edited: for example, invocation of the Virgin Mary and to the saints had to be omitted. Instead, in keeping with local needs, objects could be added against which protection was especially needed.

Moreover, there are differences in other parts of *Käsikiria* in comparison to the Swedish agenda, even though the entire structure follows its exemplar. In regards to baptism, there is a translation of the preface from Martin Luther's baptismal liturgy *Taufbüchlein* (Baptismal Booklet) meant for godparents and parish members present. In keeping with Luther, Agricola gives advice on how a good priest must act and behave when baptising a baby. A drunken fool cannot be an acceptable baptiser other than in an extreme emergency, and those leading a poor life cannot be asked to be godparents.

The chapter concerning the affirmation of baptism was not included in Swedish agendas earlier than 1548, and thus it is not found in the agendas of both the Codex Westh and Uppsala Codex B 28. The presence of this chapter proves that Agricola had updated his agenda according to the latest source of the time.

Agricola lays the foundation for marriage with the translated preface from Luther's *Traubüchlein* (Marriage Booklet). Apparently, he independently compiled the code from different sources concerning engagement, impediment to marriage and living in matrimony (Knuutila 1988). This can be considered the first juridical document printed in Finnish. There is also a Swedish translation of the code which was reportedly used until the 17th century. The first secular body of laws written in Finnish, which includes the code of marriage, was King Christopher's Law of the Realm, translated by a Finnish clergyman known as Lord Martti. Its precise year of completion is unknown. It was earlier considered that it was completed during the same period as Agricola's works, but today, there is more of an inclination to date it to after 1570 when Lord Martti worked in Stockholm as court preacher to John III of Sweden.

The wedding ceremony begins at the church door. After an instructive speech, the priest ceremoniously asks the couple if they shall take each other as their wedded spouse and love each other for better or for worse. Each one answers in turn: I do. Following this is a prayer and a ring ceremony in which the groom places a ring first on the bride's index finger, then the middle finger and finally the ring finger where it remains. The ring was placed on this finger because it was believed that there was a vein that travelled straight to the heart from it (Knuutila 1990). The congregation is requested to witness and remember this important occasion. Following this is reading a gospel and then prayer. Only after this, the bride and the groom go to the altar to pray and receive the Eucharist. During the bridal Mass, the couple to be wed stands under an ornate wedding canopy made of fabric. After the Eucharist, the bride is taken to the marital bed singing the hymn

Veni creator spiritus. Finally, the priest blesses the nuptial home so that peace and love would prevail there and its residents may live a long and happy life.

After the marriage procedures, there is a short chapter which provides instructions on the churching of women. During Agricola's time, women were considered impure after giving birth. They could not do ordinary housework nor go to church before they were received by the Church in a special ceremony. When a woman came to the church door, the priest received her, recited a prayer, took her by the hand and led her inside.

The priest's official duties also included visiting the ill and comforting, encouraging and preparing them for death. Agricola's *Käsikiria* provides detailed instructions on how this must be carried out. It was important to know how to be prepared for death in the proper way. One had to confess his sins and be forgiven and, in addition, settle conflicts and other unresolved matters with other people. Before death, one had to receive the Eucharist as given by the priest, and after this, the ill could safely leave his life in Jesus' hands. The most terrible circumstance was if someone were to die unexpectedly. The following chapters in *Käsikiria* explain how a body is taken from the home and how it is buried.

The death penalty was practised in Sweden, and thus in Finland, during Agricola's time and it was reserved for the absolute worst crimes, blasphemy, infanticide or bestiality for example. Agricola's *Käsikiria* thus provides advice on how to prepare criminals for a beheading. One situation the agenda realistically takes into account is the possibility of a sentenced person actually innocent of a crime, which employs the death penalty, who will lose his life. A good priest can thus manage to turn this misfortune around by imploring that even Jesus Christ was, at the time, found guilty and died as an innocent man for all people.

The end of Agricola's agenda no longer follows the model of the Swedish agenda as the beginning of this section has already shown. It provides instructions on comforting the immediate family of the ill and the deceased and finally describes Jesus' life. As previously noted, the last chapter should be, according to the table of contents, a litany in the same way as in the Swedish agenda, but it was completely left out of *Käsikiria*.

3.5 Agricola's Missal / Messu eli Herran Echtolinen

Agricola's next work was his missal *Messu eli Herran Echtolinen* ('Mass or the Lord's Supper'), often shortened to *Messu* ('Mass'). The first Eucharist service held in the vernacular in Finland during the Reformation was in Swedish at Turku Cathedral in 1534, and organising Finnish-language Masses evidently began in 1537. A new edition of the Swedish-language missal was printed in 1537, and composing Finnish translations for the needs of the Finnish parishes most likely began from this. However, the oldest Finnish translations were only manuscripts. It was quite a wait until there was a missal in Finnish printed in 1549. Before that, the Swedish-language missal had already had the time to be revised to some extent. Nevertheless, Agricola had no desire to completely follow the Swedish missal. Instead, he also adopted some German elements which he became familiar with when he was studying in Wittenberg.

The steps in the Finnish Mass during the Reformation can be described by examining the structure of Agricola's missal. Before the beginning of the actual Divine Service, there is a preparatory part. The priest can then, as he wishes, give common penance, in other words state the public confession of the congregation and recite a prayer. After this, he makes a short Exhortation to the congregation to partake of the Holy Communion. The Exhortation model is mainly from Martin Luther's *Deutsche Messe*, or German Mass (Parvio 1978). After this comes the priest's Confiteor in Latin, that is, his confession and absolution as passed down from the Middle Ages, but in a shortened form under the spirit of the Reformation.

The Introit – the opening song – starts the Mass. According to Agricola's instructions, the Introit can be, for example, a psalm in Finnish taken from *Rucouskiria*. There are only a few Finnish songs known from Agricola's time that were composed as true Introits, but these were from the Codex Westh, not Agricola's works.

Certain liturgical songs have traditionally been permanent parts of the Mass (see Tuppurainen & Hannikainen 2010 for more details), starting with *Kyrie eleison* ("Lord, have mercy") and *Gloria* ("Glory to God in the highest") immediately following. After the salutation, there are short prayers read at the altar known as collects. During Agricola's time, it was possible to use either collects printed specifically for the Mass text or varying prayers according to the liturgical year. Agricola provides both possibilities and refers to his *Rucouskiria* regarding the varying prayers. His prayer book contains a previously published series of Finnish collects.

After the collects, it is time for the daily Epistle reading. According to Agricola, it also has two traditions which can be followed: there is either a whole chapter or half of the Pauline or one of the other Epistles under continuous reading (*lectio continua*) or a corresponding text is chosen according to the time in the liturgical year. After the Epistle comes the Gradual, which Agricola has as the Ten Commandments (the Decalogue) and, in addition, a psalm or some other song of thanksgiving. The placement of the Decalogue is from Olaus Petri's Mass (Parvio 1978). After the Gradual, the Gospel is read, and the same alternative principles as in the Epistle reading are followed in its selection.

The next part is the Sermon. Agricola only refers to delivering the Sermon but he has no actual Sermon text. Basically, there was no sermon text in Finnish preserved from the time of the Reformation. The first Finnish-language collection of sermons was the Ericus Erici (Sorolainen) Postil which was published in two hefty volumes in 1621 and 1625.

Even though Agricola's sermons were not preserved, there are notes on sermons and their delivery in his works. The Sermon had not become established as a central part of Divine Services during the beginning of the Reformation, but in many contexts, Agricola stressed its importance. Agricola is known to have purchased the Luther Postil in Latin in which he entered hundreds of comments and explanations (Heininen 1976). It was specifically in this postil that he wrote owner's details in 1531 where, for the first time, he used the byname *Agricola*. It is evident that the name was already being used before this but there is no information about it in any older written sources.

The *Credo* – the Creed or a statement of religious belief – was not a permanent part of Mass at the beginning of the Reformation, but it was in Finnish-language Masses from the start. Agricola's *Messu* provides the possibility to read either the Nicene Creed or the Apostles' Creed but only the latter was written in full in the missal. The text of the Nicene Creed had already been published at the end of *Rucouskiria*.

At the beginning of the actual Mass – the Service of the Sacrament – first come the *Salutation* and *Sursum Corda* ("Lift up your hearts") sung in rounds, and afterwards come two optional Prefaces which comprise the words beginning the Eucharist Prayer. The longer preface concerns instructions on the Elevation, raising the Eucharistic objects with regard to both bread and wine, and the shorter prayer only refers to the raising of the bread. For this whole part of the service, musical notations were printed in Agricola's missal, but according to the instructions, reciting the lyrics is possible as an alternative to singing.

After this comes the *Sanctus* ("Holy, Holy, Holy"). Then it is time for the Lord's Prayer and the *Agnus Dei* ("Lamb of God"). A new feature of the Reformation in Agricola's *Messu* was the one-verse rhyming hymn *O Puhdas Jumalan Caritza* ('O innocent lamb of God'). It is marked with repeat signs so that like the original German, it was sung three times. The hymn was composed in 1531 by Nicolaus Decius, one of the German pioneers of Lutheran liturgical song (Holma 2010). It was translated into Swedish by Olaus Petri in 1536. It found its way into the revised Swedish missal in 1548 (Parvio 1978), so it is understandable that it cannot be found in older Finnish-language missal manuscripts.

After the hymn, the priest gives an Exhortation and following this is the Distribution of the Eucharist. There is a woodcut between the longer and shorter prefaces in Agricola's *Messu* showing one congregation member kneeling in front of the altar receiving the sacramental bread and others waiting for their turn behind him. According to the new practice adapted during the Reformation, both bread and wine are distributed to the people, not just bread as the custom had previously been.

After the Eucharist, a salutation is sung and then a prayer of thanksgiving is recited together with the congregation. After the prayer comes another salutation and then the *Benedicamus Domino*. At the closing of Mass, the priest reads the priestly blessing or priestly benediction, an addition which is specifically a Lutheran feature (Parvio 1978).

After the actual text for Mass, Agricola's missal additionally has a collection of texts from the Bible. These texts are mostly divisions from selected chapters of the Book of Isaiah which are for reading on certain days to provide variety. There are 22 of them, and in selecting them, Agricola followed the mediaeval tradition of the Turku diocese and the exemplar provided by the *Missale Aboense* (Knuutila 1987; Heininen 2007). While translating biblical divisions, Agricola did not follow any one particular source text, but rather, in his own way, he used several sources from different languages simultaneously (Tarkiainen & Tarkiainen 1985).

There is also one litany right at the end of the missal. The same prayer is basically included in Agricola's *Rucouskiria* but clearly as a shorter version that corresponds quite closely to the litany found in the Codex Westh agenda. It has been shown that these two were based on a litany added to the 1541 Swedish agenda which is itself a rather faithful translation of Martin Luther's German litany (Nordberg 1963; Häkkinen 2012b).

Agricola's *Messu* shows no direct sign of a translator or anyone who completed the work. The title page only shows that the book was printed in Stockholm and the year as MDXLIX in Roman numerals. The place of printing and the year are also shown at the end of the book, this time as 1549 in Arabic numerals. Not even the name of the printer is shown. There is no reason, however, to doubt Agricola's part in the genesis of the missal. The same pictures and textual borders as in his other works were used as ornamentation in this book.

3.6 Agricola's Passion / Se meiden Herran Jesusen Christusen Pina

Se meiden Herran Jesusen Christusen Pina ('The Passion of our Lord Jesus Christ') was Agricola's following work, shortened as *Pina* ('Passion'). Today, the spelling of the word is *Piina*, but in Agricola's time, because of no literary standard, the *i* could have been either a long or a short vowel. Easter has traditionally been the most important period of celebration in the Christian liturgical year. The events of Easter have been followed and described day to day in church services and devotions. Going through the suffering and death of Jesus Christ in the Middle Ages involved responsory and sermons that lasted for hours. Furthermore, great Passion Plays were produced and processions were organised. During the Reformation, there was a desire to focus on essential points with only the power of words, and it became customary to present the history of the Passion in services by reading shorter divisions from the Gospels according to Matthew, Mark, Luke and John appropriate for the time. The events in the four gospels of the New Testament, however, had been recounted in a somewhat different manner from each other, and consequently their content had to be rearranged and put together in order to come up with the most perfect narrative possible.

The Passion as composed by Johannes Bugenhagen, vicar of Wittenberg, gained great popularity in the Lutheran Church. It was first published in Latin in 1524 and then in German in 1526. (Heininen 1979.) There were several editions printed and it was translated into Low German, Danish and Swedish. In the preface of his 1544 German Passion, Bugenhagen explains that he had begun a comprehensive introduction to the history of the Passion while he was working as a teacher at the monastic school of Belbuck Abbey, before coming to Wittenberg. Bugenhagen continued doing his editing work in Wittenberg and also lectured on the Passion at the university.

By examining the text of Agricola's *Pina* and specifically its titles and subheadings, Simo Heininen has shown that Agricola translated his Passion from the 1544 German edition of Bugenhagen's work. As usual, he did not follow his exemplar very closely and possibly used other editions of the same work, at least the Swedish translation. Agricola shortened the piece by omitting the preface and epilogue and also Isaiah 53 that followed it, as well as the story of the destruction of Jerusalem. Regardless, he presents all of the events of the history of Christ's suffering and death in exactly the same order as Bugenhagen's work. He also included a few additions which Bugenhagen composed for his original texts so they could be logically harmonised.

Agricola's *Pina* begins with a reference to Lazarus Saturday. The true Passion text begins with the events of Palm Sunday. Then, one day at a time, there is a progression to the depiction of Good Friday and Holy Saturday. There is one chapter dedicated to the depiction of Easter Sunday and the Resurrection. Then comes the telling of how Jesus appeared to his followers after Easter. The presentation of the history of the Passion ends with Pentecost but following it is additionally a short chapter written in the form of an intercessory prayer of Christ, but there was no model for this found in Bugenhagen's Passion (Tarkiainen & Tarkiainen 1985).

Since all the gospels had already been published in Finnish as parts of his New Testament, Agricola could have copied the translations of textual sections directly from it. This, however, is not what had happened. Instead, there were many changes and corrections in the text. Words and expressions were somewhat replaced by other ones. Moreover, there are changes in grammatical tenses which can be explained as the influence of various exemplary texts. After all, Agricola had many translations of different languages in front of him when he was translating the New Testament, and these translations did not exactly correspond to each other completely.

By its appearance, Agricola's Passion is a small and unassuming book, comprising 28 leaves. In addition to a few decorative initial capitals, there is only one small picture used for embellishment showing Christ resurrected and two Marys at the edge of an empty grave. The reverse side of the title page has a picture of Christ crucified, and the title page border has an illustration of Samson's fight with the lion. Perälä, who has also studied the illustrations in Agricola's works, has shown that in the ecclesiastical tradition, Samson has been interpreted to predict the coming of Christ and that even Luther followed this interpretation. We can therefore consider that there was a conscious decision to select the picture on the title page of Agricola's *Pina*, although at first glance, it may seem to be an unexpected image and have nothing to do with the subject matter.

3.7 Agricola's Psalter / Dauidin Psaltari

Agricola's *Dauidin Psaltari* ('David's Psalter'), often known simply as *Psaltari*, is his Book of Psalms or Psalter. The standard, contemporary form of the word is *psalttari* containing a geminated *t*. As with *Se Wsi Testamenti* (today

Uusi testamentti), the marking of consonant gemination had no standard in Agricola's Finnish, so one consonant actually could have phonetically been two. After his New Testament and liturgical books, Agricola started to translate the Old Testament. There were already a few excerpts from the Old Testament in *Rucouskiria*, including 40 psalms and 85 other prayers, and at the end of *Messu*, there were altogether around 30 pages of divisions selected from the Prophetic Books and Genesis. A majority of the Old Testament at that point in time, however, had not been translated into Finnish.

Of the great books of the Old Testament, Agricola was only able to get the Book of Psalms published in its entirety. The Finnish translation was released in 1551 and it included, in addition to their introductions, all 150 psalms of the Bible in numerical order. In addition to the psalms, Agricola had planned on having a selection of the Prophetic Books in *Psaltari*, following Bugenhagen's 1544 Psalter but as a slightly expanded version. (Heininen 2007.) For technical reasons, however, Agricola was not able to publish the whole book as one volume. Instead, it was divided into three different books: Agricola's *Psaltari* and *Weisut ia Ennustoxet* ('canticles and prophecies') were published in 1551 and a volume of the books of three Minor Prophets – Haggai, Zechariah and Malachi – was published in 1552.

The Finnish word *psalttari*, in Greek *psaltērion*, has two meanings: in addition to 'Psalter', a collection of psalms, it also means 'psaltery', a stringed instrument for the accompaniment of songs. The original name of the instrument in Hebrew – the true, original language of the psalms – is *nēvel*, but there is no exact information on the nature of the instrument itself. It has been speculated to be some kind of lyre or harp. (Montagu 2004.) Both the Finnish word *psalmi* and English *psalm* stem from the Greek word *psalmós*, which itself is a derivation of the Greek verb *psállein* 'to pluck'. It reached Finnish through Swedish and Latin, and the word reached English through Old French and Latin. Psalms originally had been songs that were performed with the accompaniment of a plucked string instrument.

It is no coincidence that Agricola started the systematic translation of the Old Testament with the psalms. Since *Psaltari* comprises rather short, poetic paragraphs, it worked excellently as both a songbook and a prayer book. The psalms were meticulously read in churches and monasteries in the Middle Ages as Latin translations, and they were read especially by choralists in smaller prayers. The aim was to go through the entire Book of Psalms within a week and then start again from the beginning. For this reason, the whole collection of psalms was divided into seven sections or Nocturns – night prayers. Two priests worked together to read them so that each one read one verse in turns. Three or nine psalms were read at once in one reading or *lectio*. Agricola explained this practice in his poetic preface of *Psaltari* and hoped that it would be preserved in the Lutheran Church.

The psalms have been quite popular devotional literature throughout time. They were translated into Finnish literally but in addition to that, adaptations fit to new poetic metres and devotional songs were composed on the basis of them. Moreover, psalms have been meticulously re-translated, edited, commented on and published during the Reformation. Agricola had an abundance of source literature and background information at his disposal when he himself began to publish a collection of psalms. Consequently, it truly is difficult to say exactly what exemplars he followed in the various decisions he employed.

Agricola evidently was not the only Finnish translator of psalms in his time. His younger contemporary and follower Paulus Juusten wrote in his renowned chronicle of bishops that the psalms had thoroughly been translated into Finnish at the cathedral school in Turku at his own hand, and he was clearly bitter that Agricola took credit for the Finnish translation by publishing it in his own name. Agricola did not, however, completely disregard his partners, because at the end of the preface poem in his Psalter, he speaks of the translators in the plural: *Muistas sis Rucollesas heite / iotca Tulkitzit Somexi Neite* ('Let not, as we pray, the memory diminish, of those who hast translate these into Finnish'). Agricola specified the place of translation as the city of Turku and the Saint Laurentius building which was his home. Furthermore, he notes that his son Christian was born at the same time as he was translating the psalms. It is, however, undisputed that there is linguistic heterogeneity in the psalms which can be interpreted to refer to the use of multiple sources for the translations. Since the psalms in their time were popular ecclesiastical literature for everyday use, they were undoubtedly translated, as necessary, by other clergymen than Agricola, at least until *Psaltari* appeared in print.

Agricola's *Psaltari* turned out to be a fine-looking work with a total of 238 pages. The Swedish Realm coat of arms was printed on the reverse side of the Psalter's title page as a sign of authoritative approval. In addition to the coat of arms, there are only 14 woodcuts. This was noticeably less than what is found in *Se Wsi Testamenti*, but there were respectively much more decorative initial capitals and ornamentation. Red ink was also used on the title page for effect.

There is a 10-page, non-verse preface at the beginning of *Psaltari* whose introduction is from Luther. After this comes a description on the life of David and then the background of the psalms. Then, Agricola explains the grouping and purpose of the psalms according to Luther as well as the characteristics of the psalms according to respected Church Fathers Saint Augustine and Saint Basil the Great.

Following the first preface comes a second preface in verse, in which Mikael Agricola Torsbius greets all the Finns at the beginning and briefly reviews his earlier literary works. After this, he praises the multifunctionality of the psalms, comments on the differences between his *Rucouskiria* and *Psaltari* and urges the use of both.

After this, Agricola switches to a completely different topic: the pagan religion of the ancient Finns and the many gods of the Häme people and the Karelians. There are many amongst the Häme gods that are also mentioned in the cantos of the 1835 Finnish national epic *Kalevala*. These include, for example, shaman and creator of songs Väinämöinen, weather god and smith Ilmarinen, forest deity Tapio and water deity Ahti. It is especially interesting that Agricola notes these deities specifically as Häme gods even though elements in the *Kalevala* have often been considered Karelian poetry. At the end of his preface poem, Agricola urges the Finns to abandon the old gods and only to bow to the Father, the Son and the Holy Spirit and to also pay tribute to the Finnish translators of sacred texts.

The noticeable difference in the way the psalms are presented in comparison to the German-language Luther Bible and the 1541 Swedish *Biblia* is that in *Psaltari*, Agricola includes a short summary in prose at the beginning of each psalm depicting their content (Heininen 1992). This is what he had partly done for the psalms in *Rucouskiria*, generally using the Latin summaries of German theologian, doctor and botanist Otto Brunfels. Moreover, Luther, who had lectured on the psalms in Wittenberg, published summaries on psalms, however not as a part of his Psalter but as a separate book. Agricola used these and their Latin translations when he composed new, more extensive summaries for his *Psaltari*. He used the Latin Psalters by Georg Major and Eobanus Hessus as his true main sources. Major was a preacher at All Saints' Church in Wittenberg and Luther's student, whereas Hessus was a humanist poet who wrote his Psalter in verse. Luther's student and assistant Veit Dietrich had composed summaries in prose in Hessus' Psalter for the needs of schoolchildren. For a few sections, Agricola also resorted to historian and Hebraist Sebastian Münster's edition of the Bible with explanations by which has the Hebrew text of the Old Testament and its Latin translation side by side.

In addition to the summaries, there are glosses in *Psaltari* which explain or comment on difficult sections. Many of these are direct translations from the source text, generally from the Luther Bible or the Swedish-language *Biblia* (Heininen 1994). In places, Agricola had independently expanded the explanations by adding, for example, synonymic or semantically close expressions to his text.

There are some linguistic differences between the psalms in *Rucouskiria* and *Psaltari* but it is difficult to say if they are improvements or just different solutions to the same translation problems. Many of the differences might stem from the fact that various works were used as source texts at the various stages of translation. Generally speaking, the Latin Vulgate model can be more strongly felt in the psalms of *Rucouskiria* than in *Psaltari* which owes more to Luther's German translations.

3.8 *Agricola's Collection of Canticles and Prophecies* / Weisut ia Ennustoxet Mosesen Laista ia Prophetista Wloshaetut

Agricola also translated a selection from the Prophetic Books of the Old Testament to supplement his psalms. He named this collection *Weisut ia Ennustoxet Mosesen Laista ia Prophetista Wloshaetut* ('Canticles and prophecies taken from the Law of Moses and the Prophets'), in short *Weisut* ('canticles'), because it included canticles (from the Latin *canticulum*, a diminutive of *canticum* 'song') and prophecies from the Old Testament. We can briefly state here that in standard contemporary Finnish, the word *veisu* refers to chants and furthermore *ennustus* generally refers to predictions and forecasts. The exemplar to *Weisut* was the Psalter by Bugenhagen who was Agricola's teacher in Wittenberg. Agricola's selection is, however, somewhat more extensive. He states in his short introductory poem that if the Finns cannot get the whole Bible translated, its core parts can at least be extracted in the same way "a bumblebee sucks the nectar from the flowers".

Translating the Prophetic Books was a more difficult task for Agricola than the New Testament because the original language of the Old Testament was Hebrew, which he evidently did not know very well. We do know that Erik Härkäpää, a student younger than Agricola and possibly his pupil, was sent to Wittenberg to study Hebrew in 1547 so that he could interpret the writings of the prophets upon his return home. Härkäpää returned to Finland in the beginning of the summer of 1551, so he was able to somewhat participate in fine-tuning the translation before *Weisut* was published in November that same year. Agricola most likely did a majority of his own translation using German, Latin and Swedish source texts. Nevertheless, we do know that he also used Münster's previously mentioned translation of the Old Testament which he had supplied with an abundance of explanations. (Heininen 2008.)

Agricola's *Weisut* includes parts of Genesis and Samuel and also the books of the Major Prophets Isaiah, Jeremiah, Ezekiel and Daniel. Agricola states in the subheading of the introduction of Isaiah that the best part was chosen for translation. All of the books of the Minor Prophets were completely translated, but the last three – Haggai, Zechariah and Malachi – were not included in *Weisut* due to the suspension of printing over the winter. Freezing temperatures and harsh weather impeded the traffic of ships in the maritime region between Finland and Sweden, and so contact between Turku and Stockholm was not possible.

With the exception of Jeremiah and Ezekiel, all the books have an introduction at their beginning, giving background information on the deeds and nature of the prophets and on their lives. The introduction of Isaiah is an exception because it has a geographical account of the area inhabited by the people of Judah. We know that Agricola was especially interested in geography, and his own library had a bound anthology of three different works comprising over one thousand pages. The information for Isaiah, however, was acquired from Luther. (Heininen 2007.)

There are a great number of glosses in *Weisut*, some of which are quite long. A few were written in Latin, as all the priests were expected to understand the language. The exemplar for the glosses was mainly the German-language Luther Bible, but Agricola additionally used other sources, such as Luther's commentaries on the Book of Isaiah and Münster's Bible. With using Münster, he also interpreted the metaphoric meaning of the original.

Agricola made attempts to explain unfamiliar or otherwise difficult to understand concepts to the Finnish people by using many alternative expressions, whereupon his notes are often longer than those he used as his exemplar. He sometimes also continues and expands his notes in other ways. As the Book of Isaiah speaks about punishments by God, Agricola's marginal notes describe the famine that prevailed over Finland in 1551 and he states that it was God's punishment on the people who defied the word of God and ridiculed His priests.

The title page of Agricola's *Weisut* has the same border as *Pina*: Samson fighting the lion with his bare hands. However, the border in *Weisut* was printed in red, as are some of the letters, whereupon it looks more impressive. The fine-looking general impression is also highlighted by large, decorative initials and variation in letter size.

3.9 *Agricola's Three Minor Prophets* / Ne Prophetat Haggai SacharJa Maleachi

Agicola's final printed work is *Ne Prophetat Haggai SacharJa Maleachi* ('The prophets Haggai, Zechariah and Malachi'). We can note here that in the same fashion as in *Se Wsi Testamenti*, but in the plural, Agricola used the pronoun *ne* 'they' as an article. As previously stated, Haggai, Zechariah and Malachi were supposed to be published in *Weisut* along with the other Prophetic Books of the Old Testament, but had to be omitted as printing was being prolonged and also winter was taking everyone by surprise. They were published the following year in 1552 as an independent book. In the beginning of its long introductory poem, Agricola himself explains that these three Minor Prophets could not be published due to the obstacles of winter.

At the end of the introduction of the Book of Zechariah, Agricola expresses the hope that not only would they be diligently read and be sung in praise of God, but that also sermons would be given on the Prophetic Books because all that had been written was done as teachings for people. However, he omitted the visions of Zechariah from his translation, as their meanings were confusing and controversial even for those who were deeply knowledgeable about the text. However, he states that he selected the clearest and most essential teachings, songs and adages.

At the end of the book, there are parts from the Pentateuch concerning law and application to law. There is a section selected from Exodus which explains the Tablets of Stone and the Ten Commandments. The sentence structure of the commandments in this new translation is slightly different from the structure in *Abckiria*. The commandments in the primer are presented in a simple form in accordance with a basic Finnish construction using the negative verb in the second-person singular imperative: *Ele tapa* ('do not kill'). However, in the new translation, an auxiliary verbal, necessive construction in the negative is used in accordance with the Germanic languages: *Ei sinun pidhe tappaman* ('thou shalt not kill').

Agricola chose a section from Leviticus that explains family relations and gives details on regulations and restrictions regarding them. These regulations and restrictions concern, for example, who got to get married to whom. Based on the same source, he also lists a large group of punishments which come as a result of illicit relationships. Then Agricola explains Deuteronomy and how those who observe the law will be rewarded and those who do not will be punished. Right at the end is the priestly blessing and certain other blessings.

Agricola's last Finnish-language book is only 80 pages long, including the cover, but its introductory poem is noticeably lengthy. Agricola greets both priests and the common people in the beginning and explains why the delay in printing had occurred. Then, in quite various ways, he depicts the spiritual gifts that God has bestowed upon people. He lists natural phenomena, crops, family members and riches of the earth. He describes the human senses and other characteristics of people and also the good and bad features of spiritual life. At the end, he states that even more parts of the Bible could be translated as long as they would be well-received. Evidently disappointed in the reluctance of the readers, he predicts that soon will come a time when there will be a desire to read even more books in Finnish, however then they will be difficult to acquire. That is why it was best to seize the opportunity now, when it was available.

4. Finnish in the Works of Mikael Agricola

During Mikael Agricola's lifetime, Finnish was still not in existence as one cohesive language. The majority of the Finnish population lived in the countryside and earned its living from agriculture, hunting and fishing. Many lived in the same place their whole life, never interacting with other parts of the population. No standard language common to everyone could be developed in these circumstances. Some individual and regional linguistic features were also preserved when language users left their home towns for cities to study or work.

The Finnish used in Agricola's works is an interesting mix of Finnish dialects and a tradition of an emerging literary language. Agricola himself explains in the preface of his New Testament that he mostly used the dialect of Finland Proper as a foundation for the literary language, but in practice, the language is quite heterogeneous and has many elements which are quite alien to the Finland Proper dialects. All of the texts published in Agricola's name are not from his own pen, but rather he selected materials for his works that were also translated by others.

This chapter describes the Finnish in Agricola's works from many angles. All the various levels of language – phonology, morphology, syntax and vocabulary – will be covered in their own sections. We will start right with orthography and phonetic length, because without a basic understanding of these features, reading Agricola's original texts can even be difficult for native speakers of Finnish. A comparison will be drawn between the subsystems of the language and the corresponding system of contemporary Finnish, and thus, the changes in the language that have happened after Agricola's time will be illustratively highlighted. In most cases, the reason for a change has been the changing of a dialectical base or conscious linguistic development, for example the avoidance of features of foreign origin or a reduction in variation.

4.1 Agricola's Alphabet and its Characters

During Agricola's time, no differentiation was made between a sound and a letter. Instead, there was the idea that characters as they were also represented the sounds. The alphabet listed in Agricola's primer is divided into vowels and consonants. Compared to the contemporary Finnish alphabet, Agricola's does not have the consonant *j* or the vowels *å*, *ä* and *ö*. The Swedish letter *å* was introduced in literary Swedish at the beginning of the 16th century and it was used quite rarely in Agricola's texts. However, it was used in Finnish words to designate the contemporary *o* or diphthong *uo*, such as *nåuse* (Std. *nousee* '(he/she) rises') and *koyråho* (Std. *koiruoho* 'absinthe, wormwood') in the calendar section of *Rucouskiria*. In contemporary Finnish, *å* is known as *ruotsalainen o* ('Swedish *o*') and it is only used in Swedish words, specifically in personal and place names.

In his listing of the alphabet, Agricola states that the vowels *ä*, *ö* and *y* (correspondingly *ä* [æ], *ö* [ø] and *y* [y] in contemporary Finnish) and the letter combination *ij* are "foreign". The latter combination most likely refers to the letter *ÿ*, which is the regular Finnish *y* with an umlaut (diaeresis, tremas). It was quite a common character for the vowel [y] in manuscripts of Agricola's time. However, the umlauts were usually omitted from Finnish-language printed texts. The phonemes corresponding to Agricola's "foreign" characters in Finnish have appeared in regular Finnish words since prehistoric times, and so from a linguistically Finnish point of view, they are not foreign. What Agricola evidently meant with this note is that *ä*, *ö* and *y* were foreign in terms of Latin working as a model for orthography.

The letters listed in his *Abckiria* (see Plate 3) do not even come close to all of the characters, character combinations and punctuation used by Agricola. We will discuss this in detail soon.

Agricola also lists a few diphthongs – a combination of two vowels in the same syllable – with instructions on their orthography and how to read them. A closer inspection of this part reveals that Agricola's instructions on pronunciation and reading does not pertain to Finnish but rather they are directly adapted from the exemplary texts used for *Abckiria*. For example, the instructions on how to read the diphthong *ae* as an *e* fit with a description of Latin articulation.

There are 13 different consonant phonemes that can be seen in words included in the old traditional vocabulary of contemporary Finnish: /d/, /h/, /j/, /k/, /l/, /m/, /n/, /ŋ/, /p/, /r/, /s/, /t̪/, /ʋ/. All of these phonemes basically share the same grapheme as in the contemporary Latin alphabet. For example /j/ is written as *j* (pronounced as the initial sound of the English *yes*). However, the labiodental approximant /ʋ/ is represented by the ordinary Latin grapheme *v* without a hook, and the voiceless dental stop /t̪/ is represented by the ordinary Latin *t*. The phoneme /ŋ/ is the one exception that has no graphemic representation. This phoneme only appears in the consonant cluster /ŋk/ (written as *nk*) or as a geminated consonant [ŋ:] (written as *ng*). However, in the more recent vocabulary of contemporary Finnish, and more often of foreign origin, the written characters *b*, *c* (as voiceless alveolar sibilant [s]), *f*, *g* (as voiced velar stop [g]), *q*, *w*, *x* (as consonant cluster [ks]) and *z* (as consonant cluster [ts]) can appear in addition to the aforementioned consonants. Agricola makes no distinction between the vocabulary of Finnish or foreign origin. Instead, he uses the same characters for consonants in all types of words. The characters *š* /ʃ/ and

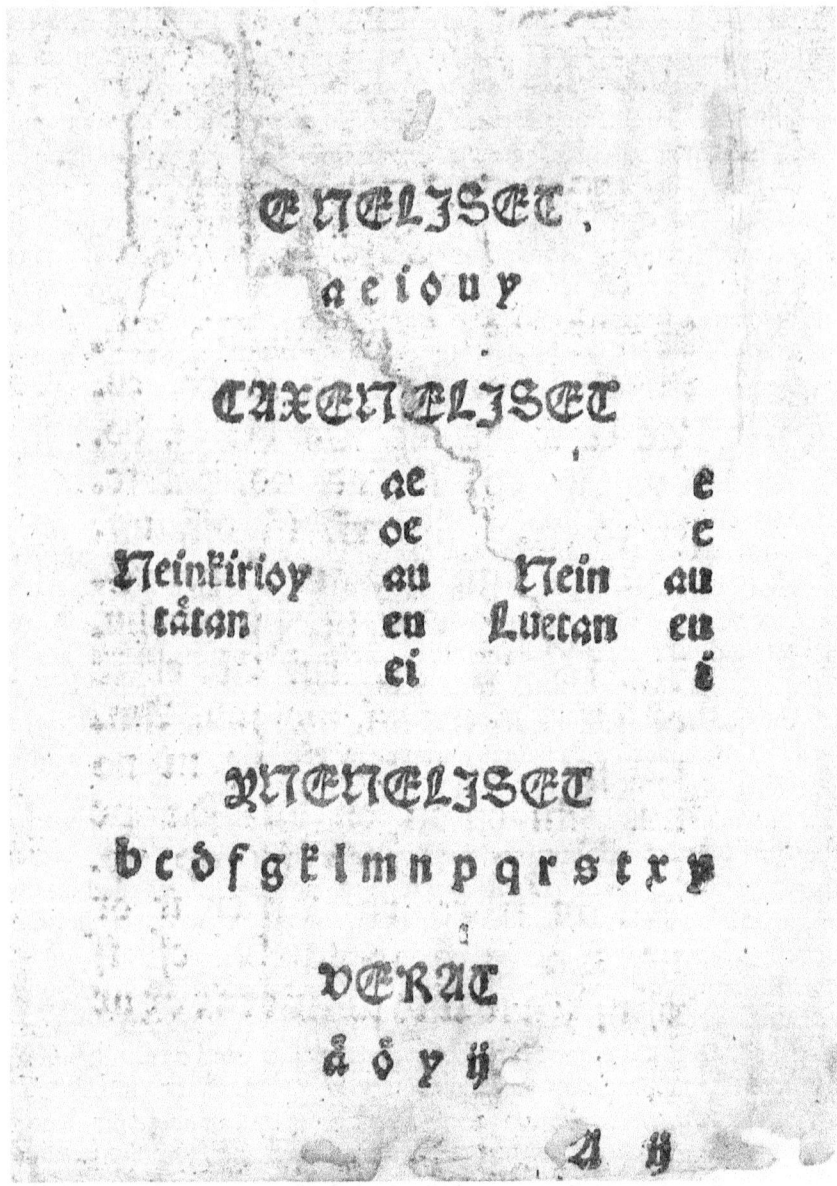

Plate 3: Agricola's alphabet: ENELJSET *(vowels)*, CAXENELJSET *(diphthongs)*, YNENELJSET *(consonants) and* VERAT *("foreign")*

ž /ʒ/, which are also used in some contemporary Finnish loanwords, do not appear in Agricola at all.

In addition to individual graphemes or characters, Agricola uses a few digraphs – set combinations of a pair of characters. These include the German ß for a double *s* or *sz*, a combination of *t* and *z*, which is probably primarily read as *ts* in Agricola's text, as well as the character ƍ (*Sanoi Jeſƍ henelle* 'Jesus said unto her' John 20:17, KJ21), that resembles the number nine in Agricola's text, which mostly replaces the sound combination *-us* or *-uus*.

A macron used to indicate nasality supplements the alphabet in running text. It is a line that is placed over a vowel normally preceding a nasal consonant character, and this macron replaces the nasal character. When coming across such a vowel, the reader should automatically be able to insert either an *m* or an *n* in terms of the context in which it is presented, for example *enēbi* → *enembi* (Std. *enempi* 'more'). The use of the macron was a generally known practice in Agricola's time, whereupon there was no need for separate explanation. Moreover, there was a great deal of use of other abbreviations in order to allow for more text in the lines of a book. For example, parts of known words or phrases could be omitted because all of the educated readers were able to fill in the textual gaps when reading it aloud.

In his introduction of the alphabet, Agricola separately lists upper and lowercase letters. The use of these letters in text somewhat differs from contemporary Finnish. Agricola uses uppercase letters at the beginning of sentences and proper names, like today, but he additionally uses them for highlighting important words or textual points whereupon a whole name, word or a part of it may have been fully written out in uppercase letters. These kinds of significant, highlighted names usually included *Herra* ('Lord'), *Jumala* ('God'), *Jeesus* ('Jesus') and *Kristus* ('Christ'). On the other hand, sometimes proper names have been written, for example in the calendar section of *Rucouskiria*, in lowercase letters or shortened because the names were easily recognisable.

There were no rules concerning compounding during Agricola's time. Instead, they were written out by gut feeling. Thus, there is no certain way to know on the basis of orthography, when Agricola meant for an expression to be a compound or when it was a collocation. Nevertheless, Agricola systematically wrote many expressions as compounds which are written separately according to the standards of contemporary Finnish. The most common examples include: *siihenasti* (Std. *siihen asti* 'until then'), *tähänasti* (Std. *tähän asti* 'until now'), *sentähden* (Std. *sen tähden* 'therefore'), *ennenkuin* (Std. *ennen kuin* 'before'), *niinkuin* (Std. *niin kuin* 'as if').

Hyphens were basically used to mark the splitting of words to a new line, in the same way as today. In practice, a hyphen could be omitted and the breakdown of syllables did not necessarily correspond to the syllabification rules characteristic to contemporary Finnish. In Agricola's time, it was important to compactly fill one page with text in a rectangular shape so that the lines would measure out to be the same, using any means possible.

In terms of punctuation marks, Agricola basically used full stops (periods) and question marks roughly in the same way as today. In practice, full stops sometimes were missing from many of such parts where they would be expected to be, and on the other hand, there could also be extra full stops. In place of commas, Agricola used slashes, but not according to the rules of comma usage of today. Instead they are used more for making the text and reading it aloud rhythmic. Commas in manuscripts of the same time were used in a similar fashion. Agricola used parentheses to distinguish additional comments and interjections from the rest of the text. Glosses (printed marginal notes) and endnotes were marked with letters or rebuses, but never by number with an index.

Contemporary Finnish has a so-called shallow orthography, in that the relationship between its orthography and articulation is relatively simple. There is a common saying that Finnish is written exactly how it is spoken. For the most part, Finnish words are pronounced the way in which they are spelt, and therefore no additional transcriptions would be required in this chapter, unless otherwise noted or to make a phonetic clarification. The articulation of consonants and to some extent the vowels has already been covered. Thus, for example, the word *köyhä* ('poor') would not need an additional phonetic transcription of [køyhæ]. Nevertheless, the shallow orthography feature for the most part means that one character logically corresponds to one specific sound, and that a conclusion can automatically be made on the correct pronunciation of practically all Finnish words on the basis of orthography. However, reaching this kind of system happened only after a lengthy development process. When Agricola began to write Finnish, he had to survey and adapt many different writing systems. He did not even attempt to achieve a system in which sounds and letters would logically and clearly correspond to one another. Thus, Agricola's texts cannot and must not be read as if the characters appearing in them would be read as they would today. We will later come back to the relationship between character and sound letter by letter.

During Agricola's time and even demonstratively much later until the 19th century, the same Finnish-language texts could be read in many different ways according to the reader's own dialectical background and Finnish language skills. Consequently, there was no one correct interpretation. Instead, the orthography in quite a few places provides the possibility to have many alternative interpretations. Furthermore, Agricola's varied spelling refers to the fact that no aims were made to write or pronounce the "same" word or form in the same text in the same way. Instead, variation was seen to be included as a natural phenomenon in both the written and the spoken language. For example, Agricola mostly wrote the Finnish word for 'world' as *mailma* with a short vowel in the first syllable, but the word with a long vowel *maailma* can be found in the earlier works. Although the latter is its standard, contemporary form, both forms can nowadays be found in Finnish. Likewise, many suffixal elements have different alternatives which can also be found as such in Finnish dialects. We will come back to these features in the section on inflectional morphology.

4.2 *Phonetic Length*

Since prehistoric times, the length of phonemes has been a phonologically relevant feature in Finnish. Apart from a few individual exceptions, both vowels and consonants can be long or short, and the difference in length determines the difference in meaning. For example, three different nouns – as lemmas or in their dictionary form – which have nothing to do with each other are: *tuli* ([t̪uli] 'fire'), *tuuli* ([t̪uːli] 'wind') and *tulli* ([t̪ulːi] 'customs').

The difference between long and short sounds in contemporary Finnish is conveyed by systematically writing short phonemes with one letter and long ones with two. During Agricola's time, this rule still did not exist and he could have used one character to represent both a long and short sound. It was rarer, but nonetheless possible, that a short sound was represented by two characters.

It was especially common both in Agricola and in other old literary Finnish works that the vowels further away from the first syllable were marked by one character regardless if in reality they were pronounced long or short. Agricola also did not always write the same word or word form in the same way, and variation, which seems to be inconsistent, can even be within the same sentence.

Since there are variants based on dialects in Agricola, in addition to orthographic variation, it is subsequently impossible to clearly know how writing and speaking corresponded to one other in terms of phonetic length. Nevertheless, the contemporary reader must remember that with his spelling, Agricola did not aim at those forms that are used in contemporary Finnish. For example, the first- and second-person plural verbal endings and their corresponding possessive suffixes also have many variants today in relation to both consonant length and vowel quality. The first-person plural form of the verb *tahtoa* ('to want') in standard, contemporary Finnish is (*me*) *tahdomme* ('we want', the personal pronoun *me* 'we' is optional), and in Agricola, it can be *tahdomma, tahdoma, tahdomme, tahdome, tahdom* or *tahdon*, but we cannot say for certain if the form *tahdome* is pronounced *tahdome* or *tahdomme*. There is still an additional problem in words with front vowels because an *e* could be read as both [e̜] and [æ]. As Agricola thus writes *meneme* (Std. *menemme* 'we go') for the verb *mennä* ('to go'), it can be read as *meneme, menemme, menemä* or *menemmä*. For these reasons, it is often impossible to determine which dialect the form Agricola used represents.

Similar variation can be seen in many other inflectional and derivation suffixes as well as in established inflectional forms. From a contemporary point of view, many words written by Agricola seem to have a typographical error. There is indeed a great deal of them in his words, but in assessing them, we must always also remember the variation in orthography and dialects. Forms that seem to have a typographical error include, for example, *armolinen, lähemäinen, kansa* (cf. *kansa* 'people'), *kiini* and *pääle*, and in contemporary standard Finnish they are *armollinen* ('merciful'), *lähimmäinen* ('neighbour, fellow human being'), *kanssa* ('with'), *kiinni* ('closed') and *päälle* ('onto'). However, these forms can truly be found in dialects and can clearly depict the true articulation of Agricola's time.

The inadequate marking of length may also cause difficulties in morphological and syntactic interpretation. Since the length of long vowels is often not indicated in a non-initial syllable, long vowels stemming from the combination of a root vowel and a suffix vowel was written with one letter. For example, *kala* ('fish') with the partitive suffix *-a* is written as *kalaa* ('fish+PART') in contemporary Finnish, but the partitive in Agricola usually looks like the nominative: *kala*. Furthermore, forms can be seen in Agricola's language in which the ending has assimilated with the final vowel in the stem. For example, the word *ruoho* ('grass') with its partitive ending is logically *ruohoa* ('grass+PART') in standard contemporary Finnish, but the ending can be assimilated in Agricola as in contemporary colloquial Finnish (*ruohoo*), and Agricola usually wrote it in a form with a short vowel *ruoho*. In these cases, the reader himself must decide on the correct form and interpretation on the basis of the translation's source text or its textual context.

4.3. Individual Characters by Phonetic Class

4.3.1 STOPS

The stops (plosives) [k], [p] and [t̪] found in words of Finnic origin appear as the characters *k*, *p* and *t* in Agricola's language the same way as in contemporary Finnish. The character for [k], however, preceding a back vowel (*a*, *o*, *u*) in Agricola is often a *c* (*cala* Std. *kala* 'fish', *cuningas* Std. *kuningas* 'king'), and before a front vowel (*e*, *i*, *y*, *ä*, *ö*) it can be a *k* (*kesä* 'summer') or sometimes more rarely the character combination *ki* (**ki**euhe Std. *köyhä* 'poor') or *ch* (*Perchele* Std. *Perkele* 'Devil'). It is important to note that it is impossible for a *c* to precede a front vowel as a character for [k] with the exception of rare loanwords in which it does not represent the velar stop but rather [s] or [ts] (e.g. *ceremonia* Std. *seremonia* 'ceremony', *palaci* Std. *palatsi* 'palace'). Mistakes are often made on precisely this feature when attempts are made to emulate Agricola's orthographic approach.

Notating the *ks* cluster and *ku* grouping has its own conventions. The character for the former is consistently written as *x* (*caxi* Std. *kaksi* 'two'). The character for the latter is often *qu*, especially **qu**in (Std. *kuin* 'as, like') for example. The word *quin* is quite common in the texts because it appears both in the function corresponding to the standard contemporary Finnish conjunctions *kun* ('as, when') and *kuin* ('as, like, than') and as a non-inflected initial word in a relative clause.

The characters for [t̪] and [p] are much simpler than those for [k]. The alternative graphemes for the voiceless dental stop can sometimes be *t*, *dt* or *tt*. Furthermore, *d* or *dh* can sometimes represent [t̪], especially at the end of a word (*annoid* Std. *annoit* 'you (sg.) gave', *muudh* Std. *muut* 'others'). Besides *p*, [p] had no graphemic alternatives other than the one seen in voiced consonant clusters which we will discuss shortly.

The characters *b*, *d* and *g* for voiced stops [b], [d] and [g] are ambiguous. Especially in non-Finnish names and words, these voiced stop consonants can be used in the same way as in contemporary literary Finnish (*Barbara*, *Daniel*, *galateri* 'Galatian'). Non-Finnish forms in Agricola can be seen in loanwords which later have fully been incorporated into the phonetic structure of Finnish. For example, the word *domari* (Std. *tuomari* 'judge') was used by Agricola quite consistently after the model of the Swedish word *domare*, using a *d* for the initial letter, even though the word begins with a voiceless stop in contemporary Finnish.

Voiceless stops in voiced surroundings within a word are regularly written with voiced stop characters, also in ordinary Finnish words. For example, Agricola's words *ramba*, *culda* and *hengi* have the same meaning as the contemporary Finnish words *rampa* ('lame, cripple'), *kulta* ('gold') and *henki* ('spirit'). Agricola evidently chose this spelling because readers who were accustomed to the Swedish orthographic system would have read consonants written with voiceless stop characters as geminates. Thus, the aforementioned contemporary Finnish words might have been read as *ramppa, *kultta and *henkki.

Word-medial voiceless stops [k], [p] and [t̪] during Agricola's time were consonants subject to consonant gradation as they are in contemporary Finnish. In practice, this means that in accordance with specific rules, stops will be replaced with weaker consonants. The most common gradations can be seen in contemporary Finnish in that the *k* either disappears or becomes *j* or *v* (*sika* : *sian* 'pig+GEN', *kylki* : *kyljen* 'rib+GEN', *suku* : *suvun* 'family+GEN'), *p* becomes *v* (*tupa* : *tuvan* 'cabin+GEN') and *t* becomes *d* (*sata* : *sadan* 'hundred+GEN'). The gradation of *t* may seem the same in Agricola (*sata* : *sadan* or *sadhan*), but in practice, the weak grade *d* or *dh* is not articulated as a stop but rather as a fricative in the same place of articulation, comparable to the initial sound in the English *this*. Correspondingly, the weak grade of Agricola's *k* can be a velar fricative written with the characters *g* or *gh* (*suku* : *sugun* or *sughun* [suɣun]). Fricatives will be discussed in more detail in the following section.

Agricola often followed a model of the donor language in loanwords and used graphemic approaches which do not appear in Finnish words. For example, the *ph* digraph represents [f] quite consistently in the word *propheta* (Std. *profeetta* 'prophet'). Agricola could write the Swedish loanword word *ryöväri* ('robber') in accordance with Swedish chancery language *röffueri*, although the more Fennicised *röueri* is more common.

4.3.2 Fricatives Not Known in Contemporary Finnish

During Agricola's time, there were two voiced fricatives that no longer exist in contemporary Finnish: the voiced dental fricative [ð] and the voiced velar fricative [ɣ]. In traditional Finnish-language phonetic transcription, the alternate term *spirant* is used for *fricative*, and the Uralic Phonetic Alphabet (UPA) – also known as the Finno-Ugric transcription system – is conventionally used, employing the Greek characters δ and γ in transcribing these sounds. In Agricola's language, the fricatives are most commonly represented by *d*, *dh* and *hd* for [ð] and *g*, *gh*, *gi* and *ghi* for [ɣ]. The [ð] is found in the week grade of *t*, for example *pitää* : *pidhen* ([piðæn] Std. *pidän* 'I keep, I hold, I consider'; the verb *pitää* has various meanings and functions, but we shall mainly discuss its use as an auxiliary verb in this chapter). Correspondingly, the [ɣ] could be seen as a weak grade of *k*, for example *vika* : *vighan* ([ʋiɣɑn] Std. *vian* 'flaw+GEN'), although this was not used as commonly and as consistently as the voiced dental fricative.

In Agricola's time, there was already a great deal of variation used in articulating the weak grade of *k* appearing in words that were written with the characters *g, gh, gi* or *ghi*. These variations (Ø, [j], [ʋ] or [ɣ]) could also be seen in Agricola's texts (e.g. *vika* : *vighan*, *vijan* or *vian* 'flaw+GEN' Std. *vian*; *suku* : *suvun*, *sughun* or *su'un* 'family+GEN' Std. *suvun*). In terms of phonetic history, all of these articulation variants of the weak grade of *k* developed from the voiced velar fricative.

Although *g* is seen in Agricola as both a character for a fricative and a voiced stop, there is no danger of getting them confused because [g] can clearly be seen only in words of foreign origin and in such positions of word in which there is no consonant gradation, such as word-initial positions. Furthermore, *g* appears in words of Finnish origin in the weak grade of the *nk* cluster, for example *hengen* [heŋ:en] ('spirit+GEN'), but as the situation today is exactly the same, the contemporary Finnish reader will automatically interpret the spelling correctly. The weak grade of *k* in this cluster was not thus a fricative during Agricola's time. For phonetic reasons, it is generally considered improbable that there would ever have been any consonant cluster consisting of a nasal and fricative [ð] or [ɣ]. Instead, the stop in consonant gradation would have been weakened in another way, partly by voicing and finally by assimilating with the nasal (e.g. [mp] → [mb] → [m:]; [nt] → [nd] → [n:]). Completely dismissing consonant gradation is common in dialects, whereupon the [k] does not weaken at all, for example *henki* [heŋki] : *henken* [heŋken] ('spirit+GEN'). It can very well be that the *nk* cluster, for the most part, was realised the same way in Agricola's time as well.

In addition to the aforementioned voiced fricatives, the voiceless dental non-sibilant fricative [θ] had existed during Agricola's time, at least in certain western dialects. This sound can be compared to the initial sound in the English *think*. According to certain researchers, Agricola's spelling of *tz* in the words *itze* (Std. *itse* 'self'), *himoitzepi* (Std. *himoitsee* '(he/she) desires') and *cutzui* (Std. *kutsui* '(he/she) invited, called') for example, may specifically indicate this fricative articulation. Interpreting Agricola's *tz* however is controversial, and no one truly knows how this fricative articulation was known in its time in such a large area. In the early 20th century, it could only be documented from certain Ala-Satakunta dialects (these dialectical differences were surveyed by Lauri Kettunen in his 1940 dialect atlas, maps 8 to 10). As Agricola's *tz* can, in some cases, clearly be interpreted as a *ts* cluster, this can be considered the primary interpretation in a broader sense as well.

4.3.3 SEMIVOWELS *J* AND *V*

The Finnish vowel-like consonants *j* and *v* are articulated in a rather weak manner. These consonants are the palatal approximant [j] and labiodental approximant [ʋ], and they can be best identified as consonants by virtue of their conditions of occurrence. In many ways, this is also reflected in Agricola's orthographic approach. Both *i* and *j* can appear as a characters for both [i] and [j] and accordingly, *u*, *v* and *w* can appear as a characters for both [u] and [ʋ]. The interpretation as a vowel or consonant can be found on the basis of syllabic position: the beginning of a syllable can have a *j* or a *v*, the middle or end of a syllable can have an *i* or a *u*.

Especially when there are closed vowels (*i*, *y*, *u*) on a syllabic boundary, it is in practice difficult to judge, on the basis of sheer auditory perception, whether [j] or [ʋ] is articulated there or not (*sia* or *sija* Std. *sija* '(grammatical) case', *lauantai* or *lauvantai* Std. *lauantai* 'Saturday'). Moreover, there are differences between dialects in this relation. As Agricola uses a consonant for this type of syllabic boundary (e.g. *kauvan* Std. *kauan* 'long', *ijankaikkinen* Std. *iankaikkinen* 'eternal, everlasting'), there is every reason to presume or to consider it at least plausible that the character is based on actual articulation, regardless of the standpoint of contemporary literary Finnish.

On the other hand, if a consonant is missing from the place where it should be according to contemporary norms of correct grammar, Agricola's form cannot be considered an error in terms of contemporary usage. For example, there was a scholarly decision made in the 19th century to always mark the *j* in the agentive suffix *-ja* or *-jä*, but this decision was made only hundreds of years after Agricola. Before this, the *j* could have well been missing from the syllabic boundary (*haltia* Std. *haltija* 'occupant', *palvelia* Std. *palvelija* 'servant', *tekiä* Std. *tekijä* 'doer, writer, factor').

4.3.4 OTHER CONSONANTS

The character *c*, which was previously discussed as a character for [k], is qualitatively ambiguous out of all the consonantal graphemes used by Agricola. It can represent [k] both in itself and as a part of many different consonant strings. In practice, in can also represent [h] or one of its allophones (*tacto* Std *tahtoo* '(he/she) wants'), and it can furthermore also stand for [s] in loanwords (*ceremonia* Std. *seremonia* 'ceremony').

The consonantal graphemes *l*, *m*, *n*, *r*, *x* and *z* ([ts]) are easy to interpret. The *z* may indeed also represent the voiceless dental fricative [θ] in *tz* clusters and furthermore it can be the character for [s] in non-Finnish words and proper nouns articulated as in Swedish (*Zebedeus* 'Zebedee'). It is also easy to identify [f] (dial. *fati* Std. *vati* 'dish, bowl') which may have been represented by the previously mentioned alternative digraph *ph* or *ffu* of Swedish chancery language (*röffueri* Std. *ryöväri* 'robber'). In terms of interpretation, the different characters for [s] are also easily distinguishable: the short *s* and the long *s ʃ* as well as the German Eszett *ß*. Due to its appearance, the long *s* can certainly be confused with the letter *f*.

Of all the consonant sounds, [h] (including its allophones [x], [ç] and [ɦ]) was proven to be quite difficult for Agricola to write. Sometimes it was omitted completely (*tadon* Std. *tahdon* 'I want'), but in addition to *h*, its graphemes could also be *c* (*tacto* Std. *tahtoo* '(he/she) wants'), *ch* (*tachdon* Std. *tahdon* 'I want'), *hc* (*tehcti* Std. *tähti* 'star') or *ck* (*tecktemen* Std. *tehtämän* third passive infinitive of the verb *tehdä* 'to do' in the instructive case). On the other hand, the letter *h* was used with voiced stop graphemes as an additional character to signify fricative articulation (*sydhen* [syðæn] Std. *sydän* 'heart'), and sometimes it bore no meaning whatsoever with a stop (*muudh* Std. *muut* 'others', *näeth* Std. *näet* 'you (sg.) see').

4.3.5 VOWEL QUALITY

When we take into account the fact that the marking of length was inadequate (as noted in 4.2), in practice, only *a* is relatively easy to interpret as a vowel grapheme. Other characters have more than one qualitative interpretation, and sometimes even an *a* may be a character for [æ] (today the grapheme

85

ä). For example, because of the vowel harmony prevalent in Finnish, we are compelled to consider that the *a* in the word *pesteistimma*, an inflectional form of the verb *päästää* ('to release, to rid, to let go'), is actually a character for the contemporary grapheme *ä* and would today be read as *päästäisimmä* (Std. *päästäisimme* 'we would let go').

Agricola's *i* can represent the vowels [i] and [y] (*ei* 'no', *syndime* Std. *syntymä* 'birth'), the character *o* can represent [ǫ], [u], [ø] or the diphthong [uǫ] (*on* 'is', *cuckola* Std. *kukkula* 'hillock', *pydon* Std. *pyydön* 'request+GEN', *nori* Std. *nuori* 'young'), *y* can represent [y] and [i] (*lyhyt* 'short', *oykein* Std. *oikein* 'correct'), *ä* can represent [æ] or [ę] (*äiti* 'mother', *käse* Std. *kesä* 'summer') and *ö* can represent [ø] or the diphthong [yø] (*söi* '(he/she) ate', *mös* Std. *myös* 'also'). Sometimes the cluster *ij* appears in Agricola as a character for [y] in the same manner as in manuscripts of that time.

The character *e* proves to be especially problematic in the interpretation of Agricola's vowels, which most often is a grapheme for either [ę] or [æ] and sometimes also [ø] or the diphthong [ię]. The fact that [ę] and [æ] are common adds to the number of problems, also in endings. It is most often possible to make an interpretation on the basis of contextual occurrence, but in some cases, it is impossible to conclusively decide what the option is, as there can be more than one logical interpretation. This is when we must resort to probabilities. For example, the stem of the negative verb in the imperative, written by Agricola as *el-* ('do not'), could be read as a Savo [ę]as in *el(e)kää* ('NEG.IMP+2PL'), but as Agricola's Finnish is mostly based on western dialects, the more probable alternative has traditionally been considered to be [æ] as in *älkää*.

The clarification between [ę] and [ø] can sometimes be hard to determine. The Finnish [ø], which today is represented by the grapheme *ö*, in many cases had developed from the vowel [ę], and the word *neure*, for example, can with good reason be read as either *neyrä* or *nöyrä* ('humble'). Nevertheless, *e* is one of the characters for [ø] in Agricola, even though the letter *ö* was also being used.

The Finnish opening diphthongs [ię], [uǫ] and [yø] had historically developed from the long vowels [ę:], [ǫ:] and [ø:]. For the latter two in particular, Agricola's graphemes often seem to refer to a long vowel, not yet a diphthong: *Somen* (Std. *suomen* 'Finnish+GEN'), *mös* (Std. *myös* 'also'). However, there is a tendency to assume that the graphemic approach indicates a diphthong because [ię] can be found in abundance (e.g. *riemu* 'joy' and *rieska*, a type of Finnish flatbread), which proves that the diphthong change already happened before Agricola's time.

The Swedish model clearly steered Agricola to use the letter *o* as one of the characters for [u]. It must, however, furthermore be noted that the derivational suffixes *-os* and *-us* in Agricola's Finnish may appear at the end of the same stem as complete synonyms (*toimitos* ~ *toimitus* 'delivery' from the verb *toimittaa* 'to deliver'). This may not be a question of orthographic variation but rather two truly alternative derivational suffixes concerning Finnish dialectical differences.

4.3.6 Phonetic Phenomenon and Inflectional Forms

For the most part, Agricola's language is both structurally and lexically similar to contemporary Finnish or it at least, in practice, equates rather easily to it. Sometimes, it is indeed more reminiscent of colloquial Finnish than normalised literary Finnish. When the text is read aloud or written as it should be read, explanations or other facts to corroborate this are only occasionally required. For this reason, it is good to consider contemporary Finnish as a reference point and single out those points in which the phonetic and morphological structure in Agricola clearly differs from today. A few differences concern several morphological groups. Of these, the loss of a word's final vowel or apocope and the assimilation changes of a word's final vowel are especially common.

From the beginning, one of the most distinguishing features of the phonetic structure of old literary Finnish has been **apocope** or the loss of a word's final vowel. This feature has strong roots in both of those dialectical groups which primarily come up as models of 16th century literary Finnish, particularly in the Turku regional and southeastern dialects (for more on apocope, see Nikkilä 1994). Apocope can most commonly be found in the southwestern dialects where the loss of a vowel depends on the word's structure, and it can be any vowel.

Apocope in old literary Finnish did not concern all vowels in the same way, nor was there a vowel loss at the end of all types of word forms in the same way. Apocope could have happened in terms of both phonetic and morphological rules, and furthermore it can be a word-specific phenomenon. The most often vocalic loss concerned [i], [æ] or [ɑ] and the loss was focused on fairly specific morphological categories. These with their main features have been put forth by Osmo Nikkilä (1988).

In the basic form of nominals, the nominative (*lacki* Std. *laki* 'law', *mercki* Std. *merkki* 'sign, mark'), apocope only appears irregularly, and it is also a rare occurrence in the translative (*ainoaxi Iumalaxi* Std. *ainoaksi Jumalaksi* 'only+TRANSL God+TRANSL'). However, apocope is common in possessive suffixes – an old special Finno-Ugric feature – for example *kätens* (Std. *hänen/heidän kätensä* 'his/her/their hand') and *poicans* (Std. *hänen/heidän poikansa* 'his/her/their son'). The vocalic loss of the second-person singular possessive suffix, -*si* in contemporary literary Finnish, was quite a regular occurrence (e.g. *kätes* Std. *kätesi* 'your (sg.) hand' and *poicas* Std. *poikasi* 'your (sg.) son'). However, both apocope and final vowel variants can be found in the first-person singular possessive suffix -*ni* (*minun käten* or *käteni* Std. (*minun*) *käteni* 'my hand', the personal pronoun *minun* 'my, mine' is optional in these possessive constructions and is usually added to stress who the possessor is in the phrase, although Agricola's use of the pronoun was often a translation loan).

It is impossible to provide clear rules on apocope specific to phonology or morphology because there are differences between Agricola's various works, and vocalic loss can also depend on the function of the form. For example, apocope can often be found in the essive case when it behaves as a temporal or locational adverbial (*sine peiuen* Std. *sinä päivänä* 'on the/that day', *tacan* Std. *takana* 'behind'). Apocope occurs in the abessive case, which signifies the absence of something, when affixed to the third infinitive – the so-called MA infinitive – formed from a verbal stem (*lackamat* Std. *lakkaamatta* 'without stopping').

Because of apocope and the word-final phonetic changes due to it, there was a merging of many suffixes in terms of their phonetic form. The effects of these changes can be seen as variation in the following sections, which discuss inflectional categories and the suffixes characteristic to them in more detail. For example, the first- and second-person personal plural endings and possessive suffixes may have become truncated to look like their singular counterparts (*isämme* 'our father' → *isäm* → *isän* "my father", *tulette* 'you (pl.) come' → *tulet* "you (sg.) come"). In practice, the fact that it is impossible to differentiate nominatives with a personal ending from those in the genitive (marked with *-n*) is an additional problem concerning the first person. For example, *Herran* in the phrase *meidän Herran tähden* ('for the sake of our Lord') can be interpreted in two ways: *meidän Herran tähden* (*Herran* 'Lord+GEN') or *meidän Herramme tähden* (*Herramme* 'Lord+Ø+1PL.PX', where Ø indicates an unmarked genitive). The noun in most postpositional phrases must always be in the genitive (e.g. *Herran tähden* 'Lord+GEN sake': 'for the Lord's sake'), but if the noun is in a state of possession (e.g. *Herramme* 'our Lord'), it should be inflected with a possessive suffix. However, a noun affixed with a possessive suffix has an unmarked genitive in a prepositional phrase (e.g. *Herramme tähden* 'for the sake of our Lord'). The latter interpretation thus would be the grammatically correct construction of the phrase.

In addition to the fact that [i] is the most common vowel that undergoes apocopic change, there could have been a vocalic loss in other places as well. As in many contemporary Finnish dialects, Agricola often had loss of the final [i] of a diphthong in the second syllable, whether the diphthong was within the word or at the end. For example, the past tense, which comprises the marker *i*, often appears as being in the present tense because of this phenomenon (e.g. *sano* Std. *sanoi* '(he/she) said', *seisotta* Std. *seisoitte* 'you (pl.) stood', *valvo* Std. *valvoi* '(he/she) oversaw'). In interpreting the form, one must resort to the source text or later translations of the same section of the text.

A common feature in Finnish dialects and contemporary colloquial Finnish is **assimilation**. Agricola's language proves that this phenomenon happened hundreds of years ago. The vowel combinations [ea], [eæ], [ia], [iæ], [ɔa], [ua] and [yæ] in particular often changed to [eː], [ɔː] and [ɔː] (*sappea* 'spleen+PART' → *sappee*, *häpeä* 'shame' → *häpee*, *poikia* 'son+PL+PART' → *poikii*, *lehtiä* 'leaf+PL+PART' → *lehtii*, *sanoa* 'to say' → *sanoo*, *apua* 'help+PART' → *apuu*, *käskyä* 'to command' → *käskyy*). The change also concerns many morphological categories. As Agricola does not often indicate vowel length in the second syllable, a conclusion on actual articulation and meaning must be made on the basis of sentential context. For example, the word *sano* could be the imperative *sano!* ('say (it)!') or the statement *sanoo* ('(he/she) says'). On the other hand, there has been an occurrence of **dissimilation** in the same vowel combinations in other dialects (*hopea* 'silver' → *hopia*, *kipeä* 'ill, painful' → *kipiä*) in which the sounds are clearly distinguishable. All of these alternatives can be found in Agricola's Finnish, for example *valkea, valkia* or *valkee* all correspond to the contemporary standard Finnish form *valkea* ('white').

All Finnish words that can be inflected – both nominals and verbs – have at least a **vowel-final inflectional stem** or a so-called vowel stem to which the necessary endings are affixed. The vowel stem on nominals are often the same as the nominative singular but not always (*kala* : *kala-* : *kala-n* 'fish+GEN', *mies* : *miehe-* : *miehe-n* 'man+GEN'). In addition, some words have a **consonant-final stem** (*mies* : *mies-* : *mies-tä* 'man+PART', *lapsi* : *las-* : *las-ta* 'child+PART'). It was more common in old literary Finnish for a word to have a consonant stem than in the standard contemporary language. Today, a consonant stem is found in especially old words whose final *i* in the nominative is alternated with an *e* vowel stem in flectional forms (*käsi* : *käde-n* 'hand+GEN' : *kät-tä* 'hand+PART').

Verbs with a consonant stem in contemporary Finnish are firstly those whose stems end in *e* (*mennä* 'to go' : *mene-* : *men-köön* 'let (him/her/it) go', *voidella* 'to anoint (with oil)' : *voitele-* : *voidel-koon* 'let (him/her) anoint'). On the other hand, verbs with a consonant stem are those that have a vowel stem with two syllables or longer and end either in *aa* or *ää* or in a vowel combination ending with *a* or *ä* (*hakata* 'to chop' : *hakkaa-* : *hakat-koon* 'let (him/her) chop', *ruveta* 'to begin' : *rupea-* : *ruvet-koon* 'let (him/her/it) begin'). It was more common in old literary Finnish for a verb to have a consonant stem than today. Forms with a consonant stem were also used alongside a vowel stem especially concerning such verbs whose stem ended with the phonetic grouping *-ta-* or *-tä-*. Certain types of these have been preserved until today, for example *tietä-ä* ('to know') : *tiede-tty* ('known') or *tiet-ty* ('certain') and *tunte-a* ('to know, to feel') : *tunne-ttu* ('known, felt') or *tut-tu* ('familiar').

4.4 Nominal Inflection

Nominals in standard contemporary Finnish are inflected in two numbers: singular and plural. The plural marker in standard Finnish is *t* at the end of a word (*talo-t* 'houses') and either *j* or *i* within a word, depending on if the marker is at the beginning of the syllabic boundary or elsewhere (*talo-j-en* 'house+PL+GEN', syllabified as *ta-lo-jen* and *talo-i-sta* 'house+PL+ELA', syllabified as *ta-lois-ta*).

Nominals in standard contemporary Finnish are inflected in 15 different cases. Two of the cases – the comitative and the instructive – are marginal: these are used only in the plural, and even then quite rarely. Moreover, the abessive case, signifying the absence of the marked nominal, is rather rare. The clearly distinguishable accusative ending with *t* can be found in only a few pronouns (personal pronouns such as *minut* 'me' and *meidät* 'us', interrogative pronoun *kenet* 'whom'), whereas other nominals have a form that looks like the genitive singular (marked with *-n*) and a form that looks like the nominative plural (marked with *-t*) which are used in an accusative function. These are classified as the genitive case and nominative cases in many grammars. A complete paradigm of examples can be found at the end of this book.

4.4.1 Declension: Case Inflection

The **nominative** case does not have an ending and it is basically the same in Agricola as it is in standard contemporary Finnish. This also applies to the nominative-like accusative. However, the nominative plural, in practice, is often different because of the fact that the changes seen in the word's stem, for both orthographic and phonetic-historical reasons, can be different from contemporary Finnish. For example, today's consonant gradation *teko* ('act') : *teot* '('acts') corresponds to Agricola's *teco* [tẹkọ] : *teghot* [tẹɣọt].

The singular **genitive** (and genitive-like accusative) in Agricola is the same as in standard contemporary Finnish, apart from possible gradation changes within the word stem: contemporary Finnish *teko : teon* and Agricola *teco : teghon* ('act+GEN'). Stems that are not subject to gradation are just simply affixed with the ending *-n*: *sielu : sielun* 'soul+GEN'.

There is a great deal of variation in the genitive plural both in standard contemporary Finnish and Agricola. It can be structured either from a stem in the singular form (*mies-ten* 'man+GEN.PL') or the plural stem formed with the plural marker *i* or *j* (*mieh-i-en* 'man+PL+GEN'). The way to form the genitive plural in contemporary Finnish depends on the type of word stem, but the first alternative was the prevailing type in Agricola. The genitive plural was thus formed by affixing *-ten* – or *-den* in a weakened grade – to the end of the singular stem. Structurally unsurprising but strange-looking in contemporary Finnish are, for example, the words in the genitive plural *kaikkeden* ('all+GEN.PL' Std. *kaikkien* 'all+PL+GEN') and *vaimoden* ('wife+GEN.PL' Std. *vaimojen* 'wife+PL+GEN') from Agricola's *Abckiria*. In keeping with phonetic rules (sound change), this ending developed into the form *-in* upon arrival at Modern Finnish (*kaikkein, vaimoin*), and as these are basically still possible, they are rare and seem outdated. Instead, forms with the plural stem are used in standard contemporary Finnish (*kaikkien vaimojen* 'all+PL+GEN wife+PL+GEN').

The fact that both word stems and endings have been involved in phonetic changes especially complicates the genitive plural. There are examples of both transitional changes over time and different mixed forms in Agricola's Finnish. For instance, *Abckiria* has the word *isä-i-den* ('father+PL+GEN.PL', Std. *isien* 'father+PL+GEN') which has an additional plural marker between the stem and the case ending. Since it is impossible to explain briefly the various ways to form the genitive plural, these previous examples should shed some light on the subject. The phonetic history of the Finnish genitive plural has been analysed in great detail by Heikki Paunonen (1975).

A dative-type genitive quite common in Agricola is a feature that stands out in the use of the genitive. This form signifies 'to' or 'for whom'. An example of this is in a question asked by Jesus.

*Sopico Keisari**n** anda wero taicka ei?*

'Is it lawful to give tribute <u>unto</u> Caesar, or not?' (Matt. 22:17, GNV)

The corresponding passage in contemporary Finnish uses the allative case (*keisarille* 'to the emperor'; the word *keisari* 'emperor', etymologically from the Latin title *Caesar*, is used in the Finnish Bible even after Agricola, whereas the title *Caesar* is used in English translations).

As our aforementioned discussion on **accusative** forms has shown, only pronouns have been marked with their own suffix. Even pronouns in Agricola's Finnish usually did not have a special accusative form with a *t* ending. Instead, they were similar to the genitive. Pronouns in the accusative case ending with a *t* are typical to the eastern dialects, and they did not reach literary Finnish until the 19th century. A few rare forms with the *t* ending (e.g. *meidhet* [mẹiðæt] Std. *meidät* 'us') in the language of Agricola and his contemporaries prove that they did exist in the 16th century, even though they were not generally used in the literary language based on the western dialects.

The **partitive** originally was a case signifying removal from something or somewhere, but in modern Finnish, it is a grammatical case which usually signifies partialness or limitlessness, for example a non-specific amount or continuous action. Its original ending was *-ta* or *-tä* (*maa-ta* 'land+PART', *mies-tä* 'man+PART', *ilois-ta* 'happy+PART'), but because of phonetic-historical development, often only a mere vowel remained (*kala-a* 'fish+PART', *kuolema-a* 'death+PART'). The partitive ending in contemporary Finnish that has a consonant mostly appears in one-syllable word stems (*puu-ta* 'wood+PART') and consonant stems (*taivas-ta* 'heaven+PART'), but in Agricola, it often also appears in vowel stems longer than one syllable (e.g. *Jumala-ta* Std. *Jumala-a* 'God+PART', *elämä-tä* Std. *elämä-ä* 'life+PART').

The **essive** case signifies a state of being and it also has a temporal meaning. The suffix is basically *-na* or *-nä*, or *-n* under apocope. The ending in contemporary Finnish is always affixed to a stem ending in a vowel, but it could be affixed to a consonant stem (see section 4.4) in old literary Finnish if the word had one, such as *colman**na*** (Std. *kolmantena* 'third+ESS') and *Wunna wonna* (read as *uunna vuonna* Std. *uutena vuotena* 'new+ESS year+ESS': 'in the new year'). This does not normally occur in contemporary Finnish, as the ending is usually always affixed to a vowel stem: *kolmantena*, *uutena*. In some cases, the form with the consonant stem has been fossilised and preserved to this day. This includes alongside *vuote**na*** the aforementioned form *vuonna* in fixed phrases such as *ensi vuonna* ('(during) next year') and *viime vuonna* ('(during) last year').

The **translative** ending, which signifies a state of becoming, is *-ksi* in contemporary Finnish, and its final vowel changes to a word-medial *e* (*poika* 'son': *poja-ksi* 'son+TRANSL', *poja-kse-si* 'son+transl+2SG.PX'). The ending has been the same in Agricola, although the consonant cluster [ks] was regularly written with an *x* (*poiaxi* Std. *pojaksi*, *poiaxes* Std. *pojaksesi*).

The **inessive** ending, which signifies a state of being somewhere (usually inside), is *-ssa* or *-ssä* in contemporary Finnish and it can also be similar in Agricola (*sielussa* 'in the soul', *edhessä* Std. *edessä* 'in front (of)'). It is however common, as in the western dialects, for the ending to only have one *s*, for example *mailmasa* (Std. *maailmassa* 'in the world'). Moreover, apocopic forms are common, for example *caupungis* (Std. *kaupungissa* 'in the city') and *hädhes* (Std. *hädässä* 'in distress'). Even words adjacent to each other can have different forms of the ending, for example *täsä Caupungis* (Std. *tässä kaupungissa* 'in this city').

The **elative** ending, which signifies removal from something or somewhere, is *-sta* or *-stä* in contemporary Finnish and the same ending is common in Agricola's texts as well. On the other hand, forms with apocope are common. The elative ending can also appear as an adverbial suffix in such cases in which contemporary Finnish has a derivative that ends in *i*, formed from the same suffix. For example, Agricola could write *ahkerasta* ('diligent+ELA') when contemporary Finnish has *ahkerasti* ('diligently'). However, adverbs that are similar to contemporary Finnish and have apocope (*ahkerast*) can be found in Agricola.

The **illative** ending, which signifies direction into something or somewhere, has multiple forms in contemporary Finnish. In the most basic of cases, it comprises the lengthening of the final vowel in the word stem and *-n*, for example *kala-an* ('fish+ILL'), but after one-syllable word stems that consist of a long vowel, an *h* is added before the vowel in the ending (*maa-han* 'land+ILL', *puu-hun* 'tree+ILL'). The ending after a long vowel in words that have more than one syllable will be affixed with the illative singular *-seen* or the illative plural *-siin* (*taivaa-seen* 'heaven+ILL', *taivai-siin* 'heaven+PL+ILL'). All of these same endings appear in Agricola but their distribution is not the same as it is today. Furthermore, the forms are sometimes difficult to interpret because of the fact that the length of vowels further away from the first syllable was not quite clearly marked. Therefore, many words in the illative appear to be in the genitive, for example *pään* (Std. *päähän* 'head+ILL'), *kylän* (Std. *kylään* 'into the village'). On the other hand, the hVn-type ending is more common in Agricola than in contemporary Finnish, and this allows for easier identification of the illative: *elemehen* (Std. *elämään* 'into life'), *ielkihin* (Std. *jälkiin* 'track+PL+ILL').

The **adessive** ending, which signifies 'on' or 'by' or signifies possession, is *-lla* or *-llä* in contemporary Finnish, and Agricola uses the same ending either as such or with apocope (*keskellä ~ keskel* Std. *keskellä* 'middle+ADE' : 'in the middle (of), amongst'). Furthermore, a variant of the ending can be found in Agricola in which the geminate [l:] has been truncated to a single consonant (*ymberile* Std. *ympärillä* 'circle+ADE': 'around'). Agricola usually uses an *e* for an ending with a front vowel, and sometimes, even on the basis of sentential context, it can be impossible to differentiate it from the allative, a case which we will return to shortly.

The ending of the outer locative **ablative** case, which signifies motion away from something or somebody, is today *-lta* or *-ltä*, and the same ending is used in Agricola, either as such or with a loss of the final vowel (*keskelde* Std. *keskeltä* 'middle+ABL', *ristild* Std. *ristiltä* 'cross+ABL': 'off the cross'). The ablative is also used as a fossilised adverb in the same manner as the aforementioned elative. Furthermore, ablative is the most commonly used case for an agent in passive constructions. These will be discussed in detail in our section on syntax.

The **allative** ending, which signifies going onto or going to something or someone, is *-lle* in contemporary Finnish, and the same ending is also used in Agricola. Furthermore, there are forms with the ending *-llen* found in Agricola's Finnish. For example, the allative of the word *puoli* ('half, side') can be *polelle* or *polellen* (Std. *puolelle* 'side+ALL'). Additionally, the geminate [l:] can be truncated in the same way as the adessive (*polelen*).

The **abessive** ending, which signifies the absence of something, is *-tta* or *-ttä* in contemporary Finnish, but the ending often has only one *t* in Agricola: *waimota* (Std. *vaimotta* 'without a wife'), *lapsita* (Std. *lapsitta* 'without children'). Consequently, it is often difficult to structurally differentiate it from the partitive. Together with the abessive ending, Agricola often uses the preposition *ilman* ('without'), an element which can make the meaning of the ending semantically clearer (*ilman waimoita ia lapsita* 'without wives and children'). This construction is considered a linguistic error in contemporary Finnish: instead, either simply the abessive (*vaimotta* 'wife+ABE': 'without a wife') or the partitive in a prepositional phrase (*ilman vaimoa* 'without wife+PART': 'without a wife') should be used. The history of the abessive case has been analysed in detail by Marko Pantermöller (2010).

The **comitative** case, which signifies being in the company of or together with someone, is rare both in contemporary and Agricola's Finnish, however it is the same in both. The affix is *-ine-* and it looks as if it is in the plural but it can semantically be either singular or plural, depending on the situation. As a modifier, the comitative is simply the ending *-ine* (*kauni-ine* 'beautiful+COM'), but as a head word in a phrase, the comitative is always affixed with a possessive suffix (*vaimo-ine-nsa* 'with his wife / their wives'). Examples of Agricola's comitative include *eitinens* (Std. *äiteinensä* 'with his/her/their mother(s)') and *caluinens* (Std. *kaluinensa* 'with his/her/their assets') with a clearly identifiable ending, but the possessive suffix has apocope.

The **instructive**, signifying 'by means of', is counted as a marginal case. In the singular, it has the appearance of the genitive (*jala-n* 'by foot'), and in the plural, it is *-n* preceded by the plural marker *i* (*jaloin* 'by feet'). The instructive in contemporary Finnish is used as a grammatical case only in the plural, and even then only rarely. The singular instructive is seen only in fossilised adverbs. Singular forms of the instructive are seen more in Agricola than in contemporary Finnish. The use of the instructive case in Finnish dialects and literary Finnish has been examined by Juha Leskinen (1990).

4.4.2 Pronouns

Pronouns belong to the category of nominals, but they are different from nouns and adjectives in terms of both form and meaning. Pronouns have no independent meaning. Instead, their meaning is determined or clarified, in practice, according to what they refer to. Moreover, their inflection is often irregular. There are rather few pronouns in all, but they are used quite frequently, and thus for this reason, their phonetic-historical development can differ from normal phonetic development. The old basic stems of the Uralic traditional lexicon have usually had two syllables, but the actual stem in pronouns is usually the first syllable, and the end comprises different suffixes. Some of the inflectional forms of pronouns have been fossilised as adverbs or conjunctions.

The most important pronouns are the personal and demonstrative pronouns. The **personal pronouns** in standard contemporary Finnish are: *minä* ('I'), *sinä* ('you (sg.)'), *hän* ('he/she'), *me* ('we'), *te* ('you (pl./form.)') and *he* ('they'). As we can see, *hän* can refer to both masculine and feminine referents. This feature of having no grammatical gender is common to all the Uralic languages. The rule in contemporary literary Finnish is that *hän* and *he* should refer to people and that the demonstrative pronouns *se* ('it') and *ne* ('they') refer to animals, objects and other inanimate referents. Agricola basically follows the same lines, but the division is not as categorical as it is today. In Agricola, a pear tree can be *hän* and a disciple can be *se*. The same type of fluctuation can be seen in dialects and contemporary colloquial Finnish. Furthermore, the second-person pronoun *te* can have a singular function today, but not in Agricola.

For the most part, Agricola uses the same variants for the personal pronouns as standard contemporary Finnish, but personal pronouns characteristic to the eastern dialects can also be found to some extent: *myö*, *työ* and *hyö* (Std. *me* 'we', *te* 'you (pl.)' and *he* 'they') which Agricola writes as *mö*, *tö* and *hö*. It is very rare to find the first-person singular pronoun variants *mie* or *miä* (Std. *minä* 'I').

In comparison to contemporary Finnish, there is a significant difference in the inflection of personal pronouns in that when they are in object form, they appear to be in the genitive with an *-n* (*Hän näki minun* 'he/she saw me'). The accusative form ending with a *t*, a feature adopted from the eastern dialects, is used in contemporary Finnish: *minut* ('I+ACC': 'me'), *meidät* ('we+ACC': 'us') and so on. Agricola also to some extent has plural accusative forms with the *t* ending but no singular forms at all.

There is a special feature in Agricola's use of personal pronouns in that they are used as certain types of reflexive pronouns affixed with possessive suffixes:

Agr. *Mite se autta rackat Welieni, ios iocu sano* **henellens** *Uskon oleuan*

Std. (1938) *Mitä hyötyä, veljeni, siitä on, jos joku sanoo* **itsellään** *olevan uskon*

'What good is it, my brothers, if someone [himself] says he has faith' (James 2:14, ESV)

Sööxe **sinus** *alaspein*

'cast thyself down' (Matt. 4:6, GNV)

The corresponding modern Finnish passage from the Epistle of James uses the pronoun *itse* inflected in the adessive case with the third-person possessive suffix as *itsellään* ('himself'), whereas Agricola uses the third-person singular personal pronoun *hän* inflected in the same way as *henellens* ('himself'). In the passage from the Gospel of Matthew, Agricola uses *sinus* ('yourself', the second-personal singular pronoun *sinä* inflected with the second-person possessive suffix) with the imperative of the verb of *syöstä* ('to throw, to cast'), whereas contemporary Finnish would use a verbal reflexive derivation, whereupon no special pronoun would be required (*syöksy* the imperative form of *syöksyä* 'to throw, to cast (oneself)', although the verb used in the imperative in the current Finnish Bible is *heittäytyä* 'to throw oneself'). The pronoun *itse* is a very old reflexive pronoun which was also common in Agricola's language, but as the abovementioned shows, it was not the only manner in which to express reflexiveness.

The **demonstrative pronouns** in contemporary Finnish are *tämä* ('this'), *tuo* ('that') and *se* ('it') and plural *nämä* ('these'), *nuo* ('those') and *ne* ('they'). All of these pronouns, or at least their stems, are very old, but Agricola practically does not use *tuo* and *nuo* at all. Instead, he has the forms *tai* (singular) and *nai* (plural) which are based on the old pronoun stems. These forms are otherwise unknown in standard contemporary Finnish.

The genitive of the plural pronouns *ne* and *nämä* is often the same in Agricola as it is today, but alongside the regular forms *niiden* ('their' ← *ne* 'they', used for inanimate objects) and *näiden* ('these+GEN' ← *nämä* 'these'), the forms *niinen* and *näinen* can be found. These forms are unknown in contemporary Finnish. There are similar forms found in the Balto-Finnic languages and they reflect different ways to form the genitive plural which we had already covered in the section on nominal inflection.

The **interrogative pronouns** *kuka* ('who'), *mikä* ('what') and *ken* ('who') are old remnants of the Uralic language family, and they are common in Agricola's language as well. In contemporary Finnish, *kuka* and *ken* are in complementary distribution in such a way that the *kuka* form is used for the singular nominative and *ken* is used for the inflectional forms: *kuka* ('who'), *kenen* ('who+GEN'), *ketä* ('who+PART') and so on. Agricola's language does not have the same kind of complementary distribution. Instead, a whole inflectional paradigm is used for both pronouns. Agricola's language also does not have such a strict dichotomy as in standardised contemporary Finnish, in that *kuka* is used when referring to humans and *mikä* is used for animals and other non-human subjects.

The **relative pronoun** *joka* ('which, that'), which begins a subordinate clause, has been common in literary Finnish since Agricola, but in addition to it, the non-inflectional word *kuin* has usually been used as a relative pronoun. Agricola usually writes *kuin* as *quin* or *cuin*. In addition to proper relative pronouns, the aforementioned interrogative pronouns were also used as relative words.

The **indefinite pronouns** (*joka* 'every, each', *jokainen* 'every, each', *jokin* 'some, something', *joku* 'someone', *jompikumpi* 'either one', *kukin* 'each', *kumpikin* 'both' etc.) for the most part have been formed from the same pronoun stems which have previously been discussed. These pronouns do not form any clear system nor is the number of them clearly restricted. Many of the indefinite pronouns in Agricola are the same as those used in contemporary standard Finnish. The most notable exception is the word *eräs* ('certain, one'), which is not found in Agricola whatsoever. It was not introduced into literary Finnish until the 19th century. Instead, Agricola used the numeral *yksi* ('one') as a pronoun for signifying indefiniteness.

One indefinite pronoun differing from contemporary Finnish is Agricola's *eijkengän* ('nobody, no one'). This pronoun is found in contemporary Finnish as an expression comprising two different word forms: *ei kukaan* ('nobody, no one'). Indefinite pronouns in Agricola have been examined by Matti Suojanen (1977).

4.5 Conjugation: Finite Verbal Inflection

Verbs in contemporary Finnish are inflected in two main classes: active and passive. There are four moods: indicative, imperative, conditional and potential. Moreover, there are four tenses: present, past, perfect and pluperfect. Finnish verbs are inflected in person in both singular and plural. A special feature of Finnish in comparison to the Indo-European languages is that the negative is a verb, and so negative forms are, in practice, verbal constructions consisting of at least two words. A complete paradigm of examples can be found at the end of this book.

All of the same inflectional categories can be found in Agricola as in contemporary standard Finnish. However there are categories, forms and constructions in Agricola that are not a part of contemporary literary Finnish. These include, for example, reflexive forms and a passive that is inflected in person. Moreover, there is a more extensive amount of imperative forms in Agricola than there are in contemporary standard Finnish.

4.5.1 MAIN CLASSES

There is no special marker for **active** forms. The **passive** voice differs in comparison to the Indo-European languages because in Finnish, it is a monopersonal main class, a certain kind of non-specific third person, and it cannot even express an agent with any agent-type construction. For example, *Kirja luettiin* ('a/the book was read') means that some unmentioned person or group of people read a book. Agent constructions however are possible in Agricola, and the agent is most commonly expressed by a constituent either in the ablative or elative. We will return to this topic in the section on syntax.

The passive form both today and in Agricola normally has the marker *-(t)ta* or *-(t)tä* and a special personal ending (the lengthening of the final vowel in the stem and *-n*), for example *sano-ta-an* ('is said, one says, let's say'), *sano-tti-in* ('was said, one said'). However, there are also passive forms appearing rarely in Agricola which have a person-specific personal ending (*me temma-ta-**mme*** Std. *meidät temmataan* 'we shall be caught up'; *te caste-ta-**t*** Std. *teidät kastetaan* 'you (pl.) shall be baptised').

In addition to the active and passive, there is a third main class in Agricola that appears quite rarely. This is the **reflexive**, meaning that the agent itself undergoes the action of the verb. Reflexive inflection can be found in some of the eastern dialects in the Finnish vernacular. Reflexive forms are also common in the Finnish national epic *Kalevala*, through which they have been adapted, to some extent, to general use, but they remained in the language only as fossilised forms. The common Finn nowadays cannot analyse the structure of these forms. A common example in *Kalevala* is the past tense form of the verb *luoda* ('to create') → *loihe* which literally means 'threw oneself, began'. Reflexive forms are more common in the third-person singular (*hen kiennexen* 'he/she turns', *kiensijn* 'he/she turned'). In contemporary standard Finnish, semantically reflexive derivational suffixes are used for reflexive inflectional forms.

4.5.2 MOODS

Of the four verbal moods, three are common both in contemporary Finnish and in Agricola. The indicative is the unmarked basic form, the imperative signifies a command or request and the conditional indicates possibility. The **indicative** is noteworthy due to the fact that it is the mood with the broadest paradigm, in other words including, in practice, all the tenses and persons. The other moods include only the present and perfect tenses.

There are three **imperative** markers in contemporary Finnish. In practice, the most common is the second-person singular, which on the surface is written with no marker, but in articulation, there is a closure of the larynx which is a remnant of an earlier [k]. This marker causes consonant gradation, for example the imperative of the verb *antaa* ('to give') is *anna!* ('give!'). If a word beginning with a consonant follows an imperative form, the marker assimilates with it: for example *Anna pois!* is articulated as [ɑnːɑp pɔis] ('Give (it) away!'). The other imperative markers are *-ka-* or *-kä-* and *-ko-* or *-kö-*. These are in complementary distribution in contemporary Finnish in that the latter is used in the third-person and the former elsewhere, for example (*te*) *anta-ka-a* ('(you pl.) give'), (*hän*) *anta-ko-on* ('let him/her give'). Agricola's language did not have this complementary distribution of imperative markers. Instead, the markers can appear as alternatives in the same person. For example, *-ka-* or *-kä-* in the third-person is common (*hen andacan* 'let him/her give') in the same way as in the Savo dialects. Finnish imperative forms have been examined in detail by Heikki Leskinen (1970).

The **conditional** marker in contemporary Finnish is *-isi-*, for example *minä anta-isi-n* ('I would give') and *hän anta-isi* ('he/she would give'). It is basically the same in Agricola, for example *racasta-isi-t* (Std. *rakastaisit* 'you would love'), but in practice, it at least loses its final vowel that would be at the end of the word: (*hän*) *ottais* (Std. *ottaisi* '(he/she) would take'), (*hän*) *sanois* (Std. *sanoisi* '(he/she) would say'). Moreover, the first vowel in the conditional marker might be lost: *hen mactas* (Std. *hän mahtaisi* 'he/she might'). The conditional does not cause consonant gradation in contemporary Finnish, but there is often a weak grade preceding the marker in Agricola: (*hän*) *annais* (Std. *antaisi* '(he/she) would give'), (*hän*) *tiedeis* (Std. *tietäisi* '(he/she) would know').

The **potential** mood, signifying uncertain action, is rare both in both old literary and contemporary Finnish. The mood is as such old, and its marker is *-ne-*. In Agricola, it appears to some extent in, for example, questions of uncertainty: *Lienengö mine se?* ('Might it be me?'). The potential marker assimilates in stems ending in consonants *l*, *r* and *s*, for example *tulleco* (Std. *tulleeko* 'might (he/she/it) come?'). The potential of the verb *olla* ('to be') in contemporary standard Finnish is formed by the special stem *lie-* which can be seen in Agricola in the aforementioned example *Lienengö mine se*, but it is possible for the potential to be formed by the regular consonant stem of *olla*: *olleco* ('might (he/she/it) be?'). The potential met a conscious revival in 19th century literary Finnish, but regardless of this, it has remained a marginal mood.

4.5.3 Tenses

The **present** (*minä sanon* 'I say') and **past** (*minä sanoin* 'I said'; this tense is called *imperfect* in Finnish-language grammars) can be called simple tenses. There is no special marker for the present tense, and the past tense marker *-i-* is of old, Uralic origin. The **perfect** and **pluperfect** tenses are clausal constructions including *olla* ('to be') as the auxiliary verb either in the present or past tense: *minä olen sanonut* ('I have said'), *minä olin sanonut* ('I had said'). There is no actual **future** tense in the inflectional paradigm of Finnish verbs, but a clausal future can be used with *olla* as the auxiliary verb: *minä olen sanova* ('I shall say'). The style of this construction is contextually solemn. All equivalent forms also appear in Agricola. The *minä olen sanova* clausal type in the Finnish vernacular, the so-called clausal present construction, is a form expressing continual action, but it took on new meaning in literary Finnish to refer to the future, apparently from the influence of exemplary texts in translation. This change has been examined by Marja Itkonen-Kaila (1997).

The clausal future construction *minä tulen sanomaan* ('I will say' lit. "I come to say") formed with the verb *tulla* ('to come') also can be seen in contemporary Finnish. However, this form does not exist in Agricola. Instead, Agricola certainly has other auxiliary constructions having the function of a future tense. The most common of these is, without a doubt, the construction that includes the auxiliary verb *pitää* ('to keep'): *minun pitää sanoman* ('I will say'). The verb *tahtoa* ('to want') in the first-person singular can also be seen as an auxiliary verb, whereupon the future tense is *minä tahdon sanoa* ('I will say'). Verbal future tense constructions in Agricola have been examined by Osmo Ikola (1949).

4.5.4 Personal Inflection

As there is in most other languages in the world, Finnish has three persons both in singular and in plural. Each person in verbal inflection has at least one ending characteristic of it. If there are alternatives, the choice of ending depends on mood and tense.

The first-person singular ending is normally *-n*: *sano-n* ('I say'), *sanoi-n* ('I said'), *sanoisi-n* ('I would say'), *sanone-n* ('I might say'). The ending is the same in Agricola. There is no form for a first-person singular imperative at all.

The second-person singular ending for the most part is *-t*: *sano-t* ('you say'), *sanoi-t* ('you said'), *sanoisi-t* ('you would say'), *sanone-t* ('you might say'). There is no ending specifically for the second-person singular imperative, the most commonly used person used in the imperative. When articulated, the command *sano* ('say (it)', historically ← **sanok*) includes an imperative marker only realised due to so-called boundary lengthening. The end of imperative forms, especially in colloquial Finnish, might have an *s* ending, which developed from the pronoun *sinä* ('you (sg.)'). This ending has been categorised as a clitic in contemporary Finnish: *katsos* ('have a look'), *sanos* ('so say (it)'). Corresponding endings have also been in Agricola (*catzos, sanos*).

There are several endings for the third-person singular. The ending for the present indicative and potential mood in contemporary Finnish is usually a lengthening of the final vowel: *sano-o* ('(he/she) says'), *sanone-e* ('(he/she) might say'). However, neither the past indicative nor the conditional mood has an ending: *sanoi* ('(he/she) said'), *sanoisi* ('(he/she) would say'). Moreover, there is no ending for the present tense if the stem ends in a vowel combination: *saa-da* : *saa* ('(he/she) receives'), *tupakoi-da* : *tupakoi* ('(he/she) smokes'). The corresponding endings can be found in Agricola, but the present indicative can also appear with the ending -*pi*: *saa**pi*** ('(he/she) receives'), *sano**pi*** ('(he/she) says'). This ending has no special meaning. It is a historical remnant of the same ending from which the most common present tense ending – vowel lengthening – developed (*sano-pa → *sano-pi* → *sanou* → *sanoo*). All the stages of this development can be seen in Agricola, although the *sanou* type is quite rare.

The ending of the third-person singular imperative is -*n* which is preceded by a lengthened vowel. The ending in contemporary Finnish, in practice, is always -*on* or -*ön*, for example *sanokoon* ('let him/her say') and *tehköön* ('let him/her do'), but following the alternative imperative -*ka* or -*kä* marker in Agricola, the vowel is lengthened accordingly: *sanokaan* ('let him/her say'), *menkään* ('let him/her go'). The ending is historically the same root as the pronoun *hän* ('him/her'), and sometimes the *h* can even be seen in Agricola's endings: *tulcohon* (Std. *tulkoon* 'let him/her come'), *sopicahan* (Std. *sopikoon* 'let him/her reconcile').

The first-person plural ending in all moods and tenses is -*mme* in contemporary Finnish: *sano-mme* ('we say'), *sanoisi-mme* ('we would say'), *sanokaa-mme* ('let us say'). The same ending is also common in Agricola, but there are other alternatives alongside it and there is no clear distribution amongst them. The ending's vowel can be *a* or *ä*, for example *tule-mma* (Std. *tulemme* 'we come') and *mene-mmä* (Std. *menemme* 'we go'), and a single consonant can take the place of the nasal geminate, for example *tunne-me* (Std. *tunnemme* 'we feel') and *tei-me* (Std. *teimme* 'we made'). The vowel can be completely lost, for example *kelpasi-m* (Std. *kelpasimme* 'we sufficed') and *saisi-m* (Std. *saisimme* 'we would receive'), and the -*m* at the end of the word could change to *n* as in *me tahdon* (Std. *me tahdomme* 'we want'), whereupon the form looks like the first-person singular (see page 98).

In contemporary Finnish, the monopersonal passive voice (*sanotaan* 'is said, one says', *tullaan* 'one comes') is usually used as the first-person plural imperative or as a request (*sanotaan* 'let's say', *tullaan* 'let's come') and especially as the first-person plural indicative present in contemporary colloquial Finnish (*me mennään* Std. *me menemme* 'we go'). However, these uses do not exist in Agricola.

The second-person plural ending in contemporary Finnish is -*tte* (*sano-tte* 'you say', *sanoisi-tte* 'you would say'). We can note here that the contemporary second-person plural (personal pronoun, personal endings

99

etc.) can also have a formal function, however this function does not exist in Agricola. The one exception to the -*tte* ending is the imperative whose ending is a lengthening of the final vowel in the stem: *sanoka-a* ('say (it)!'), *tehkä-ä* ('do (it)!'). The same endings are found in Agricola, but there are additionally even more alternatives and there is no clear distribution amongst them. The vowel, in addition to *e*, can be *a* or *ä* (*sanotta* Std. *sanotte* 'you say', *menettä* Std. *menette* 'you go') or it can be completely lost (*te wihastut* Std. *te vihastutte* 'you get angry', *iloitkaat* ← *iloitkaat(te)* Std. *iloitkaa* 'rejoice!'). There can also be a short *t* where there would be a geminate [t̪ː], for example *näete* (Std. *näette* 'you see').

The ending of the third-person plural in contemporary Finnish is most often -*vat* or -*vät*, for example *sano-vat* ('they say'), *meni-vät* ('they went'). The imperative ending is the plural marker -*t* preceded by the lengethening of the final vowl in the stem: *sanoko-ot* ('let them say'). The present indicative in Agricola is the same as in contemporary Finnish (*catso*wa*t* Std. *katsovat* 'they look'), but the past indicative and conditional endings simply have a -*t*: *he sanoit* (Std. *sanoivat* 'they said'), *he sanoisit* (Std. *sanoisivat* 'they would say'). Agricola's past and conditional -*t* represents an original form historically, whereas the form today is analogically based on the present tense. The structure of the third-person plural imperatives in Agricola is the same as in contemporary Finnish: the plural *t* marker is preceded by a lengthening of the final vowel in the stem: *langetkaat* ('let them fall'), *menestykööt* ('let them prosper').

The same *h* as in the third-person singular can appear before the ending (*tulcohot* 'let them come'), and sometimes the third-person singular form (*tulcohon* 'let him/her come') is used for the plural, the same way as in contemporary colloquial Finnish.

The passive personal ending both in contemporary and Agricola's Finnish is -*n* which is preceded by a lengthening of the final vowel in the stem (*sano-ta-an* 'is said, one says', *sano-tt-i-in* 'was said, one said'). It is historically the same ending which appears in the third-person singular imperative and is etymologically connected to the pronoun *hän* ('he/she'). The *h* of the original ending can still be seen in Agricola, for example *iloitahan* ('is rejoiced, one rejoices'), *lopetetahan* ('is ended, one ends'). The passive voice is in a way a non-specified third person that has no connection to a subject in any way. However, the passive syntactically behaves as a third-person voice in many respects.

4.5.5 Two Important Features

The most common verb in Finnish is **olla** ('to be') which is not only used as it its but also in the formation of many clausal inflectional forms and verbal constructions. The stem of the verb is rather old but there are many special features concerning its inflection. Thus *olla* differs from all other verbs in terms of these features.

The verbal stem in the present indicative changes within the paradigm: *ole-n* ('I am'), *ole-t* ('you (sg.) are'), *o-n* ('he/she/it is'), *ole-mme* ('we are'), *ole-tte* ('you (pl.) are'), *o-vat* ('they are'). The old word stems of the Uralic languages usually had two syllables and ended in a vowel, but the original stem of the 'to be' verb seems to have had one syllable *(v)o-. The stem ole-, as seen in the first and second person today, is evidently a derivation of this. This duality can be seen in Agricola in the same was as in contemporary Finnish.

The personal ending of the third-person singular is also irregular in the paradigm of the present tense. As we already discussed in the section on personal endings, this ending can indeed in some forms be -n preceded by a lengthening of the final vowel. However, in terms of the verb *olla*, it is not a question of this ending but rather that the infinite form of the old *o* stem, whose original form was *oma*, was adopted as a third-person form included in the paradigm and it phonetically developed into a simpler form (*oma* → *om* → *on*). Moreover, the third-person plural *ovat* ('they are') developed from the same *oma* form which was affixed with the plural marker *t*, but in this case, there was a change due to the analogical influence of other verbs *omat* → *ovat* (cf. *sano-vat* 'they say', *teke-vät* 'they do'), whereupon the ending looks the same as in other third-person plural forms.

The third-person singular in Agricola can be exactly the same *on* as in contemporary Finnish, but the form *ombi*, affixed with a clitic, can quite commonly be found alongside it. The same *-pi* ending is also quite common in other verbs in Agricola, apart from modal verbs. Sometimes the form *onopi* can also be found in Agricola's language, whose stem *ono* is also known in certain dialects. It was originally most likely used in especially stressed positions, but in Agricola, it seems to be a complete synonym of *on* and *ombi*.

One special feature that also pertains to *olla* is that the potential mood is formed from a completely separate one-syllable stem *lie-* which also is included amongst the old traditional lexicon of the Uralic language family. This form is used as the normal 'to be' verb in many Finno-Ugric languages, such as Sámi and Hungarian, but its use in standard contemporary Finnish is limited to the rare potential mood only. The potential mood is also quite rare in Agricola, but preserved examples prove that the potential form could have been formed from both the *ole-* and *lie-* stems. The forms *ollee* ('be+POT+3SG') and *lienee* ('might-be+POT+3SG') appear in Agricola as synonyms, both meaning '(he/she/it) might be'. Moreover, the *ollee* type can be found in Finnish dialects.

Knowing the inflectional paradigm of *olla* is important because normal clausal tenses (*minä olen sanonut* 'I have said', *hän oli mennyt* 'he had gone') was constructed in Agricola's time and is still constructed with this verb. Furthermore, the normal existential possessive construction is formed with the possessor in the adessive case and *olla* in the third-person singular: *Minulla* **on** *kirja* ('I have a book'), *Hänellä* **oli** *talo* ('He/She had a house'). Both Agricola and contemporary Finnish has *omistaa* 'to own', a verb that corresponds to the 'to have' verb in the Indo-European languages, but it has never been the primary choice for expressing possession.

The second important, yet special verb is the **negative verb**. It too is included in the old traditional lexicon of the Uralic language family, and it had two stems from the beginning: the basic *e-* and the imperative *el-* or *äl-*.

The negative verb gets inflected in person as in all verbs: *e-n* ('NEG+1SG'), *e-t* ('NEG+2SG'), *ei* ('NEG+3SG'), *e-mme* ('NEG+1PL'), *e-tte* ('NEG+2PL'), *ei-vät* ('NEG+3PL'). However, it by itself has no other tense than present. When forming negative phrases, the tense is expressed with a head verb and a second auxiliary verb, *olla*: *minä en sano* ('I do/will not say'), *minä en sanonut* ('I did not say'), *minä en ole sanonut* ('I have not said'), *minä en ollut sanonut* ('I had not said'). A special connegative form is used for the head verb in the present tense which, in practice, has the same form as the second-person singular imperative (*minä en mene* 'I do/will not go', *me emme mene* 'we do/will not go' etc., cf. *mene!* 'go!'). Historically, the connegative form used together with the negative verb however is not in the imperative, but rather the verbal stem with the present tense marker **k*. It is only by chance that it looks like the imperative. The original **k* ending of both is only represented by boundary lengthening in contemporary Finnish, which has no orthographic depiction.

Negative forms in Agricola's language are mostly the same as in contemporary Finnish. Alongside the third-person plural form *eivät* is the otherwise rare *evät*, which is not grammatically surprising, that is, it just includes the negative verbal stem *e-* and the personal ending *-vät*. Contemporary Finnish only has *eivät* and it is more common in Agricola than *evät*. The form *eivät* is actually formed by affixing the personal ending to the third-person singular form *ei*. Ilkka Savijärvi (1988) has stated that the form *evät has* not been consistently distributed in all of Agricola's works, but rather it is more commonly found in his later works: *Psaltari*, *Weisut* and *Ne Prophetat*.

There is a feature in the use of negative forms in Agricola differing from contemporary Finnish in that although the negative verb usually complies in number and person, it may also appear in a non-inflected form. In this case, it is in the third-person singular form in all persons: for example *mine ei ole*, *me ei tiedhe* in comparison to contemporary Finnish *minä en ole* ('I am not'), *me emme tiedä* ('we do not know'). The non-inflected *ei* is especially common when it precedes the subject and it is affixed with the clitic *-pä*, for example *eipe mine taidha sinulle site anda* (from Agricola's footnote on Matthew 15:5) which would be *minä en taida antaa sitä sinulle* ('I do not believe I shall offer it to you') in contemporary Finnish. This non-inflection of the negative verb can be seen in Finnish dialects, and this special feature of Agricola's Finnish is most clearly from the vernacular.

A negative word may be compounded with a conjunction or interrogative adverb in Agricola just as in contemporary Finnish: *ehkei* (*ehkä* + *ei* 'perhaps|no': 'perhaps not'), *ellette* (*ellä* + *ette* 'unless|NEG+2PL': 'unless you (pl.)'), *mixengä* (*miksi* + *en* + *kä* (clitic) 'why|NEG+1SG+CLT': 'so why can't I?'). It should be noted that the initial component *ellä* in the forms *ellen* ('unless I'), *ellet* ('unless you (sg.)'), *ellei* ('unless he/she/it') cannot be used on its own as an independent word any more in Agricola than in contemporary Finnish, even though it can mean 'if' in some dialects.

In addition to the aforementioned negative forms, there are also a few special negative forms found in Agricola, although rarely, which were sometimes considered linguistic errors or proof of the fact that Agricola's

Finnish-language skills were lacking. There are cases in which a personal ending is affixed to the main verb in addition to the negative verb or in place of it: *en woijn* compared to contemporary Finnish *en voi* ('I cannot'), or *ettei me olisimma* compared to contemporary Finnish *ettemme me olisi* ('that we would not'). Many of these irregular forms can be found at the end of *Rucouskiria* and some of them can indeed be explained as linguistic errors. The same types of errors can also be found in manuscripts of the same time, so it is possible that Agricola took these structures from texts translated by others.

In his study on Agricola's negative phrases, Savijärvi (1988) has stated that there is no one common explanation for Agricola's odd-looking negative forms. Instead, they are explained in different cases in different ways. One explanation concerns orthographic fluctuation, especially the fact that the boundary lengthening at the end of the connegative form was marked with a consonant according to actual articulation. For example, Agricola's phrase *en olen nijn tehnyt* spoken out loud sounds quite correct, even though the corresponding expression today is written as *en ole niin tehnyt* ('I did not do so'). The boundary lengthening assimilates with the initial consonant of the following word, in other words *en ole niin* in this case is articulated as [ẹn o lẹ n niːn].

Furthermore, the choice of form could have been influenced by analogy and especially the vernacular model for the third-person plural. In the southeast Häme dialects, right in Agricola's home region, it is still possible for the third-person plural ending to be affixed to the head verb in the negative form, for example *ei ihmiset tiärävät* (Std. *ihmiset eivät tiedä* 'people do not know'), although this is completely impossible in standard Finnish.

4.6 Infinitive Verbal Forms

In addition to personal forms inflected in mood and tense, Finnish verbs have several forms which are used as a part of various verbal constructions. These forms have some of the same characteristics as nominals, and they have even been called nominal forms.

The nominal forms of different languages are often divided into three classes according to their syntactic behaviour. Those that act like nouns are called infinitives, those that act like adjectives are participles and those that act like adverbs are gerunds. However, there has not been a practice to differentiate gerunds as their own group in Finnish. Instead, they have been called infinitives. This is why Finnish grammars have several different infinitives that are differentiated from each other by numbering or by referring to their markers.

There are normally three different distinguishable infinitives in contemporary Finnish. Older grammars usually have four or sometimes even five. The abundance of nominal forms is an old feature of the Finno-Ugric languages, so they appeared in literary Finnish beginning with Agricola.

The **first infinitive**, also known as the A infinitive, is the basic form of the verb both in contemporary Finnish and in Agricola (*sano-a* 'to say', *juos-ta* ('to run'). In addition the actual basic form, or the so-called short form, a translative form is used which is always affixed with a personal possessive suffix: *sano-a-kse-ni* ('as far as I say'), *juos-ta-kse-mme* ('in order for us to run'). The basic form is semantically neutral. The translative form often expresses aim or purpose of action.

In comparison to contemporary Finnish, there is a clear difference in Agricola in that the first infinitive can also be accompanied by the passive marker, for example *antaa* ('to give') and *syödä* ('to eat') in the active voice are *annettaa* ('to become given') and *syötää* ('to become eaten') in the passive. It is quite apparent that passive forms and structures in the texts to be translated prompted the formation and use of passive infinitives, as the Finnish vernacular virtually does not have them. Passive infinitives were removed from literary Finnish through conscious development in the 19th century because they were considered quite un-Finnish.

The **second infinitive**, also known as the E infinitive, appears both in contemporary Finnish and in Agricola in two cases, the inessive and the instructive: *sano-e-ssa* ('when saying'), *sano-e-n* ('by saying'). The inessive structure can be formed with the passive voice: *sano-tta-e-ssa* ('while one says/is saying'). The inessive mostly expresses simultaneous action as the predicate verb of the phrase, the instructive typically expresses simultaneous action or manner of action.

The original form of the second infinitive marker was *-te* and this can be seen even in contemporary Finnish following certain consonant stems: *juos-ta* ('to run') → *juos-te-ssa* ('when running'), *juos-te-n* ('by running'). The consonant of the original marker can be seen in several instances in Agricola, as in contemporary Finnish, although the *t* is replaced by the weak fricative, for example *sanoden* (Std. *sanoen* 'by saying') and *antades* (Std. *antaessa* 'when giving'). An *i* may also be the vowel in Agricola's second infinitive, as the consonant that originally was included in the marker had disappeared: *culkeisa* (Std. *kulkiessa* 'when walking'), *iaghetaisa* (Std. *jaettaessa* 'while sharing').

The **third infinitive**, also known as the MA infinitive, comprises the marker *-ma* or *-mä*. This marker is an old, multipurpose nominal derivational suffix. Regular nouns can be derived from verbal stems with the suffix, for example *elää* ('to live') → *elämä* ('life') and *kuolla* ('to die') → *kuolema* ('death'). The form is categorised as an infinitive when it employs special syntactic uses. In contemporary Finnish, these are forms in the inessive, elative, illative, adessive and abessive (*sano-ma-ssa* 'saying', *sano-ma-sta* '(from) saying', *sano-ma-an* 'to say', *sano-ma-lla* 'by saying', *sano-ma-tta* 'without saying'), but in addition to these, Agricola also has an instructive form which is possible to be used in both the active (*sanoman* 'say+INF3+INSTR') and passive (*sanottaman* 'say+PASS+INF3+INSTR') voices. Constructions formed with this and the verb *pitää* in the third-person singular can express compulsion or necessity (*hänen pitää sanoman* 'he/she has to say', *pitää sanottaman* 'has to be said'), but on the other hand, they can also be semantically neutral future forms.

The third infinitive inessive, elative, illative and abessive are in essence morphologically and semantically the same in Agricola as in contemporary

Finnish. There are, however, forms that can be sporadically found in Agricola which were formed from passive stems, for example:

palio cansa cocounsi - - hänen cauttans **parattaman**

'great multitudes came together...to be healed by Him' (Luke 5:15, KJ21)

Such passives are not possible in contemporary Finnish.

The use of the third infinitive adessive is different in Agricola than in standard contemporary Finnish. The structure today primarily expresses a manner of action, but in Agricola, it specifically means an action that is about to happen, for example *oli colemallans* ('he/she was about to die'). This type of practice in contemporary Finnish is known only in dialects. All in all, the form was rare in old literary Finnish, and other manners were used to express the same meaning.

A **fourth infinitive** is noted in older Finish grammars. Its markers are *-minen* in the nominative and *-mis-* in the partitive. In affirmative phrases, it signifies compulsion or suitableness, for example *minun on antaminen* ('I must give'), and in negative phrases, it signifies something that should not or must not be done, for example *sinne ei ole menemistä* ('one should/must not go there'). These forms are completely possible today, but in practice, they are rare. However, they are quite common in Agricola's Finnish.

In addition to the infinitives, Finnish has three participle structures. Of these participles, the first two have a complete inflectional paradigm of nominals, formed both with active and passive stems. The **first participle**, also known as the VA participle under new terminology (*sano-va* 'say+PCP1', *sano-tta-va* 'say+PASS+PCP1'), is a present participle which can be used as an adjective and partially also as a noun, and additionally as an element in different verbal constructions. The so-called clausal present, indicating future, the *on tuleva* type, in which the head verb is represented by the VA participle, has already been discussed. In Agricola, the derivational suffix *-inen* can be affixed to the participle with no effect on the meaning: *on tuleva* and *on tulevainen* are thus, in practice, synonymic expressions. Today, the latter, longer participle form is no longer in use other than as an archaism or a dialectical form.

The original form of the vA participle was -PA (*-pa* or *-pä*) which is only possible in contemporary Finnish in participles fossilised as nouns, such as *syöpä* ('cancer' lit. "(human) eating (disease)" ← *syödä* 'to eat'). However, -PA is a common ending in Agricola. Its variants originally were distributed in that -PA appeared after a stressed or secondary stressed syllable (in practice, the third syllable), and -VA in non-stressed positions. However, they no longer had a clear distribution in Agricola. In contemporary Finnish, -VA has been standardised in all positions.

The VA participle is used in grammaticalised verbal constructions. Of these, one is a necessitive construction, in which the passive marker precedes the participle: *on sano-tta-va* ('has to say'), *on men-tä-vä* ('has to go').This was also common in Agricola. Another important construction is the participle structure which replaces a subordinate clause in which the participle form takes the place of an object: *Hän sanoi **minun menevän*** ('He said that I was going'). Agricola's language has such participle structures which can be found today, but it also has forms that differ from contemporary Finnish, representing the interphases of development. These forms prove that the participle construction was only in a development stage during Agricola's time. An irregular construction can be, for example a type such as *Siellä kuultiin **hevoset hirnuvat*** ('one heard the horses neighing there', today *hevosten hirnuvan* with both words in the genitive) in which the word *hevoset* ('horses') can be classified as the object of the main clause and *hirnuvat* ('neighings') is classified as its postmodifier in the participle structure.

The **second participle** is the Finnish past participle. This participle is *-nut* or *nyt* in the singular active (*sano-nut* 'said', *teh-nyt* 'done') and *-neet* in the plural active (*sano-neet* 'said', *teh-neet* 'done'). The past passive participle is *-t(t)u* or *-t(t)y* (*sano-ttu* '(something) said', *teh-ty* '(something) done'). According to new terminology, the form has been called the NUT participle, regardless if the term illustratively covers all the ending variants or not. Because of this, there has sometimes been discussion on a separate TU participle as well.

The same exact participle forms appear in Agricola as in contemporary Finnish, but in addition, there are also other ending variants which originate from different dialects. The forms *-nehet* or *-nuet* or *-nyet* (*antanehet* and *antanuet* ← 'given', *tehnyet* 'done') appear alongside the plural *-neet* ending, and furthermore *-nut* and *-nyt* can function as a plural participle. The final *t* can be lost from the ending (*oppinu* Std. *oppinut* 'learned', *nähny* Std. *nähnyt* 'seen') as well. Moreover, *-nu(v)at* or *-ny(v)ät* is possible. The NUT participles are quite common forms in the texts, because apart from being used as nominals and parts of different verbal constructions, they are also used as the head verb of normal clausal tenses, that is, in the perfect and pluperfect tenses (*minä olen teh**nyt*** 'I have done', *he olivat sano**neet*** 'they had said').

The third participle in contemporary Finnish is the so-called **agent participle**. Its marker is the same -MA as in the third infinitive but the differentiating factor is that it has complete case inflection and its own syntactic usage: it signifies action completed by someone, for example *Tämä talo on isän rakentama* ('This house was built by my father', *rakentama* 'build+AGT') and *Me asumme isän rakentamassa talossa* ('We live in a house my father built', *rakentamassa* 'build+AGT+INE'). The one completing the action is always expressed as a modifier in the genitive with the agent participle (*isän rakentama* 'father+GEN build+AGT': 'built by father'). However, the participle cannot be expressed by itself.

The agent participle is an old Finno-Ugric feature, but it was not normally used in Agricola or in any other old Finnish writtings because there was no exact equivalent to it in the source languages used for translating old texts. Consequently, the translators who strived to be as exact as possible did not need to resort to it. Instead, they could resort to the conventional past participle (NUT/TU).

There is a structure comprising the -MA marker and the caritive derivational suffix -TON which can be used as a negative equivalent of all the participles. The structure can be semantically active or passive, for example *sanoma**ton*** ('non-saying, unsaid'). This **negative participle** also appears in Agricola and the suffix might include a diphthong: *sanomaton* or *sanomatoin*. However, it can be understood more as an adjective derivational suffix than as a participle included in true inflectional morphology.

4.7 Possessive Suffixes

Possessive suffixes are characteristic of Finnish and many of its related languages. They are elements referring to person, which can be affixed to both nominals and the infinitive forms of verbs. Historically, they have the same origin as the personal pronouns and personal endings of verbs, but morphologically, they are not completely identical to verbal personal endings even though there are similarities. There are different dialectical variants of the possessive suffixes and the same diversity can also be seen in Agricola.

The possessive suffixes in standard contemporary Finnish are as follows: *talo-ni* ('my house(s)'), *talo-si,* ('your (sg.) house(s)'), *talo-nsa* ('his/her house(s)'), *talo-mme* ('our house(s)'), *talo-nne* ('your (pl./form.) house(s)'), *talo-nsa* ('their house(s)'). As we can see, the third-person possessive singular and plural suffixes are identical, and with the exception of the nominative and the illative, the ending can be a lengthening of the final vowel and an -*n* in the other cases (*talo-lle-en* 'to his/her/their house', *talo-ssa-an* 'in his/her/their house'). This alternative form is more common today than the -*nsa* or -*nsä* ending. However, -*nsa* or -*nsä* in practice is the only alternative in Agricola, either as is or with apocope.

The first-person singular possessive suffix is the same in Agricola as it is in contemporary Finnish, although the final vowel might be lost. The same applies to the second-person singular in which the loss of the final vowel is more common. In addition, the alternative -*ti* can appear quite rarely for the second-person singular, which is historically the more original suffix than the regular -*si* ending.

The same kind of variation in the first-person plural possessive suffix can be seen as in its corresponding personal ending (see page 99). Its vowel can be *a* or *ä, e* or it can be altogether lost, and the *m* can be long or short or has changed to an *n* at the end of the word (*meidän leipämmä, leipämme, leipäme, leipän* 'our bread'). In addition, there is an ending variant in Agricola in which the consonant is an *n* within the word: *meidän syntinne* ('our sin(s)'), *meidän Herrana* ('our Lord'). These are complete dialectical forms, but in the eyes of the modern Finn, they misleadingly look like the second-person plural.

The second-person plural possessive suffix in Agricola includes -*nna* or -*nnä,* -*nne* or -*n* (*teidän leipännä, leipänne, leipän* Std. *leipänne* 'your bread'). Historically, the variation in the plural possessive suffixes can be explained by the fact that there was an *n* marker originally with them that could be used to demonstrate that there was more than one possessee. In addition, there used to be a third grammatical number alongside the plural: the dual. The dual can still be found in some languages related to Finnish, for example in Sámi (*mon* 'I', *moai* 'we two', *mii* 'we (more than two)'), but as it disappeared from the Balto-Finnic languages, its ending integrated with the plural endings. The history of inflectional morphology from this aspect has been examined by Julius Mark (1925) and Erkki Itkonen (1955).

4.8 Special Syntactic Features in Agricola

Being faithful to an original text was an important principle in translation work during Agricola's time. The structure of the text was changed as little as possible while translating, and in literal translation, word order and phrasing after foreign models were unconsciously passed on to Finnish. Consequently, the literary Finnish Agricola used clearly differed from the idiomatic colloquial Finnish of the time.

There is very little that Agricola would have completely written freely in his works, regardless of the exemplars. This can, to some extent, be found in his glosses and introductory poems. The glosses, however, are short and the introductions are written in verse. We therefore cannot draw a trustworthy conclusion on what Agricola's prose by his own hand would have been like judging from these texts.

4.8.1 WORD ORDER

The basic word order in the Finno-Ugric languages had historically been subject–object–verb (SOV). In other words, the modifiers preceded their head words and the positioning of the predicate was at the end of the clause. However, the basic word structure over time changed in that the object in regular, contemporary Finnish clauses usually comes after the verb (SVO). Nevertheless, verb-final clauses were still rather common in Agricola's Finnish. This has sometimes been speculated to be an influence of the exemplary languages – especially German – on his translated texts, but it could also be based on old Finno-Ugric conventions. There is quite a great deal of alternatives in the choice of word order because, for instance, thanks to a rich inflectional system, the relationship between words can be determined not only by mere word order.

The modifiers of nominals in contemporary Finnish traditionally come before its head word, but the order in Agricola's translated texts may be in line with the source language. For example, the *Pater Noster* (the Our Father prayer, commonly known as the Lord's Prayer) was translated as *Ise meiden* (lit. 'father our') in Finnish, although the idiomatic expression in contemporary Finnish would be *Meidän isämme* ('our father+1PL.PX': 'our father'). In addition to opposing word order, the idiomatic expression would include the possessive suffix as well. Basically, the structure *Isämme* ('father+1PL.PX': 'our father') simply with the possessive suffix would suffice. However, the construction chosen at the beginning stages of literary Finnish is still in use: *Isä meidän*. Other old means of expression in the fossilised constructions of liturgical Finnish have been preserved until today.

Negative clauses in Agricola are special because having a verb at the beginning is common even in ordinary propositions. A negative word inflected in person is, by word class, a verb, and it is normally positioned after the subject as a predicate of the clause. If a negative clause begins with a negative verb in contemporary Finnish, the clause is interpreted as a counterargument or insistence. However, it is a normal negative clause in Agricola:

Agr. *Emme me leipie ottaneet cansam*

Std. *Me emme ottaneet leipiä mukaamme*

'we didn't bring along any bread' (Matt. 16:7, CEV)

Finnish adpositions were historically postpositions for historical reasons: the postpositional construction for the most part developed from a head word that inflected in a local case and its modifier in the genitive, for example *kive-n pää-lle* ('stone+GEN head+ALL': 'onto a stone') and *isä-n jälke-en* ('father+GEN trace+ILL': 'after father'). In word-for-word translation, the model of the source languages, however, prompted postpositions to precede its head word, whereupon they became prepositions:

Agr. *Techti - - langesi* **päle** *colmanen osan Kymeiste ia Wesilechteistä*

Std. tähti - - putosi virtojen ja vesilähteiden kolmasosa**n päälle**

'star... fell on a third of the rivers and springs of water' (Rev. 8:10, CEB)

Agr. ***ielken*** *walmistuxen peiuen*

Std. valmistuspäivä**n jälkeen**

'after the day of Preparation' (Matt. 27:62, RSV)

Agricola's adpositions and their non-Finnish exemplars have been examined by Heidi Salmi (2010).

Relationships that are expressed with prepositions in the Indo-European languages can often be expressed with case endings in Finnish. In word-for-word translation, it often happened that prepositions were semantically translated with a corresponding adposition, and this is how non-Finnish expressions came about: for example, Agricola's expression *Minä uskon Jumalan pääle* has a postposition phrase (*Jumalan pääle* 'God+GEN head+ALL') and today, the expression *Minä uskon Jumalaan* has a case ending (*Jumalaan* 'God+ILL'), both expressions meaning 'I believe in God'. A word form that is more of a calque than a similar original expression in Finnish could have been chosen as an adposition. Agricola and contemporary Finnish employ a postpositional construction, but as we can see from the following examples, they use different postpositions: Agr. *hebrein tekstin jälkiin* (postp. *jälkiin* 'trace+PL+ILL') and Std. *heprean tekstin mukaisesti* (postp. *mukaisesti* 'according+ADV') → 'according to Hebraic text'; Agr. *teidän edestän* (postp. *edestän* 'fore+ELA+2PL.PX') and Std. *teidän puolestanne* (postp. *puolestanne* 'half+ELA+2PL.PX') → 'on behalf of you (pl.)'.

Several of Agricola's adpositions are the same as in contemporary Finnish. A significant exception however is that *alle* ('under+ALL') is completely missing from Agricola, and the postposition *ala* is used instead, something entirely unknown in contemporary Finnish (however, the word *ala* 'discipline, field, subject' is a known noun in contemporary Finnish):

Agr. *Henen Kädhens warion **ala** hen minun peitti*

Std. *Hänen kätensä varjon **alle** hän peitti minut*

'<u>under</u> the shadow of his hand hath he hid me' (Isa. 49:2, GNV)

4.8.2 Passive Constructions and Reflexive Expressions

The source languages of Agricola's translated texts have a genuine passive category and passive clause, whereupon the target of action is a grammatical subject and the performer of action is expressed, if expressed, by a thematic structure with an agent. Contemporary Finnish does not have a similar passive. Instead, the Finnish passive is a certain kind of non-specified third person, and when using it, the target of action is the object of the clause, but it is completely missing a clearly stated subject, for example *Koulussa opetetaan englannin kieltä* ('English is taught at school'). The agent can be thought of as some person or group of people, but a word classified as a subject is missing from the clause. Finnish also has no dummy subject, thus simply a predicate in extreme cases can form a clause. In addition to a passive verbal structure, a monopersonally used verb can be the predicate of this kind of clause that has no subject. For example, *Sataa* ('It is raining') is a grammatically complete sentence. All of these characteristics are old features common to the Uralic language family.

When translating, being faithful to an original text has brought genuine passive structures along in old literary Finnish as well. For example, the clause *hen petettin* ('he was betrayed', with *hän* 'he' in the nominative) in Agricola is comparable to *hänet petettiin* (with *hän* in the accusative) used today. Agricola also uses passive verbal structures which are completely missing from contemporary Finnish, for example the passive of the first infinitive in its basic form. Passive infinitive forms have been used in expressions such as:

*teme olis taittu **myte** - - ia **annetta** waiuasten*

'it might have <u>been sold</u>...and <u>been given</u> unto the poor' (Mark 14:5, GNV) in which *myte* (read today as *myytää*) means 'to become sold' and *annetta* (read today as *annettaa*) means 'to become given'. The colophon at the end of *Abckiria* has a passive structure with the passive past participle (the so-called second or TU participle) of the verb *painaa* ('to print') with an agent expressed by the ablative: *paynettu Amund Lauritzen poijalda* ('printed by Amund Laurentsson'). Today, the MA agent participle construction is used for such expressions (see page 106).

Rare but nevertheless possible in Agricola are passive forms that are affixed with something other than its normal passive personal ending (a lengthened vowel and *-n*). Of these, the first-person plural forms are the most easily identifiable: *me eroijtetaisim* ('we would be separated') and *me sinusta wirghotetaijsim* ('we would be refreshed by you (sg.)'). The performer of action (*sinusta*) in the latter passive construction is the agent of the clause, which is expressed by the elative in this case.

Expressions of reflexivity in Agricola are partly different than those in contemporary Finnish. Reflexive expressions in the Germanic languages evidently were a model to these structures in which the target of action is expressed with a personal pronoun structure affixed with a possessive suffix: *käenne **sinuas** minuhun pein* ('turn (yourself) unto me') and *pane **sinus** mata* ('put yourself to bed'). The idiomatic expression *panna maata* ('to lie down, to go to bed') can be found in the reflexive structure of the latter example. This kind of expression cannot be formed on the basis of any kind of grammatical rule. Instead, it is a special feature which is included as such in genuine Finnish phraseme inventory.

The only true reflexive pronoun in Finnish is *itse* ('self') which is often affixed with a possessive suffix. It was also common in Agricola, for example *itseni* ('myself')

*mine annoin **itzeni** wietelte*

'I allowed myself to be misled' (Jer. 20:7, NLT)

This passage has the passive verb *vieteltää* which means 'to become misled, to become persuaded'. There is an alternative to *itseni* with the same reflexive meaning. Agricola had used personal pronouns affixed with a possessive suffix, for example *minuni* ('myself') formed from the first-person singular pronoun stem *minu-* and the first-person singular possessive suffix *-ni*:

*Mine olen quitengi **minuni** tehnyt iocaitzen Palueliaxi*

'I have made myself a servant to all' (1 Cor. 9:19, ESV)

4.8.3 Congruency
There is a basic rule in Finnish that when the subject comes before the predicate in a clause, the predicate complies in number and in person: ***minä** menen* ('I go'), ***sinä** menet* ('you go'), ***hän** menee* ('he/she goes'), and so on. The same rule, for the most part, applies in Agricola, but morphologically

singular but contextually plural words are a significant exception, for example *perhe* ('family'), *kansa* ('(a) people') and *väki* ('crowd'). In these words, Agricola usually complies with a similar, logical congruency which also appears in dialects, having the predicate in the plural even when the subject is in the singular: *canssa san***ouat*** ('the people say'), *palio weki cul**it*** ('a great crowd heard'). The predicate is in the plural because the subject refers to a number of people, even though the word itself is morphologically singular. This plural incongruency can be compared to a normal instance, for example *mwtomat loopuuat* ('some shall depart') in which the subject in the plural complies with the predicate in the plural.

In terms of congruency in Agricola, there is also irregularity involving the negative verb. It can inflect in person normally but it can also be uninflected. Non-inflection in Agricola is especially common in the third-person plural and when the negative word precedes the subject:

Agr. *Catzocat taiuain lintuin päle, sille **ettei he** kylue, **eike** nijte **eike** mös cocoa rijhen*

Std. Katsokaa taivaan lintuja, sillä että **ne eivät** kylvä **eivätkä** niitä **eivätkä** myös kokoa riiheen

'See the birds of the sky, that they don't sow, neither do they reap, nor [do they] gather into barns' (Matt. 6:26, WEB)

The word *ettei*, a contraction of the conjunction *että* ('that') and the negative verb *ei* ('no, not'), can be found in the same way as in contemporary Finnish. The negative verb can be uninflected in other persons, especially when the clitic -*pä* is affixed to it:

Agr. ***eipe te*** *tadho cwlla, Mine hwdhan, ia **eipe te** taidha wastata*

Std. **ette** tahdo kuulla, minä huudan, ja **ette** tahdo vastata

'but ye heard not, and I called you, but ye answered not' (Jer. 7:13, KJ21)

As regards congruency, special cases include possessive and modal constructions but they are special, specifically in comparison to the Germanic languages, and most often there is no difference in them between Agricola and contemporary Finnish. The possessor or the logical subject in these constructions is not a grammatical subject. Instead, it is inflected in a specific case, most normally in the adessive or genitive, and the predicate is always in the third-person singular: *minulla on talo* ('I have a house'), *hänellä on talo* ('s/he has a house'), *meillä on viisi taloa* ('we have five houses'), *minun täytyy mennä* ('I must go'), *sinun täytyy mennä* ('you (sg.) must go') and so on. An especially common monopersonal construction in Agricola is the *pitää menemän* ('shall go') type, comprised of the verb *pitää* ('to keep, to have to') in the third-person singular and the main verb in the third infinitive instructive. This type can express, among others, necessity, obligation or future:

*Minun **pite oleman** henen Isense, ia henen **pite oleman** Minun Poicani.*

'I will be his Father, and he shall be my Son' (Heb. 1:5, GNV)

This construction is virtually no longer used in standard contemporary Finnish at all, but it is indeed known and understood.

The predicate in contemporary Finnish is usually also in the singular when the subject is in the partitive plural, expressing a non-specific amount. In these examples, the predicate is in the third-person singular: *Ihmisiä tuli paikalle joukoittain* ('people came to the place in droves'), *Sinne tuli paljon ihmisiä* ('many people came there'). This is how it was most often done in Agricola as well.

The rule of congruency also concerns adjectival modifiers and their head word: the modifier is in the same number and case as the head word. This rule is just as valid in contemporary Finnish as it is in Agricola: *swrella iouckolla* ('with great company'), *caikista Makunnista* ('out of all the lands'), *surkiat sielut* ('sorrowful souls'). Pronouns that behave as modifiers also have congruency in the same way: *telle aijalla* ('at this time'), *teste peiueste* ('from this day').

4.8.4 CONJUNCTIONS

Conjunctions express relationships between clauses or constituents, and it is often crucial to understand their function in terms of interpreting a whole expression. Consequently, it is good to especially note such cases in which Agricola's conjunctions or their usages differ from contemporary Finnish.

Coordinating conjunctions – those that join two entities of equal value together – in contemporary Finnish are *ja* ('and'), *sekä* ('and, as well as') and the correlative *sekä–että* ('both–and'), and these have been common starting with Agricola. Moreover, *-kä*, a clitic that expresses coordination together with the negative verb, has appeared in literary Finnish starting with Agricola:

*Mine wihan ninen pahain Seuracunda, **enge** istu ninen Iumalattomain tykene*

'I hate the assembly of evildoers, and I will not sit with the wicked' (Ps. 26:5, ESV)

This passage can be found in contemporary Finnish with the same conjunction, but written as *enkä*. On the other hand, Agricola also uses *ja* and a separate negative verb associated with it:

*Coruillan pite teiden cwleman, **ia ei** ymmertämen*

'By hearing ye shall hear, and shall not understand' (Acts 28:26, GNV)

Today, this would be considered a linguistic error. The more uncommon coordinating conjunction *ynnä* is mostly an adverb in Agricola, meaning 'together with someone':

*Nin Petari ia Iohannes **ynne** ylesastuit Templin.*

'Now Peter and John went up <u>together</u> into the temple' (Acts 3:1, GNV)

Disjunctive coordinating conjunctions *eli, elikkä, tai, taikka* ('or'), *joko–tai* ('either–or'), *vai* ('or', in questions) have been in use starting with Agricola. However, many other pairs with the same meaning have been used alongside *joko–tai* which are no longer possible in standard contemporary Finnish. These correlative conjunctions were: *ehkä–eli, eli(kkä)–eli, eli–tai(kka), tai(kka)–eli, joko–eli, taikka–eli, taikka–taikka*. The conjunction *eli(kkä)* ('that is, in other words') signifies similarity in contemporary Finnish, but it can also mean an alternative in Agricola:

*Iohannesen Caste, olico hen Taiuahast **elicke** Inhimisilde?*

'The baptism of John, was it from heaven, <u>or</u> of men?' (Mark 11:30, GNV)

Adversative coordinating conjunctions *mutta* ('but') and *vaan* ('but rather, instead') have appeared in literary Finnish starting with Agricola, and they were used as synonyms. In contemporary Finnish, *vaan* has become specialised to express a correct alternative that comes after a negated clause, and many times in English translations, it must be expressed by the word *instead* in a new sentence immediately after the initial claim: *Minä en ole sairas vaan terve* ('I am not ill. Instead, I am well.'). However, the corresponding example could have had the conjunction *mutta* in Agricola.

There are three different types of subordinate clauses in contemporary Finnish: conjunctive clauses beginning with a subordinating conjunction, relative clauses and indirect interrogative clauses. We have already discussed relative pronouns in section 4.2.2. Indirect interrogative clauses in themselves are similar to direct questions but they have syntactically been subordinated to a main clause. In Finnish, a polar question cannot be formed by merely switching word order. Instead, the first word of the interrogative clause must be affixed with the interrogative clitic *-ko* or *-kö*, for example the second-person singular of the verb 'to be' *Oletko sairas?* ('Are you ill?'). The same clitic is used in indirect interrogative clauses: *En tiedä, olet**ko** jo kuullut tästä asiasta* ('I don't know <u>if</u> ~ <u>whether</u> you already heard about this matter'). This was also applied to Agricola's Finnish:

*Olle**co** hen syndinen, em mine tiedhe*

'<u>Whether</u> he <u>is</u> a sinner, I do not know' (John 9:25, RSV)

Agricola sometimes uses a subordinate clause beginning with *jos* ('if') in place of an indirect polar question:

[Pilatus] *cutzui tygens Pämiehen ia kysyi henelde,* **Ios** *hen io Amu coollut oli*

'and [Pilate] called unto him the Centurion, and asked of him whether he had been any while dead' (Mark 15:44, GNV)

Should this construction be used in contemporary Finnish, it would be considered a type of translation loan, taken from the Germanic languages, and a linguistic error.

The types of subordinate clauses found in Agricola are the same as in contemporary Finnish, but the conjunctions starting these clauses are partly different. Furthermore, the functions of these conjunctions can be different, even though they themselves would be the same conjunctions. We should present the most important of these cases, since the relationships between the clauses can otherwise be easily misunderstood.

The most common and most diverse of the subordinate conjunctions in contemporary Finnish is *että* ('that'). Starting with Agricola, *että* has been used in an explicative (expressing a general explanation), consecutive (expressing consequence) and finalising (expressing intent) function, for example:

Ei quitenga Opetuslapset tiennet **ette** *se Iesus oli*

'However, the disciples did not know that it was Jesus' (John 21:4, LEB)

Nin he laskit, ia tuli nin palio caloia **ettei** *he woineet site wete*

'They did, and the net was so full of fish that they could not drag it up into the boat' (John 21:6, CEV)

mine wloswien henen teille, **ette** *te tiedheisit,* **etten** *mine leudhä ychten Syte henen cansans*

'I bring him forth to you, that ye may know that I find no fault in him' (John 19:4, KJV)

Deviating from contemporary Finnish, the adverb of degree *senpäle* (lit. 'unto it') often precedes *että*, signifying reason or intent:

hen pane sen Kyntelen ialghan päle, **Senpäle ette** *sisellemeneueiset näkisit walkiudhen*

'setteth it [a candle] on a candlestick, that they that enter in, may see the light' (Luke 8:16, GNV)

The word *jotta* ('so that') in contemporary Finnish generally appears as a conjunction expressing intent, but this is extremely rare in Agricola. The reason is quite evidently that the finalising *jotta* conjunction is known mostly in the Savo dialects (found amongst the eastern dialects) which were not the foundation for Agricola's literary Finnish. It was not until the end of the 19th century that *jotta* consciously became established as the primary finalising conjunction.

In Agricola, *että* also appears as a causative (expressing reason, 'because') and a temporal (expressing time, 'when') conjunction:

Ettes *neit minun Thomas, nin sine uskoit*

'Thomas, because thou hast seen me, thou believest' (John 20:29, GNV)

Teme ombi nyt se colmas kerta **ette** *Iesus ilmestui henen opetuslapsillens*

'This is now the third time that Jesus showed Himself to His disciples' (John 21:14, KJ21)

In contemporary Finnish, this first passage has the word *koska* ('because'). Although the second example uses the word *that* in the English translation, it has a temporal meaning, and in contemporary Finnish, the word *kun* ('when') is specifically used. As we can see, contemporary Finnish uses other conjunctions in these functions for the purpose of clarity. The clictic *-s* in *ettes* of first passage developed from the second-person singular pronoun (*että sinä* 'that you' → *että sä* → *ettäs*).

A great difference in comparison to contemporary Finnish is the fact that the conjunction *koska* in Agricola is primarily temporal (expressing time, 'when'), but it is causative (expressing reason 'because, since') in contemporary Finnish. Thus, the word *kun* ('when') in contemporary Finnish texts corresponds to Agricola's *koska*:

Agr. *Mutta* **coska** *Iesus siselmeni Capernaum, tuli yxi Pämies henen tygens*

Std. (1938) *Ja* **kun** *hän saapui Kapernaumiin, tuli hänen tykönsä sadanpäämies*

'When Jesus had entered Capernaum, a centurion came to him' (Matt. 8:5, NIV)

Agricola had left the name of the city uninflected (cf. *Kapernaumiin* 'Capernaum+ILL') in this example as he rather often did with words and proper nouns not of Finnish origin.

The temporal conjunction of standard contemporary Finnish *kun* ('when') does not appear in Agricola at all. Instead, he used either the aforementioned *koska* or the conjunction *kuin*. In contemporary Finnish, *kuin* ('as, than') primarily signifies comparison. The most common orthography of *kuin* in Agricola is *quin*:

*Ia **quin** hen siseltuli Jerusalemijn, hämmestui coco caupungi*

'And <u>when</u> he entered Jerusalem, the whole city was stirred up' (Matt. 21:10, ESV)

It was not until the late 19th century that the distinction between *kun* and *kuin* was defined for modern Finnish by scholarly decision.

A concessive conjunction (expressing concession) *es* appears in Agricola which does not exist in contemporary Finnish at all:

*Eipe heiden pidhe woittaman eli ylikädhen saaman, **Es** quinga corkiasti he lendeuet*

'they shall not win or achieve exhalation, <u>though</u> they fly however high'

(Biblical gloss in *Psaltari*, for Psalms 66:7)

The conventional concessive conjunction in contemporary Finnish is *vaikka* ('although, even though') which also appears in Agricola. Agricola's most common concessive conjunction, however, is *ehkä*:

*caiki hyuet Tööd, ilman wscota tehdhyt, **echke** quinga hyuet ne näkyuet, ouat syndi*

'all good work practised without faith, <u>even though</u> it seems however good, is a sin'

(Footnote in *Se Wsi Testamenti*, for Matthew 7:24)

Today, *ehkä* cannot be used as a concessive conjunction at all. Instead, it is an adverb signifying possibility ('maybe, perhaps').

The polysemantic *kuin* in old literary Finnish was consciously established in the late 19th century as a conjunction expressing comparison. It has had this same function, in addition to many others, starting with Agricola. Moreover, the set phrase *niin kuin* ('as if, as though') has been common starting with Agricola, even though he usually writes it as one word: *ninquin*. Furthermore, the word *kutta*, an unknown word today, appears in Agricola as a comparative conjunction: *eij mw ole **kutta** sula pahuus* ('nothing else <u>than</u> wickedness'). Preceding this can even be the adverb *niin* ('so, as'): *tee, **ninkuttas** puhuijt* ('do <u>as</u> you have said'). The comparative conjunction *kuten* ('as, like') does not appear in Agricola at all and was not in use in literary Finnish until the 19th century.

4.8.5 NON-FINITE CLAUSES

There are several established constructions in contemporary Finnish which contextually correspond to complete subordinate clauses but in which there is a non-finite form of the predicate, not inflected in person as in normal clauses. The most important types include: a participle construction (*Isä* *sanoi **pojan lähtevän/lähteneen*** 'Father said that his son is leaving/that his son left'), a temporal construction (***Pojan lähtiessä/lähdettyä*** *isä katseli ulos ikkunasta* 'While his son was leaving/After his son left, his father looked out the window') and a finalising construction (*Ostin kirjan **voidakseni opiskella*** 'I bought a book so I could study'). The verbal structures used in these constructions have previously been discussed in section 4.6.

The word representing the subject of the non-finite predicate in these clauses is usually in the genitive. If a personal pronoun is being used for the subject, a possessive suffix must be affixed to the non-finite form (*sinun lähdettyäsi* 'after you left'): the personal pronoun itself can be omitted if the subject is the first- or second-person (*lähdettyämme* 'after we left'). The third-person pronoun can be omitted when the subject of the main clause is the same as the subject of the non-finite clause (*Hän sanoi lähtevänsä* 'He said that he was leaving'). Should the non-finite clausal subject be shown (*Hän sanoi **hänen** lähtevän* 'He said that she was leaving'), it is understood as a different person than the one in the main clause (even though as a gender-neutral pronoun, *hän* and its genitive *hänen* refer to either a male or a female, the latter example differentiates 'he' and 'she' just to make a distinction between the two subjects of the two clauses).

Temporal and finalising constructions in Agricola are basically the same as in contemporary Finnish. However, phonetic variation characteristic to dialects can be seen in the forms, and also the word order is often different than in contemporary Finnish. The present in the temporal construction expresses action occurring at the same time as in the main clause. This is, in Agricola, for example:

*Neite mine olen puhunut teille, **ollesani** teiden tykenen*

'I have said these things to you while I am still with you' (John 14:25, NRSV)

The past in the temporal construction depicts action which occurred previous to the action of the main clause, for example:

*Nin iloitzit sis Opetuslapset Herran **nechtyens***

'Then were the disciples glad when they saw the Lord'

This example was taken from *Pina*, but the corresponding construction to this passage with a subordinate clause appears in Agricola's New Testament (*Nin Opetuslapset jhastuit, ette he HERRAN neit*, with the verb *ihastua* 'to be thrilled' synonymic to *iloita* 'to be cheerful'), whereupon the English translation is John 20:20 (GNV). The finalising construction, in the basic case, expresses intent of action, for example:

*Nin he sis poimit kiui **laskettaxens** hende*

'Then they picked up stones in order to throw them at him' (John 8:59, LEB)

The participle construction has also been called a referative non-finite clause because it most often expresses what someone has said, thought, wanted or felt. The same kind of participle constructions in contemporary Finnish can be found in Agricola, for example:

Agr. *Mine soisin **oleuani** nyt teiden tykenän*

Std. Minä soisin **olevani** nyt teidän luonanne

'Would that I were with you now' (Gal. 4:20, AMP)

The passive participle is a part of the predicate of the participle construction in the following example, which would work in contemporary Finnish so long as the orthography and the form of the predicate structure would be appropriately adapted:

Agr. *he lwlit Iumalan Waldakunnan cochta **ilmoitettauan***

Std. he luulivat Jumalan valtakunnan kohta **ilmoitettavan**

'they thought that the kingdom of God was going to appear immediately' (Luke 19:11, NET)

The formation and usage of non-finite clauses can be rather complex. Since subordinate clauses can usually replace them, Finnish language learners and speakers of Finnish as a foreign language particularly aim at avoiding them. It is specifically for this reason that we should note that idiomatically constructed non-finite clauses appear in Agricola. For example, there is a combination of participle and temporal constructions skilfully formed in the introductory poem of *Rucouskiria*, written by Agricola himself:

Oij sine surckia Locasecki / etkös neite Mieleses ecke
*Haiseuva Raato **oleuas** / ia Matoin Eues **cooltuas**.*

'Oh you miserable rotter / does it not suddenly come to mind
that you are a putrid carcass / and a meal for the maggots after you die'

If Agricola would not have had a command of Finnish as a native speaker, he hardly would have been able or wanted to use such complex clausal constructions in his own poetry.

However, there are also cases found specifically amongst Agricola's participle constructions in which the relationships of the constituents in the non-finite clause were designated differently than in contemporary Finnish and even differently within the same expression:

*Sille sijnä cwllan ne Rooskat winise**pä** Ja ne Pöret kitise**uen**, Orhijt hirnu**uat** ia Rattat wieryu**uet***

'You can hear the sounds of whips [crack<u>ing</u>] and the noise of wheels [rattl<u>ing</u>].You can hear horses gallop<u>ing</u> and chariots bounc<u>ing</u> along!' (Nah. 3:2, ERV)

This passage using the conventions of contemporary Finnish would be *Sillä siinä kuullaan niiden ruoskien vinise**vän** ja niiden pyörien kitise**vän**, orhien hirnu**van** ja rattaiden vieri**vän*** where the verbs with the present active participle would be in the accusative and their modifiers in the genitive. These examples do not, however, disprove Agricola's language skills because these features can be found in other examples of old literary Finnish. They just prove that the system of participle constructions was not yet developed and had not assumed its present structure during Agricola's time.

4.9 Vocabulary in the Works of Agricola

It is impossible to calculate the precise number of words in the works of Agricola. In addition to Finnish, the works also had Latin as well as sporadically a few other languages, such as Swedish, Greek and Hebrew. Moreover, the non-Finnish words were used amongst the Finnish-language text. It is impossible to know if Agricola had thought that they were acceptable loans in Finnish or if he had resorted to language replacement when there was a lack of a Finnish expression. Furthermore, some inflectional forms are such that they essentially could be included in the inflectional paradigm of at least two different words. Therefore, we cannot say for certain what basic form they represent.

4.9.1 Statistics on Agricola's Vocabulary

In older 20th century studies (e.g. Rapola 1962), it has been estimated that there might be approximately 6,250 different words in Agricola. Calculations based on a digital corpus have, however, shown that it greatly exceeds over 8,000 words. There was a publication entitled *Index Agricolaensis* created on Agricola's works. This index contains all of the word forms found in the works and where they appear, listed in alphabetical order according to their original orthography. This corpus has not been lemmatised, in other words the textual words found in it have not been analysed nor linked to a specific search word or dictionary unit. Instead, each form has been identified solely on the basis of its orthography. Therefore, the orthographic form <nein>, for example, can represent the adverb *näin* ('like this, thus') or the verbal structure *näin* ('I saw'). The same possibilities for interpretation can be included for the orthographic form <näin>. In extreme cases, one and the same form could have been written in a few dozen different ways, and one orthographic form could have more than ten different grammatical interpretations. Consequently, the index cannot directly provide a word count or even the number of word forms from the texts. Nevertheless, based on the corpus in the index and based on a manually lemmatised dictionary sample concerning the beginning end of the alphabet, it is estimated that the entire word count in Agricola's works may be approximately 8,500 (Jussila 2000). In addition to this, there are approximately 500 proper nouns.

The word count of Agricola's works does not seem so large if we compare it with, for example, the number of entries in the dictionary of contemporary Finnish *Nykysuomen sanakirja* (approximately 207,000 words). On the other hand, there are rural district vocabularies – collections of dialectical vocabularies compiled from one rural district – that strive for concise lexical coverage, and they usually do not include more than 20,000 to 24,000 entries. So in this regard, the word count in Agricola's works must be considered to be rather abundant, especially when the one-sidedness of the subjects discussed in his works are taken into account. Nevertheless, there is roughly the same amount of words in Agricola as in *Kalevala*, a book considered linguistically rich and colourful (Jussila 2009).

Since the subjects in Agricola's texts are limited, they do not provide a reliable image of Finnish 16th century vocabulary on the whole. They contain an abundance of non-Finnish words and temporary expressions formulated under the circumstances of translation, which at no stage became established in literary or colloquial Finnish. Another point is that the texts are lacking in vocabulary pertaining to normal Finnish daily life: for example, words which, thanks to comparative Finno-Ugric studies, can indeed be proven to be very old but for one reason or another have not proven themselves to be necessary when translating spiritual literature into Finnish (for example *koivu* 'birch', *leppä* 'alder'; *hiihtää* 'to ski', *suksi* 'ski').

Furthermore, different Finnish dialects did not have the same opportunity to be showcased in Agricola's texts. The translator himself explained in the introduction of his New Testament that he gave priority to "the Finnish language", in other words to the Varsinais-Suomi or Finland Proper dialects. It was these dialects which he had become familiar with while living in Turku. He based his choice on the fact that Turku was the land's spiritual and administrative centre. Leaning on his own and his fellow students' language skills, Agricola may have also made use of the reserves of expressions from the southeast Häme dialects spoken in Pernå and its neighbouring regions. He learned the vocabulary of the southeastern dialects spoken in the Vyborg region while he was there studying. However, the percentage of Savo and Ostrobothnian dialects, for example, rested on possible assistants and other sporadic sources. We will discuss dialectical vocabulary later.

When comparing Agricola's lexical reserves to contemporary Finnish, we must remember that a large part of the vocabulary in modern standard and literary Finnish is a result of conscious lexical development work, which was at its most active in the 19th century. Thus, Agricola was lacking an abundance of ordinary words found in modern Finnish which were not adopted as neologisms until after the 16th century. Some of these neologisms were formed from Finnish elements (e.g. *ala* 'discipline, field', *eräs* 'certain, one', *henkilö* 'person') and some were borrowed from other languages (e.g. *moottori* 'motor, engine', *normaali* 'normal', *prosentti* 'percent'). Some of the gaps were random (e.g. *aihe* 'subject, theme', *airo* 'oar', *ihminen* 'human, person'), and some were missing because of the fact that referents of these neologisms were not even known to the Finns during Agricola's time: *amerikkalainen* ('American'), *auto* ('automobile, car'), *elokuva* ('cinema, movie').

4.9.2 BASIC VOCABULARY

The significance of the vocabulary used by Agricola cannot be assessed solely on the basis of the number of words because a notable part of the vocabulary that became established in literary Finnish through Agricola's works is a quite common basic vocabulary, necessary at all times and everywhere. There are only three words missing from Agricola's works out of the one hundred most common words in contemporary Finnish (Saukkonen et al. 1979): *eräs* ('certain, one'), *eri* ('separate, various') and *esittää* ('to present'). Of these three, *eräs* is an eastern Finnish dialectical word which was not adopted into literary use until the 19th century, and *esittää* was a consciously formed neologism which was noted for the first time in Daniel Europaeus' Swedish–Finnish dictionary in 1853. However, the lack of the word *eri* in Agricola may be pure coincidence because the first appearance of the word was in the hymnal of Hemminki of Masku in 1605. Furthermore, there are derivations and inflectional structures found in Agricola with *eri* as an initial component (e.g. *erinänsä* 'separately', *erittää* 'to take apart, to make different') as well as compound words which have *eri* as a modifier (e.g. *erimaa* 'separate|land': 'uninhabited region', *eriseura* 'separate|region': 'sect')

Raimo Jussila (2000) analysed the first instances of entries in *Nykysuomen sanakirja* that were found in the vocabulary of old literary Finnish between 1540 and 1810 and noted that there was no balance in the development of the vocabulary. Certain writers and works have had a clearly more significant role than others in making lexical contributions to literary Finnish, and in these statistics, the indisputable top name is Mikael Agricola with 5,228 first instances. The runner-ups are Christfrid Ganander (4,102 new words) and Daniel Juslenius (2,676 words), both of whom made an impact in the 18th century and created Finnish-language dictionaries. There was a conscious aim to compile vocabulary for these dictionaries from both standard and colloquial Finnish, from all possible areas of life.

As a contributor to the vocabulary of literary Finnish, Agricola holds a special position because he was the first producer of printed Finnish literature. Indeed, a few manuscripts composed by different authors of Agricola's time are known, but the size of their vocabulary is extremely small, and the kind of vocabulary would not even be found in Agricola. Examples of these kinds of words not found in Agricola include *kauhistella* ('to be horrified'), *känsä* ('callus'), *lukita* ('to lock'), *muori* ('old mother, grandmother') and *tupa* ('cabin') from an excerpt from the Uppsala Evangelion (Penttilä 1943); and *haluta* ('to want', *halata* in Agricola which today means 'to hug'), *hypellä* ('to hop', *hypätä* in Agricola which today means 'to jump'), *kiistellä* ('to argue, to dispute'), *kumppanuus* ('partnership'), *kyteä* ('to smoulder'), *lykky* ('luck'), *päättyä* ('to be concluded'), *suo* ('bog'), *vaade* ('demand') and *valkaista* ('to whiten') from the Codex Westh (1546/2012). The word *sairastupa* ('infirmary'), also not found in Agricola, appears both in the Codex Westh and in the Uppsala Evangelion, and the word *vuo* ('flow, flux') appears in the Codex Westh, the Uppsala Evangelion and also the Uppsala Missal.

4.9.3 Word Formation

Since there are no printed sources older than Agricola, and moreover, any baselines of approximately the same time are extremely limited, it is impossible to figure out conclusively some questions involving the words Agricola used: these issues concern what his own formations or borrowed neologisms were, what the creations of his contemporaries were and what were used more commonly before the emergence of older literary sources.

New words are usually always created, in one way or another, on the basis of a previous vocabulary. The acquirement of new word stems happens most often by borrowing from other languages. On the basis of the features within a language, new vocabulary is, in practice, mostly formed by derivation, compounding or phonetic modification. Hence, it is best to search for Agricola's own words amongst the derivations and compounds. Two good examples on attempts at neologisms based on old vocabulary are Agricola's terms for vowels (*eneljiset* read as *äänelliset* "those that are voiced") and consonants (*yneneljset* read as *ynäänelliset* "those that are articulated together (with vowels)") (see Plate 3 on page 78). These words, however, did not remain in use. Moreover, Agricola's original neologism referring to letters or graphemes *kirjanrahtu* ("iota of a book") already lost the competition with the loanword *bokstavi*, a word of Swedish origin found the author's own text. Agricola also offered the compound *ajanrahtu* ("iota of time") as a synonym to the word *minuutti* ('minute'), but this did not become established either.

The distribution and establishment of a new word usually takes some time, whether it be a question of written or spoken language, and in the meantime, speakers end up having to actually be, in a number of ways, temporarily satisfied with acute needs of expression. Consequently, both the non-establishment of form and the existence of parallel alternatives can be seen as indicators of the young age of a concept and its name. When it comes to individual words, this is not, however, conclusive proof of how young they are, because both new and old expressions can run side by side in the competition.

Of the derivational types characteristic to Agricola, there are those which are no longer used today in the formation of new derivations. These are particularly distinctive to the modern reader, including action nouns (nomen actionis) with the suffix *-mus* or *-mys* (*häätämys* 'banishment'; *vedenpaisumus* "swelling of water" → 'flood myth, deluge myth') and agent nouns (nomen agentis) formed with the suffix *-uri or -yri* (*nisuri* 'suckling', *pilkkuri* 'mocker', *sikuri* 'swineherd'), for example. Agricola also had diminutive derivations which do not appear in today's standard language, for example *jalopeurukainen* ('young lion'← *jalopeura* 'lion', today *leijona*) and *vaimokainen*, a hypocoristic derivation for the word *vaimo* ('wife').

A few of Agricola's derivational types are clearly dialectical, such as the caritive derivations *häpiämättyys* 'shamelessness, impudence' and *kiittämättyys* 'ungratefulness, ingratitude'. These exist only in the southeastern dialects. For the most part, the derivational suffixes Agricola used were generally known, productive elements of word formation that any Finn could, in essence, have used in the same way and are still in use today.

The names of many foreign peoples and languages can most likely be counted as formations by Agricola. This is because the inconsistency characteristic to their manner of formation refers to the fact that they were not established. Furthermore it is a question of the fact that there hardly was a need for this vocabulary other than for translation purposes. A translator had to convey everything he came across when translating scripture. As there were many concurrent source texts, there were differences in the models provided by the source languages as well. For example, Agricola used the terms *edomi, edomiti, edumeeri* and *edomiteri* (today *edomilainen*) for the Edomites. The terms Agricola used for Hebrew were *hebraica, ebrea* and *hebrea* (today *heprea*), and he expressed 'in Hebrew' as *hebreiten* and *ebreitten* with an adverbial suffix ("in a Hebrew way"): today, either *heprea* is used as a modifier in the genitive with the word *kieli* ('language') in the adessive (*heprean kielellä* 'in the Hebrew language') or by itself in the translative (*heprea**ksi** 'in Hebrew').

In the case of verbal word formation, Agricola's compound verbs were a particular favourite of his. In these verbs, the initial component was most often an adverb signifying direction (*alas|polkea* 'downwards|trod+INF1': "to trod downwards", *edes|astua* 'forth|step+INF1': "to step forth", *ulos|tulkita* 'outwards|translate+INF1': "to translate outwards"). In most cases, they were modelled after prefix verbs from the source languages, but a comparison to the source texts shows that they were not all direct calques. Furthermore, Agricola's language has compound verbs that seem self-made, whose initial component is not an adverbial prefix but a noun inflected with a case ending, for example *eloa|leikata* ('life+PART|cut+INF1': 'to mow'), *kivil|surmata* ('stone+ADE|kill+INF1': 'to stone') and *suuta-antaa* (mouth+PART|give+INF1': 'to kiss'). Compounding in Finnish has traditionally been a means of word formation characteristic only to nominals, so the abundant use of compound verbs has given the literary language a solemn style, deviating from the vernacular. It appears that Agricola had consciously used this to his advantage.

The system of degrees of comparison of adjectives is also a part of the sphere of word formation. It is often presented as a special subcategory along with nominal inflection. The degrees of comparison in Agricola are basically the same as in contemporary Finnish, in other words, it has the positive, the comparative and the superlative: *suuri – suurempi – suurin* ('large – larger – largest'). The comparative marker *-mpi* is an old Uralic derivational suffix expressing opposition or an alternative, and it also appears in certain pronouns (*kumpi* 'which, which one', *jompikumpi* 'either, either one'). In Agricola, it is written, according to the common orthographic practice, with a voiced stop character *-mbi* (*swrembi* Std. *suurempi* 'larger', *ialombi* Std. *jalompi* 'nobler'). The difference, however, in comparison to contemporary Finnish is that as the final vowel of two-syllable adjectives with an *a* or *ä* in the stem today regularly changes to an *e* before the comparative suffix (*paha*

– *pahempi* 'evil – more evil'; *enä – enempi* 'many, much – more'), it may not change at all in Agricola (*paha – pahambi, enä – enämbi*).

The superlative marker *-in* is an old specifying derivational suffix whose original form, depending on vowel harmony, was *-ma* or *-mä*. Its current form has been affected by phonetic-historical changes and the analogy of the comparative, but the original form of the marker can be slightly better seen when inflected (*suurin* 'largest' : *suurim**m**an* 'largest+GEN'). There is often only one nasal consonant in the inflected form of the superlative in Agricola (*suuriman*), but it is impossible to tell if this stems from the general truncation of geminate nasal consonants or whether the original form of the superlative marker was preserved in his language. Superlative forms such as *jaloimain* ('noblest+PL+GEN') and *makeimita* ('sweetest+PL+PART') are case examples of those which were not affected by the analogy of the comparative, since they only have a nasal consonant and not the word-medial *mp* cluster (today *jaloi**mp**ien* and *makei**mp**ia*).

The true morphological superlative is not used in all Finnish dialects. In fact, it is not found, for example, in many Häme dialects. A comparative form provided with a special intensifier *kaikkein* or *kaikista* ('of all') may appear in its place. A few such cases can be found in Agricola in which superlativeness is expressed by the positive with an intensifier: **caikein***corckia Herra Iumala* ('the Lord God the highest').

4.9.4 Dialectical Vocabulary

Agricola chose to use the dialects spoken in the Turku region as a basis for literary Finnish, so it is not surprising that the vocabulary in his works was mainly taken from the western dialects. For example, *ehtoo* ('evening'), *nisu* ('wheat') and *suvi* ('summer'), anomalous words in terms of contemporary standard Finnish, are common in Agricola and other older Finnish texts. The dialectical words *ilta* ('evening'), *vehnä* ('wheat') and *kesä* ('summer') from eastern Finland, which are the standard words for these concepts today, did not replace the former set of words until the 19th century. A very common postposition in Agricola's Finnish is *tyge* ('to') which is a variant of the western dialect word *tykö*. The eastern dialectical *luo ~ luokse* ('to') later replaced *tyge* or *tykö*, which was thus completely removed from literary Finnish.

The boundary between literary and colloquial Finnish was just taking shape during Agricola's time. The clearest distinction of literary Finnish included words and constructions that never appeared in the true vernacular, those formed by loaning and translating. However, when it comes to the original vocabulary, there really was no boundary. Literary Finnish could accept any dialectical word, provided it was semantically fitting. It was easy to adapt the phonetic structure, as needed, to have more of a southwestern quality, the dialect that dominated literary Finnish.

There are some dialectical words in Agricola which no other cultivator of literary Finnish used. These include, for example, *eres* ('in a different way than') derived from the word *erä* ('quantity, item, entry, set') and *ihdoillansa* ('on the loose') formed from the stem of unknown origin *ihta* referring to space, freedom or possibility. The verb *hierata* in Agricola refers to defiling (today *liata* or *tahrata*) and *pydertää* refers to making something cloudy or confusing (today *samentaa*). Agricola's *kastinen* or *kastikka* refers to a grasshopper (today *heinäsirkka*) and *tirkatti* refers to a veil (today *huntu*).

An interesting detail in Agricola is the word *kymi*, which refers to a large river, in essence the Euphrates. This appears as a Finnish dialectical word in only a very narrow region within the southeastern Häme and Kymenlaakso dialects, thus appearing practically in the vicinity where the great Kymi River (Fin. *Kymijoki*) flows, rather close to Agricola's home region of Pernå. The word is only known elsewhere in Finland as a proper noun or understood through literary Finnish as a term for a river with a large amount of water.

4.9.5 LOANWORDS AND CALQUES

A new vocabulary can be acquired by forming it on the basis of a language's previous lexicon or by borrowing from other languages. There were stages in the development history of literary Finnish when there was a desire, as a matter of principle, to refrain from borrowing, but the 16th century writers did not take a clear ideological stand on borrowing. The problems were solved on a case-by-case basis.

It is easy to resort to a direct loan, especially when it is not so impossible for the word of the foreign language to be phonetically or structurally used in Finnish. Borrowing is also a useful immediate solution when the translator himself does not know the meaning of the word to be translated. Many of Agricola's words are clearly Latin, for example *agrimonia* (today known as *maarianverijuuri* 'common agrimony, sticklewort'), *betonika* (today *rohtopähkämö* 'betony, bishop's wort') and *lactuca* (today *salaatti* 'lettuce'). The plant *nardus* is used both in Agricola and today, both in Finnish and English. Latin words may have also seemed more stylish and more terminological than their Finnish counterparts, thus they may have also been used even when it would not have been necessary.

Agricola often phonologically adapted a loanword to sound Finnish by at least adding a final vowel or a Finnish derivational element. These slightly Fennicised words include, for example *finni* (today *suomalainen* 'Finn'), *funtti* (today *kastemalja* 'baptismal font') and *glosu* (today *reunahuomautus* 'gloss, marginal note'). Other examples include Finnish verbal derivational suffixes in the words *förbannattu* (← Swe. *förbanna*, today *kirottu* 'cursed') and *värkkyä* (← Swe. *värka*, today *särkeä* 'to break').

Many compounds were formed by translating the words of the source language component by component: Swe. *av|gud* – *epä|jumala* ('non|god': 'false god'), Swe. *väl|signad* – *hyvästi|siugnattu* ('well|blessed': 'blessed'), Swe. *före|bild* – *esi|kuva* ('fore|image': 'role model, exemplar'), Swe. *predik|stol* – *saarna|stuoli* ('sermon|chair': 'pulpit'), Swe. *ut|tyda* – *ulos|tulkita* ('outwards|translate+INF1': 'to translate').Words were also updated by providing an old one with a new meaning after foreign models, for example the word *jäsen* ('limb, extremity') was also given the meaning of 'member' and the verb *langeta*, which originally referred to falling or dropping, began to mean sinning. It is often impossible to know which language was the model for a Finnish expression because there was an increase in Swedish and German vocabulary in the same way by forming calques and semantic loans after Latin.

4.9.6 REMNANTS OF THE PAST IN AGRICOLA'S VOCABULARY

There are words or word forms in Agricola and the language of his contemporaries which are somewhat unknown in contemporary Finnish. They seem to have still been in active use in the 16th century but soon afterwards fell into oblivion. By following the lines of development in language history, we can deduce that some of them are quite old. For example, Agricola's *inhiminen* is evidently a more original form than today's *ihminen* ('person, human'). This is because phonetic changes are usually reductive, and it is not possible to construct a normal line of deduction between variants going from shorter to longer. The derivation *inhimillinen* ('humane') has the longer stem preserved even to this day. The word *ihminen* does not appear in Agricola at all, even though it demonstrably was already in existence at that time. It was namely noted in the word list in Sebastian Münster's 1544 *Cosmographia*. Both *ihminen* and *inhiminen* concurrently appear in Lord Martti's Finnish translation of the Law of the Realm at the end of the 16th century, but over the 17th century, *inhiminen* was completely omitted from literary Finnish use.

Another example of the truncation and structural fading of a word form is Agricola's adverb *vaivoin*, which evidently is the same word as *vain* ('only') of contemporary Finnish. The same *vaivoin* also appears in Westh's text, so it is neither a question of something exclusively typical to Agricola nor a question of a word formed by Agricola. In grammatical terms, it is the instructive plural of the word *vaiva* ('trouble'), thus a structure corresponding to the adverb *tuskin* ('hardly') from the word *tuska* ('agony'). The contemporary-like *vain* was not adopted into literary Finnish until its appearance in Juhana Wegelius' 1747 postil.

A third example of an interphase of historical development is *vanhurskas* ('righteous') which also appears in Agricola as *vaanhurskas*. The initial component has been explained to be the genitive form of the word *vaka* ('upright, steady'), but after the change of the *k* to a fricative ([vaɣan]) and its loss ([va.an]), it became a one-syllable word and structurally more indistinct. In a slightly similar fashion, the genitive of the word *ikä* ('age') changed into something unidentifiable in the word *iankaikkinen* (← *[iɣænkaik:inen] 'eternal, everlasting'). In this case, Agricola replaces the consonant with a *j* for the syllabic boundary: *ijankaikkinen*.

There are also examples of words in Agricola whose stem is even unknown in contemporary Finnish. For instance, Agricola has the verb *niedellä* ('to despise, to desecrate, to ostracise'), a derivation of the root *nietää* ('to curse') which is a verb of unknown origin that has appeared in Finnish and also Estonian. Neither one is used in contemporary Finnish any longer. The verb *luhdata* or *luhtia* ('to defend, to prove innocent') appears both in Agricola and old legal Finnish, and it has been speculated that this verb is quite an old Swedish loan (Hakulinen 1964). Derivations such as *luhtaaminen* ("defending"), *luhtaavainen* ("defensive") and *luhtimus* ("defence") were also in use, all of which are today unknown to the modern Finn.

The particle *ma(a)* is quite puzzling. It appears in both Agricola and the Codex Westh, and judging from its context, it means 'as' or 'as one says'. It has often been placed in parentheses along with the name of a person being cited, for example in the health advice for August in *Rucouskiria*:

*Tällä kuulla ei sovi ottaa sisäliset lääkitykset (**ma** Seneca se mestari sanoo)*

'It is not good to ingest medicines this month (as sayeth Master Seneca)'

Many theories have been presented on the structure and etymology of the word form. One possibility is that it is a truncated form of the pronoun *minä* ('I'), the same which can also be found in poetic Finnish and in Estonian (Häkkinen 2010). Whatever the history of this form may be, it has only been in use in 16th century literary Finnish and then disappeared without a trace. It evidently had already been so structurally and semantically obscure in the beginning stages of literary Finnish that it was not considered necessary to use and preserve it.

Concepts preserved from Catholic times and the words that went with them are not surprisingly relics. These concepts and words were no longer required during the Reformation. They include, for example, a day of fasting referred to as *himmurtai* ('Ember days') and *mariankakko*, probably a type of gingerbread, baked in honour of the Virgin Mary, Queen of Heaven.

In addition to words that were later lost, there are also meanings found in Agricola that were lost. The meanings of words in most cases change from concrete to abstract through metaphoric use, and there are a great number of words appearing in 16th century texts whose meanings are in a more original state than in contemporary Finnish. A good example of this is the verb *käsittää* ('to understand, to comprehend'), derived from the word *käsi* ('hand'), which means 'to take by the hand' in Agricola. The word *harras* ('pious, devout') of Germanic origin, which stems from the same root as the Swedish word for 'hard' *hård*, appears in Agricola still in the meaning of 'hard, harsh, strict' (Vartiainen 1988).

Agricola's language also provides examples on instances in which development has led to different directions than those in standard contemporary Finnish. For example, the word *huone* ('room') has quite a loose meaning in Agricola, referring to a house and everything that goes along with it – including people and movables. The adverb *irrallisesti*, derived from the stem *irta-*, means 'light-spiritedly, grievelessly' in Agricola, but the contemporary Finnish adjective *irrallinen* concretely means 'loose' and its aforementioned derived adverb 'loosely'.

4.9.7 CULTURAL-HISTORICAL EVIDENCE

Even though words as such are part of an abstract language system, they have clear connections to the context and environment in which they are used. Roughly speaking, there are two types of words: function words and content words. The former expresses the internal relationships of a language, the latter refers to the extralinguistic world, either to a concrete world of beings or objects or more abstract conceptual or relational systems. A change in the extralinguistic world forces a change in language as well. When, at any time, there is a need to speak about something, language must offer ways of expression to do so.

The basic vocabulary in Agricola concerning religion and legality seems to be well-established, and some of the same vocabulary also appears in manuscripts of his time. These fields most clearly had a tradition of oral standard Finnish that took shape during the Middle Ages. Agricola's language offers evidence on mediaeval secular innovations as well, for example cities and stone constructions (*holvata* 'to vault', *kamari* 'chamber', *katu* 'street', *lukko* 'lock', *muurata* 'to mason', *muuri* 'wall', *sali* 'hall', *tiili* 'brick', *tori* 'market', *torni* 'tower', *uuni* 'oven'), social and administrative organisation (*marski* 'Lord High Constable', *monarkki* 'monarch', *patruuna* '(property) owner', *pormestari* 'mayor', *porvari* 'bourgeois', *raati* 'council', *vouti* 'bailiff') and practitioners of various professions (*huora* 'prostitute', *lääkäri* '(medical) doctor', *mestari* 'master', *nikkari* 'carpenter', *tuomari* 'judge'). The words referring to these innovations can be considered mediaeval purely on an etymological basis: they are Swedish loans, a language from which borrowing was not earlier possible. The same holds true for words that stem from Latin and Greek as well: the vocabulary was acquired both directly from Latin and Greek literature and through Swedish and German.

Even though the language of Agricola does not show all the words and phenomena that existed in the 16th century, the vocabulary can give insight at least into what was in existence and what people knew about. As Agricola gives an explanation on the crops of the Finnish people in the introductory poems of *Psaltari* and *Ne Prophetat*, we can deduce that at least peas, cabbage, turnips, beans and onions could be found on the 16th century Finnish table. As the words *aasi* ('donkey'), *kameli* ('camel') and *jalopeura* ('lion', today *leijona*) appear in Agricola, we can deduce that at least some of the 16th century Finns were in some way aware of the existence of these animals, even if they would never have been found in Finnish nature. The nomenclature of beneficial herbs and other plants is proof of a tradition of herbalism. Furthermore, the names of the zodiac signs in the calendar section of *Rucouskiria* convey that writing and reading horoscopes were an important undertaking even during Agricola's time.

5. Mikael Agricola's Networks in Finland and Abroad

In the Middle Ages and the beginning of modern history, it was common for a profession and social status to be passed down from father to son. A son of nobility became a nobleman, a son of a merchant became a merchant and the son of a farmer became a farmer. An important exception to this common rule was the Church and its system of officials. Roman Catholic clergymen could not enter matrimony nor start a family, thus there was a constant search for a new group of young people outside the clergy for serving the spiritual estate.

Clergymen were not bound by family and assets, thus they were free to move about from one place to another. The Church offered representatives of the different estates of the realm the opportunity to be schooled and to progress from a modest start to a significant social status. Mikael Agricola is an excellent example of this. He was born the son of a farmer, but thanks to his talents and many significant supporters and partners, he advanced to the top of an ecclesiastical career in his homeland.

Great figures are often thought of as exceptional individuals who have achieved something quite worthy and significant, solely with their own work and owing to their personal talents. However, even great figures have their role models, assistants and partners, without whom their fate may have been shaped quite differently and their achievements may have been much more modest. A great deal also depends on the time, the circumstances and fortunate or unfortunate coincidences that one comes across on the road of life. This chapter examines the connections and contacts Agricola shared in, in both his homeland and abroad, making him a significant figure in Finnish history.

5.1 Agricola's Teachers, Assistants and Supporters

As stated earlier, Mikael Agricola's first teacher and supporter was most likely Vicar Bertil of Pernå. He must have taken notice of Mikael Olavinpoika's giftedness and desire to read. Mikael was the son of farmer who was just one of the common, uneducated people. Thanks to his own educational background, Bertil had the opportunity to assist Mikael in setting off on the road to learning. It is otherwise difficult to comprehend how the only male heir to a wealthy farmhouse could have escaped from staying on his family farm and taking over the responsibilities of a landowner. Since there were other boys sent to school in Vyborg from Pernå at the same time, it is logical to presume that a vicar trained in theological education would have actively been influential in this. However, there is no specific proof of this nor is there any information on what kind of elementary education the vicar may have given the boys before leaving for school. At the very least, he most likely taught elementary skills in reading and writing and the basics of dogmatics and Latin. These basic studies were useful in the initial stages of school.

Bertil also could have possibly had an influence because there was no other person known that could be given the attribute of sending boys from Pernå on the road to learning. There was no one else in Mikael's family that had any schooling at this time either. However, Agricola's sister later got married to Klemet Krook, a man born in the neighbouring rural district of Finnby (Fin. *Suomenkylä*). He was schooled to at least some extent, and it is possible that he too was a schoolmate of Mikael. Nevertheless, Krook became a scribe in the 1530s in the King's office in Stockholm, and in 1542, he was appointed as bailiff of Nyslott County (Fin. *Savonlinnan lääni*). He put taxation in order and organised settlement in this position with such stringent measures, that the people complained about him, and within a few years, he was dismissed from his post. Agricola might not have been very close to his brother-in-law, although they met a few times and Agricola gave Krook a certain valuable book as a gift as a sign of kinship. Agricola possibly also got information from Krook on the pagan ways practised in eastern Finland, which he described in the preface of his Psalter. The kinship ties ended when Agricola's sister died and Krook remarried. In 1551, Krook sold his share of the farm in Torsby to Agricola. He lived the rest of his life in Stockholm, and it is known that he died there before 1562. (Tarkiainen & Tarkiainen 1985.)

Johannes Erasmi, headmaster of the school in Vyborg, took Mikael under his wing. There is no exact information on the duration of the young boy's schooling, but it might have been approximately a good eight years. Johannes Erasmi and Agricola moved to Turku in 1528 and were appointed with different positions in the Bishop's office. It is more difficult to assess the significance of Reformation-spirited Johannes Block, preacher at Vyborg Castle, because he came to the city just when Johannes Erasmi and Agricola were leaving for Turku.

Agricola's long-time superior and supporter was Bishop Martinus Skytte, known for his pious and helpful nature. He was quite a world-travelled individual. Before he was appointed as Bishop of Turku, Skytte studied and taught in Germany and Naples for a total of about ten years. He also worked in Sweden as a Prior in the Dominican monastery in Sigtuna, as an inspector of all the Dominican monasteries in the entire Swedish Realm and as head of Dacia, the ecclesiastical province of Scandinavia. As early as 1513, he represented Dacia in the General Chapter of the Dominican Order held in Genoa. (Paarma 1999.)

With Skytte's support, Agricola got to study at the University of Wittenberg, just as some other talented young men of the diocese. While he was working in the Bishop's office, Agricola became closely acquainted with the matters pertaining to the entire, vast diocese, and since Skytte was already an elderly man, he needed an assistant in many practical matters, such as carrying out visitations. Skytte negotiated on retiring in 1544, but as no settlement was reached in the negotiations between the parties, he continued on in his duties until his death. Consequently, more and more assistance was needed. Canutus Johannis, Vicar of Turku and Agricola's closest colleague, was tending to many of these responsibilities. He presumably supported Agricola in translating literature into Finnish as well.

Agricola also had friends and acquaintances who were members of the gentry. A nobleman by the name of Erik Fleming was one of the lead secular figures of the eastern territory of Sweden, and his name is often noted amongst those men of power who were presumed to have supported Agricola's literary work. In his letter to Georg Norman in 1543, Agricola himself noted that Fleming had promised him, in writing, that he would proclaim his stand on publishing the New Testament at the Diet of Västerås. However, he allegedly did not fulfil his promise. Fleming is known to indeed have been in support of the Reformation and the confiscation of Church possessions which was carried out with it, but evidently his most important motive was to get the Fleming property previously ceded to the Church back into his family upon the appropriate circumstances. (Lahtinen 2007.)

Agricola received true support from Swedish nobleman Nils Bielke and his Finnish-born wife Anna Hogenskild. When Agricola's home, the prebendy house of Saint Laurentius, suffered great damage in the fire of 1546, Bielke helped Agricola acquire the former official residence of the Dean of Turku. He also forwarded Agricola's other requests to the King or to authoritative officers working in the King's office. A study by Anu Lahtinen (2007) on the rhetoric in Agricola's letters has shown that judging from the wording of the letters, the relations between Agricola and Bielke were cordial and there was no strict hierarchy between them. However, having a commoner background, Agricola could not act as if he was on quite the same level as his friend of nobility.

Anna Hogenskild's mother Anna Tott was the owner of many manors in Finland, and after her death in 1549, they were passed down to her daughter. Agricola represented Anna Hogenskild in matters of estate inventory and otherwise assisted her in overseeing her best interests. His assistance was necessary because in 1550, Bielke also died. Their son Hogenskild Bielke was already accepted into the cathedral school in Turku in 1547 as Agricola's student, and he remained in Turku under Agricola's supervision even after Agricola himself wound up transferring from the headmaster's post to other duties.

In 1552, Anna Hogenskild received a copy of Olaus Petri's chronicle from Agricola, evidently prepared by him himself. He composed a playful, poetic inscription on the cover. Olaus Petri, one of the leading figures of the Reformation in Sweden until the early 1530s, subsequently wound up withdrawing from his position because his sermons had a critical tone, addressing the secular exercise of power and the manner in which the King collected the Church's resources to the crown. The chronicle discussed the history of Sweden and was written in the spirit of humanism, and it added even more to the King's unpopularity. In the chronicle, Olaus Petri depicted the merits of the country's earlier rulers in a way that could have been understood as being critical towards the King himself and his governance. King Gustav Vasa did his best to confiscate all copies of the chronicle in circulation. Olaus Petri and Archdeacon Laurentius Andrae, his longtime partner from the cathedral chapter, were sentenced to death, although the verdict was never carried out. (Arffman 2008.) Agricola was familiar with the chronicle and used it as a source when he wrote about the Christianisation of Sweden and Finland in the preface of his New Testament. Copying and donating this banned book was a clear critical statement towards the King.

Agricola had approached the King by letter by the time he was studying in Wittenberg. He also became personally acquainted with the prominent men in Sweden at different stages in his career. Upon his return from Wittenberg in 1539, he travelled via Stockholm when he and Georg Norman got a call to meet the King. He most likely also met Olaus Petri on the same journey who, at the time, worked as the preacher of the Church of St Nicholas (Storkyrkan, the great church) in Stockholm and as the city scribe. Later, in 1551, Agricola wrote to printer Amund Laurentsson, requesting him to appeal exclusively to Olaus Petri so that he would assist in printing books that the Finns needed and would come up with a way to help the Finnish people in the dreadful poverty and famine the country was enduring at the time. (Tarkiainen & Tarkiainen 1985.) Agricola received no clear response to these appeals. Olaus Petri had limited facility and he himself died the following year in 1552. Nevertheless, Agricola's Book of Psalms and its two subsequent and complementary books were published after minor delays in 1551 and 1552.

Agricola also met the King even later. In regard to his official career, the most significant of these meetings was his bishop inauguration in 1554. A bit later, the King was visiting Finland for almost a year between 1555 and 1556 to lead acts of war and to inspect the conditions of the region. He was also Agricola's guest when he was in Turku during this journey. On the King's orders, Agricola took his final journey in 1557 to the peace negotiations in Moscow with Archbishop Laurentius Petri, Olaus Petri's brother.

Lesser in the secular hierarchy of power but an especially valuable connection in regard to Agricola's literary work was Amund Laurentsson, the Stockholm royal printing house master and overseer. Agricola noted Laurentsson as a dear friend in both his letter to him in 1551 and in his books. As Anna Perälä (2007) has shown in her studies on the typography and illustrations in Agricola's works, Agricola was the most industrious client of Laurentsson's printing house in the 1540s. It is difficult to imagine how Agricola would have pulled through in his publishing career if particularly the Stockholm royal printing house and its master Laurentsson would not have tended to the printing of his books. Producing nine books alongside other tasks in less than ten years is no small achievement even by today's standards, especially if the books were to be published in a language hardly used up to the time as a language for literature at all.

Of all the influential people abroad in connection with Agricola, Erasmus of Rotterdam is always mentioned, but he was only acquainted with Erasmus through his writings and they never personally met. However, Agricola got to get acquainted with another true great man while studying in Wittenberg: Martin Luther. Agricola evidently had already came across both Erasmus' and Luther's works during his schooling in Vyborg. In addition to this, Agricola's Luther postil with its hundreds of comments is evidence of his familiarity with Luther's works. Later, in translating parts of the Bible, Agricola considered the German-language Luther Bible to be a central exemplar to his own work.

In Wittenberg, Agricola got to see Luther in person. However, there is no precise information on the extent to which the men were associated with each other. Luther went on leave from his regular lecturing responsibilities at the university right when Agricola arrived in Wittenberg. However, Luther continued his duties as the university dean and also gave lectures, provided his health and other urgent matters allowed. During the time Agricola stayed in Wittenberg, Luther was only able to lecture on roughly ten chapters of Genesis. (Tarkiainen & Tarkiainen 1985.)

Students freely got to come to listen to Luther's sermons, and Luther also had a custom of organising debating exercises for more advanced students and received students at his home. Visiting students got to eat with their master and listen to his famous table talks. It is possible that Agricola also participated in these functions. This is because in April 1539, Luther wrote to King Gustav Vasa saying that he would be sending Norman to the Stockholm royal court to be a tutor and also recommended Agricola as his travelling companion. Luther noted Agricola as a young but outstanding man in terms of knowledge, talent and manners. These words have been interpreted to infer that Luther personally was acquainted with Agricola. (Tarkiainen & Tarkiainen 1985.)

As mentioned before in section 2.4, there were also other teachers at the University of Wittenberg alongside Luther who were significantly influential as role models. They provided Agricola with different ways of thinking and many kinds of elements for the content of his own published works. An especially important teacher was Philipp Melanchton who regularly saw to his educational duties when Agricola was in Wittenberg. On the other hand, Melanchton's restrained and factual lectures interested such a big audience that it was impossible to differentiate an individual student from the group without special merit. Nevertheless, Melanchton also sent King Gustav Vasa a recommendation on behalf of Agricola and Norman, stating their devotion and knowledge, and hoping that the ruler would grant them support and care. This recommendation, however, reached its destination through a proxy, so it does not prove that Agricola and Melanchton might have been acquainted with each other. (Heininen 2007.)

Since Agricola had studied theology and he had already been ordained a priest before going to Wittenberg, he probably benefited the most from university lectures that concentrated on subjects other than religious matters and the Bible. In this sense, Melanchton in particular was an extremely beneficial teacher for him because he lectured on the sciences of classical antiquity, such as natural sciences, philosophy and rhetoric, as well as classical literature. Luther took to the culture of classical antiquity selectively and, for example, rejected Aristotle, but Melanchton lectured on Aristotle's ethics and brought his works to print, after having them thoroughly checked. His teaching method was such that he translated Greek texts into Latin and explained their content. Consequently, in addition to substance, his lectures also offered Agricola the opportunity to study Greek better, a language he needed to know while translating the New Testament. (Tarkiainen & Tarkiainen 1985.) Reading Latin, however, came easier to Agricola. Before leaving Wittenberg, he purchased a two-volume book with nearly 1,500 pages that comprised a large number of Latin translations of Aristotle's works.

5.2 Agricola as a Representative of Finland

Since prehistoric times, Finland had been a point of contact between the East and the West. It had been conquered and Christianised from both directions with its territories alternatingly joined to both Sweden and Russia. The Finnish people, particularly in older times, only had the role of bystander, goods or military strength as the powers of the neighbouring countries fought over the ownership and administration of Finland. However, certain Finnish prominent men actively got to participate in the realm's organisation of circumstances. One of these prominent figures was Agricola.

Clergymen during the Middle Ages and at the beginning of the modern era were needed for the service of secular authority and tasks between different lands for many reasons. The best of them were prudent, experienced and schooled men, they could speak different languages, they had the ability to draw up official documents and they knew how to discuss, negotiate and debate. Moreover, thanks to their status, they were members of a network of authority and knowledgeable about such matters and background information which one had to know how to take into account in negotiations. For example, Vicar Bertil of Agricola's home rural district was a member of a four-man mission to Novgorod in 1513. The last Catholic Bishop of Turku, Arvid Kurki, sent him to the border discussions that revised the peace treaty between Sweden and Moscow that was signed and confirmed in March 1510 for a total of 60 years (Pirinen 1956).

During the Middle Ages, when all of Finland formed one single diocese, the Bishop of Finland was also a great man in a secular sense. His background support was a multi-tiered Church organisation of many lands which was above all secular authority. The bishop had his own castle, a large staff and his own conscripts at his service. He received one-third of the tithes collected by the Church, and he accumulated assets with which he could trade, even with foreign countries. The bishop had land, farms and valuables, for example books. The bishops were learned, respected individuals who represented the best of society and science. The bishops were responsible for the finances and administration of their diocese, they served as the highest judges and travelled in a brilliant convoy of up to 200 horses at governing assemblies. The bishops were high-ranking members in the King's council and represented their entire diocese in the ruler's favour.

Circumstances, however, changed along with the Reformation. The Church lost its financial might as the King became its head and a majority of its riches were taken over by the crown. Moreover, a significant part of the hallmarks of the Church's authority were lost. The bishop's responsibilities as a leader, organiser and organisational operator of his diocese were preserved, but his rights and wages were decreased considerably. The originally 12-member cathedral chapter that served as a support to the bishop shrunk down, as no new members were appointed to take the place of those who had died. During his career, Agricola as a chapter member wound up following up close the changes in the balance of power between the Church and secular authority.

King Gustav Vasa developed secular administration and his office's actions. He surrounded himself with learned assistants and minions, many of whom came from Germany. One of them was Norman. He was later promoted as the highest overseer of the Swedish Church. The Church's influence in administration was intentionally decreased even though it still retained its role as an educator of officials. The King preferred appointing non-nobility to positions in both Church and secular administration because they did not have the same kind support system from influential family ties as noblemen had. Thus, officials themselves understood that they had to thank the King alone for their position and serve him to the best of their abilities.

When Skytte died in1550, the King was in no hurry to appoint a new bishop. In May 1554, he invited the four remaining cathedral chapter members to Gripsholm Castle, including Dean Petrus Ragvaldi and three canons – Canutus Johannis, Mikael Agricola and Paulus Juusten. After the initial negotiations on matters concerning the care of Finnish issues, the King announced that there was no longer a need for Swedish cathedral prelates to go to a Roman curia in order to receive confirmation for an episcopal post because the King had the right to provide that same confirmation at home in Sweden. Furthermore, he announced that Finland would be divided into two dioceses: the Turku diocese and the Vyborg diocese. Agricola was entrusted with running the Turku diocese, and the younger Magister Juusten was appointed with the Vyborg diocese. Bishop Botvid Sunesson of Strängnäs accepted Agricola and Juusten's episcopal oaths because, as Juusten's chronicle of bishops describes, Archbishop Laurentius Petri was unpopular with the King and he was not thought necessary to be invited.

Agricola and Juusten were consequently not ordained as bishops in a mediaeval manner. The King did not even use the title *episcopus* except for special instances. The episcopal duties were indeed for the most part the same as before, but the official title was *ordinarius* ('ordinary'). Thus, it was concrete proof that the position of the new ordinaries was weaker than that of the former bishops. Nevertheless, the Turku diocese was larger and more distinguished than the Vyborg diocese, and so, despite a demotion of rank, Agricola could now finally think of himself as being at the top of the Finnish ecclesiastical hierarchy.

The declining of the position of bishops was actively influenced by Norman who originally came to Sweden to be tutor to Prince Eric. In a few years, however, he had risen to a significant official position in the King's office and council. In 1543, when nearing completion of the translation of the New Testament, Agricola approached Norman with a superfluously eloquent letter in Latin requesting to persuade the King to be favourable towards a printing endeavour and its financing, for example, in such a way that Agricola would be granted some unused, midsized prebandry earnings. (Tarkiainen & Tarkiainen 1985.) This appeal did not produce any results, and the endeavour was postponed for many years still. Norman had chosen his side and strictly represented the interests of the King at the expense of the Church.

Under the King's wishes, Agricola circulated the parishes, saw to the local conditions and itemised the Church's assets. The unrest with the Russians however increased, and in 1555, war broke out on the Karelian Isthmus. Vicar of Turku, Magister Canutus Johannis was sent to Moscow the following year to inquire if Tsar Ivan IV Vasilyevich would receive Swedish peace negotiators, and after been given a positive response and a warrant of safe conduct – a letter of protection – Gustav Vasa sent an exalted convoy of approximately 100 men on a journey led by his brother-in-law Sten Eriksson Lejonhufvud. Archbishop of Uppsala Laurentius Petri and representative of Finland, Ordinary Mikael Agricola of Turku were included in the convoy. It was an appropriate point in time, in the sense, that the Livonian Order in the Baltics was dissolving and conditions in the Baltic Sea region were expected to become more uneasy than before. While awaiting new conflicts, Gustav Vasa and Ivan did not want to waste their forces on clashing with each other (Tarkiainen 2004, 2007).

The original documents on the Russo-Swedish peace negotiations have disappeared, but there are copies preserved in both Russian and Swedish archives. Some of the Russian documents were published in Swedish in the 19th century, and the whole set of documents was published in Russian in 1910. The documents became a subject of more accurate research than before together with the preparations for Agricola 2007 – a national commemoration in Finland of the 450th anniversary of Agricola's death – whereupon a part of the Russian documents was released in Finnish (Kovalenka 2004). The essential points in the Swedish and Russian documents were somewhat similar, but the Russian documents more expansively and vividly depicted other issues concerning the negotiations, for example celebrations and gifts given at meetings. The Swedish reports contain a meagre but detailed depiction of the travelling routes and stopovers of the mission. This depiction is not found in the Russian documents.

The Swedish convoy journeyed to Novgorod and Moscow by a total of 37 sleighs through snow-covered landscapes, and on the Russian side of the border, the Russians accompanied the Swedes with a total of 150 conveyances. There had never before been such a grand travelling convey that left from Finland on a mission to the East. It was quite apparent that the size of these convoys gave emphasis to the great significance of the negotiations on both sides.

The Moscow negotiations covered many important issues. There had to be a reassurance that the negotiations were handled by mediation between appropriate representatives of correct rank. The points that had to be clarified were: who were the parties that were guilty of boundary clashes and continual warfare, how damages done should be repaired and to what extent to do so, how prisoners of war were to be exchanged and how the borders between the realms were to be placed in the future. As a sufficient amount of good will and flexibility was found on both sides, a compromise on the issues was reached without having either party be needlessly disgraced. Furthermore, there was already confirmation beforehand that the same treaties would be approved in Novgorod as well. It might have earlier been the case that there would have been a requirement to later constrict the treaties already once signed in Moscow.

There is no certain record on Agricola's role in the official negotiations. It was obvious that he must have participated in the mission because a sufficient number of high-ranking individuals for the parties had to be available in these negations, carried out with a tsar who was aware of his own status. Finnish representation was also important because border conflicts were happening where Finland and Russia met, far from the core region of the Realm of Sweden. In keeping with the old custom, the Bishop of Turku was a dignified enough individual to represent all of Finland.

Since Agricola had gone to school in Vyborg, he knew the conditions on the Karelian Isthmus. It is possible that his diverse linguistic skills were assumed to be of some help. Nevertheless, interpreters were specifically hired to assume the role of mediators in the true negotiations. Many of the Russian interpreters spoke German and at least one spoke Swedish as well. The main interpreter of the Swedish mission was a *frälseman* nobleman (Fin. *rälssimies*) by the name of Bertil who normally worked in Vyborg and spoke Russian. Documents were quickly translated as the negotiations progressed. The most authoritative members of the negotiating parties had no common language. The Swedish clergymen and nobility knew no Russian and the Russians did not speak the languages the Swedes knew: as Russia belonged to the sphere of the Orthodox Catholic Church, Latin – the common language amongst the West European learned people – was not spoken there, not to mention Swedish.

Agricola is in no way predominately featured in the preserved documents on the negotiations. He evidently only participated in the drafting of one rejoinder submitted to the Tsar. Due to Archbishop Laurentius Petri becoming ill, the Swedish delegation in writing requested some of the documents in the negotiations, and the Swedes reciprocated to the statement received, outlining the actions of King Gustav Vasa and the previous Russian rulers in a positive light, depicting damage done in reciprocal warfare, war scenarios and the reasons for them. Finally, an appeal was made on behalf of peace and for the release of prisoners, and a picture of a better future was painted, whereupon commoners got to tend to their fields in peace with no fear of enemy attacks.

Based on the aforementioned facts, there is no need to exaggerate Agricola's merits or diplomatic skills in the imperial policies of the time. He participated in that one important mission and did his part in the authoritative line-up, and that is all. He indeed settled small border disputes in his homeland but he did not have previous experience in political discussions on other lands nor was his nature evidently very diplomatic judging from the fact that many times in his career, he knowingly aggravated King Gustav Vasa by going against his wishes. In the prefaces in his books, he sometimes reproached his adversaries and defended his translation work in quite an aggressive tone. Agricola did not have time to give any information on his experiences on the journey to Moscow and his possible part in the negotiations because of his sudden illness and then death on 9 April 1557 on the journey back.

The Swedish and Russian documents on Agricola's precise place of death provide slightly differentiating information from each other. According to Russian sources, Agricola died in the rural district of Uusikirkko (later Kuolemajärvi) at Kyrönniemi when the convoy journeyed towards Vyborg along the icy Gulf of Finland. According to Swedish documents, his death occurred on the same coastline but slightly more east in the village of Seivästö, located in the rural district of Äyräpää.

Agricola achieved his most important diplomatic triumphs in his homeland. Considering the circumstances, he succeeded well in his duties as leader of the Finnish Church. At no point did the Reformation in Finland break out into such bloody revolts which were felt in its homeland Germany. Agricola did not abruptly destroy all which was traditionally considered a part of Christian life during Catholic times. He combined the new and the old, and the most central dogmas and prayers were preserved the same as they had always been, up to and including Ave Maria. Despite difficult conditions, Agricola brought the basic literature required by the Church to the pages of books. The literature could then be distributed in the same form for all the parishes to use. The people remained peaceful in religious matters and had the chance to experience the benefits brought by the Reformation themselves: it was the first time each Finn could understand what the priest was saying and chanting to them from beginning to end, and personally benefit from the good news of faith and mercy which the new Lutheran faith expressly highlighted.

5.3 Agricola as a Provider of Information and Influence from Abroad

It is impossible for the contemporary person to imagine how difficult and coincidental it was for the ordinary person of Agricola's time to attain information on issues and events of the other parts of the world. There were no schools or textbooks in existence for the common people, no newspapers or radio, not to mention other forms of media. Books were written in foreign languages and the ordinary people would not have been able to read them, even if they would have been in Finnish. Information was passed on orally from person to person and changed upon its transmission. Information travelled better in harbour cities, where ships and merchants from abroad arrived, than in the secluded countryside, but it was even difficult to separate fact from fiction even there. Those who travelled abroad boasted with the wonder they saw and exaggerated their stories in order to make a bigger impression upon those who were listening. In these conditions, the clergymen were in a key position as teachers and educators of the people.

The fundamental task of the clergymen of the Reformation era was to distribute new Evangelical teachings purely and clearly in the people's own language. In addition to this, they also passed on other types of information. A part of it was strictly related to the Bible. The Good Book had a great deal of strange words and concepts which were impossible to comprehend without explanations. Agricola appended a great many glosses (marginal notes) and summaries in which he explained the text with the support of source materials from outside Sweden and Finland.

Agricola carried out a majority of his literary life's work by translating literature composed in other languages into Finnish. At the same time, he brought Christian tradition, culture and ways of thinking from abroad into Finnish consciousness. As for some of his works, he could also independently make some choices concerning content. For example, neither *Abckiria* nor *Rucouskiria* followed any one, specific exemplar. Instead, there was a selection of elements from various sources chosen for them. *Rucouskiria* in particular is an especially interesting book in view of scientific thought of Agricola's time because the information found in its calendar section features many branches of science.

Agricola himself lists his most important sources and exemplars at the beginning of *Rucouskiria*. Immediately following the Bible, he notes Martin Luther, Philipp Melanchton and Erasmus of Rotterdam. As previously stated, Agricola met Luther and Melanchton in Wittenberg, but he never personally met Erasmus. However, he quite evidently was familiar with Erasmus' works starting from his schooldays and started to consider him his important literary mentor. An important book that provided general education was, for example, Erasmus' collection of proverbs *Adagia*, accompanied by annotated commentaries. This work inspired Agricola to compile proverbs and use them as elements in his own works.

We can get a picture of Agricola's literary preferences by examining his personal library. There is a considerable amount of information on his collection of books still available today. Agricola tended to write his name in the books he purchased as well as information on when it was acquired. Sometimes it was also marked with when, to whom and for what price it was resold. On the basis of this information, many works preserved in Swedish and Finnish libraries have been able to be identified as belonging to Agricola. Many learned librarians, theologians and literary researchers have participated in the reconstruction of Agricola's personal library. Amongst them include concrete researchers of Agricola, especially Viljo Tarkiainen (1948) and Simo Heininen (1996) whose studies have shown that Agricola's collection had a great deal of other books than just spiritual works.

Agricola also wrote many kinds of entries in the books he owned, and from this, we can deduce where his interests lay. For example, he wrote the Latin words *Amicus Chato, Amicus Plato, magis amica Veritas* ('Cato is a friend, Plato is a friend, but the greatest friend is truth') in his Lutheran postil in 1531. Thus, he reworded the saying which is usually considered to be Aristotle's. Agricola possibly thought of these words in his citation in that it was good to be familiar with the opinions of authorities but still it was it was necessary to think for oneself. He had the opportunity a few years later to become acquainted with the philosophy of Aristotle through Melanchton's lectures at the University of Wittenberg.

In 1532, Agricola purchased an anthology which included many works of different writers. There was a small book printed in Basel amongst them which included two writings by Erasmus: one praised marriage and the other praised medical science and medicines in particular. According to the way of the humanists of the time, learned people of antiquity and their works were noted as exemplars of medical science, for example the natural sciences by Pliny the Elder and medical writings by Galen of Pergamon. Erasmus himself translated Galen's Greek writings into Latin. Agricola later got to hear more at Melanchton's and other teachers' lectures in Wittenberg.

There was no education or research on the field of natural sciences offered in Finland in Agricola's time. The country did not even have one schooled doctor. Empirical natural science was just at its beginning stages elsewhere in Europe. Antiquity philosophers in their time indeed had got far in many different fields, but during the Middle Ages, the interest towards the natural sciences had diminished and knowledge attained had, for the most part, been forgotten. Knowledge concerning phytotherapy was cherished at monasteries, but even there, botany and medicine shrank down, in practice, to merely lists depicting medicinal plants and their uses. The influence of humanism finally started to revive and develop the rich tradition of antiquity. Expeditions had great significance, through which one was able to become familiar with the continents, plants and animals. Particularly new plants beneficial to humans and those used for decoration rose great interest both in learned people and in wealthy nobility and bourgeoisie circles. They gladly sought out these new phenomena for their own gardens.

Finland saw the decline of monasticism in the 16th century due to the influence of the Reformation. Some of the tradition regarding phytotherapy, however, was preserved, thanks to the materials included in the *Rucouskiria* calendar section. The sources for the calendar cannot be clarified in detail, but information pertaining to health specifically represents a pan-European tradition of phytotheraphy which could have come into Agricola's hands via many different paths. The majority of the information regarding the actual calendar and its chronology evidently originates from Erasmus Reinhold (Harviainen et al. 1990). Reinhold was a professor of mathematics in Wittenberg at the time Agricola was there. In his chronicle of bishops, Juusten wrote that *Rucouskiria* spent time in the hands of all the Finns every day. The book possibly interested the people because of the calendar section specifically and the instructions that went along with it. The bountiful selection of prayers was largely compiled for the needs of the priests.

Agricola's interest in medicine can be seen from the fact that he purchased *Libri de Rustica* ('Book of country affairs') in 1538 in Wittenberg. It too was an anthology, including knowledge from both antiquity and the Renaissance on rural life and matters regarding the practice of agriculture. In addition to entries describing careful reading, Agricola wrote Latin instructions in it on how to tend to horses and sheep. As the duty of the priests still hundreds of years later was to also distribute knowledge to the people on practical matters regarding life and health, there is no reason to doubt that even Agricola would not have orally passed on the knowledge he had attained.

Agricola was also interested in history. In addition to Erasmus' writings, the anthology Agricola acquired in 1532 also included the work *Dictorum et factorum memorabilium libri novem* ('Nine books of memorable deeds and sayings') by Valerius Maximus. It was an extensive collection of information on general education which had hundreds of narratives and anecdotes selected from classical sources. They gave brief and concise depictions of significant figures in Greek and Roman history and important events in antiquity.

Moreover, geography was clearly one of Agricola's interests. In the preface of his New Testament, he makes a direct reference to Jacob Ziegler's depiction of Finland and its division into different provinces. In 1539, he purchased another anthology in Wittenberg comprising a total of four geographical works. The most extensive of these was a nearly 600-page commentated edition on geography by Strabo (*Strabonis geographicorum commentarii*) which thoroughly depicted the parts of Europe, Asia and Africa during antiquity. Furthermore, the tome included Julius Solinus' *Rerum toto orbe memorabilium thesaurus locupletissimus* which was a compilation of information concerning the whole world from the works of many different writers such as Pliny the Younger. The third work was Pomponius Mela's *De situ orbis libri III* which included a depiction of Late Antiquity geography. Fourth was Joachim Vadian's *Epitome trium terrae partium, Asiae, Africae et Europae, compendiarum locorum descriptionem continens* which was a depiction of the regions in the New Testament using the view of systematic geography. Knowing these was understandably important to the Finnish translator of the New Testament. Agricola thus wrote a comment on the first page in Latin, according to which the anthology was "quite an illustrative and magnificent depiction of the globe".

Agricola used the information he acquired as background support and a source of explanations and comments added to his translations, but in addition, the knowledge of many fields was also required for his work as headmaster. As stated before, there is no direct information on what and how Agricola taught at the cathedral school in Turku, but his own personal library and university studies guaranteed that he knew much more than the schoolboys studying at his hand were able to take in. Perhaps he himself thought that his knowledge was sufficient because he sold or gave away a part of his collection of books. While serving as headmaster, he came into possession of Sebastian Münster's book *Cosmographia: Beschreibung aller Lender* which was first printed in 1544. This book was closely associated with Sweden and Finland because Georg Norman had promised to bring information the book needed on Sweden when he visited Münster in Basel in 1542. (Heininen 2007.) The book contained geographical, historical and ethnographic depictions of the whole known world. It also had a description of Finland and a sample of the Finnish language: a list of words and The Lord's Prayer in Finnish. In terms of its composition and linguistic form, the prayer was interesting because it was clearly of eastern dialect and the final words (*For thine is the kingdom, the power, and the glory, for ever and ever*) were missing. These missing words were not added until the time of Reformation. It can be interpreted as a representation of an older stratum of translation than The Lord's Prayer (*Isä meidän*) found in Agricola's works (Ojansuu 1904). Might this be the reason why Agricola abandoned the work almost right away? There is no information in the book on how he attained it or its price, but there is, however, a marking according to which, it was the book that Agricola gave to his brother-in-law in 1545 "as a sign of kinship". Perhaps he was also slightly disappointed in Norman who served as a spokesperson for the book, and who in his new ascendancy did not seem to be of any use to his former travelling companion.

For nearly ten years, Agricola was in charge of leading the most important educational institution in Finland and serving as its governing teacher. Furthermore, thanks to his printed works, he became an authority and a role model in the field of Finnish literary use. It is a great shame that not even one of his students had recalled their teacher and his activities in writing, especially in his educational duties, but on the basis of his position and literary merits, Agricola must have significantly influenced the following generations of Finnish scholars.

6. The Legacy of Mikael Agricola

Mikael Agricola was not an unknown person in his lifetime but he was no national hero either. The preface poems he himself wrote show that he encountered difficulties and opposition in his work and that his works were not as revered as he would have hoped. In his era in the 16th century, it was never taken for granted that Finnish would someday become a fully respected, cultivated language or that Finland would someday in the future become an independent state whose language and culture should be developed. Even during its mid-19th century autonomy as part of the Russian Empire, Finland had many leading figures in society and in the scholarly world who believed that the work done for the good of the Finnish language was just a waste of time and effort.

Circumstances changed dramatically in the late 19th and early 20th centuries. Finnish was given official language status in Finnish society, and Finland gained its independence in 1917. In these contexts, there was an aspiration to highlight those prominent social and cultural figures that initiated and achieved this great change. Today, virtually every Finn recognises Mikael Agricola's name and knows that it was he who was the founder of literary Finnish.

6.1 The Literary Legacy of Mikael Agricola

Mikael Agricola was the only Finn during the Reformation who succeeded in translating literature required by the Church into Finnish and bringing his works to print. It was possible to circulate printed works everywhere where the word of God was taught and preached in Finnish. Thus, Agricola's works became the foundation of Finnish literature and the literary language. There is no exact information on the number of copies, but generally speaking, there were a few hundred printed in those times. This quantity was sufficient for the needs of Finland. There were only 102 parishes at the time when Agricola was finished with publishing books, and the only ones who required books in Finnish were, in practice, clergymen. The language of nobility and the wealthy bourgeoisie was Swedish or German, and the ordinary Finnish-speaking people still did not know how to read.

The works Agricola produced fulfilled nearly all the needs of the Church. By using them, it was possible to tend to services and ecclesiastical ceremonies in Finnish, and one could find materials in them at will for preaching, teaching and different devotional needs. The only clear shortcoming was the fact that Agricola did not print a Finnish hymnal. This shortcoming was partly relieved by lyrics in *Rucouskiria* and the psalms in *Psaltari*. German-type hymns in verse indeed began to be inducted immediately from the beginning of the Reformation, but the Finnish congregations in Agricola's time were still not used to singing hymns together. The first Finnish hymnal was not published until 1583 by Jacobus Finno.

There are eight hymns in today's Finnish-language hymnal *Virsikirja* ('Hymnal', lit. 'hymn book') of the Evangelical Lutheran Church of Finland, which, in one way or another, are connected to Agricola's translated texts (Tuppurainen 2007). Apart from one, they found their way into *Virsikirja* through Finno's hymnal. None of them is exactly in a form following Agricola's original text. The poetic hymn *Oi Jumalan Karitsa* (*Lamb of God, Pure and Holy, O Lamm Gottes, unschuldig*) found in Agricola's missal is most reminiscent of the modern hymn. Today, it is hymn number 65 in *Virsikirja*. Its text in Agricola, however, is just one verse long. Finno added two other verses to the hymn which are still being sung in its modernised wording.

The liturgical books and parts of the Bible Agricola translated were put into rigorous use. Proof of this is that the text in many later works was directly borrowed from Agricola. Paulus Juusten published a Finnish-language missal in 1575, and its content shows that a majority of it was copied verbatim from Agricola. Juusten did not quite slavishly duplicate Agricola. There were sections in which he attempted to slightly improve Agricola's format, but later translators generally returned to Agricola's take on them. Juusten's book, however, included a few excerpts which are not in Agricola. Therefore, we can say that he too had his own minor merits in translation work. The relationship between Agricola's and Juusten's missals has been examined in detail by Martti Parvio (1978). A special achievement of Juusten is that he combined all the material required for a missal in the same book. Thus, a priest did not need to switch to another book in the middle of the service, and instead he could read the gospels, epistles and required prayers from the missal.

Although Agricola himself did not publish a hymnal, the psalms he translated were used by singers both as they were and as elements in later anthologies. Michael Bartholdi Gunnærus, a headmaster in the unassuming little town of Helsinki, composed a collection of 95 missal introits for a manuscript in 1605, whose Finnish-language texts were formed from verses of psalms selected from Agricola's works (Hannikainen 2006). There were some minor linguistic and orthographic changes which evidently came about without the author realising it because his own dialectical background was different from Agricola, but the linguistic structure remained unchanged and was easily recognisable. These linguistic differences have been examined in detail by Kaisa Häkkinen (2010).

Agricola's New Testament was on the desk of Bishop of Turku Ericus Erici (Sorolainen) when he was drafting the first Finnish-language postil published in two volumes in 1621 and 1625. Osmo Ikola (1949) has noted that the gospel texts for the various holidays during the year were usually copied straight from Agricola's New Testament. This is an interesting observation because Ericus Erici is known to have led a translation committee whose task it was to translate the whole Bible into Finnish. The work of this first Bible translation committee was never finished, and in its toil of many years, it evidently did not focus on the New Testament because there had already been a printed translation in existence. If the committee would have retranslated the New Testament, Ericus Erici would have without a doubt used the output of his committee's work for his postil.

The entire Bible was published in Finnish in 1642: *Biblia: Se on: Coco Pyhä Ramattu Suomexi* ('Biblia: it is: the entire holy Bible in Finnish') or *Biblia* for short. A four-man committee led by Swedish-born Aeschillus Petraeus saw to its translation. The three other members were native-speaking Finns. The committee was instructed to use pure and proper Finnish so that it would be understood by everyone in the country. These instructions were interpreted to edit out certain features in Agricola, for example eastern dialectical accusative personal pronoun forms ending in *t* (*meidät* 'us', *teidät* 'you (pl.)', *heidät* 'them') alien to the western Finns as well as loanwords and structural features clearly from Swedish. Interesting documentation on the translation committee's work has been preserved: a copy of the New Testament with the first part full of corrections found at Skokloster Castle. This copy belonged to Vicar Henrik Hoffman of Masku, one of the committee members.

Martti Rapola (1963) has examined Hoffman's notations and attested that they were evidently entered right at the beginning of the translation work. Hoffman went through Agricola's texts and marked down sections where he himself wanted changes. He replaced parts of words written with one vowel pronounced as a long vowel with two-vowel strings. He added vowels to the ends of words in those nominal case endings that normally had apocope in Agricola, but on the other hand, he removed final vowels from possessive suffixes and certain verbal forms. For the most part, he removed the third-person singular -*pi* ending completely. Hoffman replaced many of Agricola's postpositional structures, which emerged when he was translating German or Swedish original texts verbatim, with plain case endings. He replaced Agricola's preferred prefix verbs with set phrases comprising verbs and adverbs, such as *alas|astua* ('downwards|step+INF') → *astua alas* ('to step down') and *pois|hakata* ('away|chop+ INF') → *hakata pois* ('to chop down').

Even though Petraeus' committee did not approve of Agricola's translations quite as they were, it nevertheless considered them the foundation for its own work. The committee worked for such a short time that it in no way would have even been able to retranslate all the books of the Bible based on the original texts. It remains a mystery how Petraeus' committee benefitted from the results of Ericus Erici's working group. Ikola (1949) has noted that the most important exemplar to Petraeus' committee while doing revision work was the Swedish translation of the Bible – the 1618 Gustav II Adolf Bible. The 1642 *Biblia* is also reminiscent of this translation both in its artwork and its overall appearance. Agricola's translations were linguistically finished to be more cohesive, and the orthography changed to be more consistent. Because of this, *Biblia* is essentially easier to read than Agricola's texts, although its orthography is also still far off from contemporary Finnish. A majority of the changes only cover orthography and minor details regarding phonetic structure. The forms and structures Agricola used were, for the most part, preserved as they were. Linguistic comparison between Agricola's biblical translations and *Biblia* has been examined by A. F. Puukko (1946).

Biblia became the definitive work of Finnish spiritual literature for a long time. During the following centuries, there were revised editions, but plans for a completely new translation directly from the original texts did not get started until the 19th century. Even then, the translation took decades. The new Finnish translation of the Old Testament was not officially approved until 1933, and the New Testament in 1938. Agricola's mark can be seen in all other Finnish translations of the Bible that were used before this. In actuality, Agricola's influence can be seen in all the spiritual literature after the release of the new translation as well, because a basic religious vocabulary and many fundamental features and the wording found in spiritual texts originate from his works. Religious language is characteristically conservative, and there is a desire to preserve its features even when they disappeared from other areas of a literary language.

The modern-day person is prone to think that when an important book is revised and improved, the revisions will, in practice, immediately be adopted and they will be used by everyone. However, there is proof in the history of a literary language that this may not always be the case. Information on revisions cannot reach all language users at the same time, and sometimes there is opposition to revisions on a matter of principle. For example, the use of the 1776 edition of the Finnish Bible, the so-called *Vanha kirkkoraamattu* ('Old Church Bible'), has been preserved to this day in the circles of certain Finnish Christian revival movements (the Laestadians and the so-called "prayer movement" – *rukoilevaisuus* – in Southwest Finland), even though the translation officially approved by the Church had been thoroughly revised two times after its publication. There is a desire to preserve the old translation because people in the circles of these revival movements are used to hearing the word of God and deeming it correct specifically in the form of what was in *Vanha kirkkoraamattu*. Only the orthography has slightly been modernised.

We can come across Agricola's texts in other contexts as well. The first musical composition appearing in Finland depicting the suffering of Jesus Christ was German composer Melchior Vulpius' 1613 *St Matthew Passion*, whose text came straight from the Gospel of Matthew. The oldest Finnish translations of the *St Matthew Passion*, *Matteus-passio*, are manuscripts from the late 17th century (Urponen 1999), in other words, from the time when *Biblia* and its 1685 revised edition were available. Still, there are details in the text of *Matteus-passio* which could only be originally from Agricola's translation of Matthew, for example the special imperative form *pidäksi* ('hold on!') which has been replaced by other expressions in later translations of the gospel. The same details are repeated in 18th century manuscripts as well. As the text for *Matteus-passio* was originally taken specifically from Agricola, it was not considered necessary to change it, even though it was not in accordance with 18th century Finnish biblical translations.

6.2 Research on Michael Agricola and His Life's Work

Although his books were put into immediate, rigorous use after being published and their content was used as material for new publications, Agricola, as a person, was no longer given any great attention after his death. Agricola's merits as a groundbreaker of literary Finnish and producer of manuscript literature faded into oblivion, especially after the printing of *Biblia* for the first time in 1642 and other literature required by the Church was published. Indeed, the preface in *Biblia* mentioned that the first Finnish printing of the New Testament was in 1548, but there was no mention of the translator. Paulus Juusten's chronicle of bishops included a few details on Agricola's publications and was published for the first time in Sweden in 1728. There were indeed a few manuscript copies in existence but they were only known amongst small circles. Agricola was not rediscovered until the late 18th century when a critical study of Finnish history began and material was collected, shedding light on the beginning stages of literary Finnish.

Finnish-born scholar Carl Fredrik Mennander was the first who began raising Agricola's work to public awareness. In his old age, he became Archbishop of Sweden. Before this, he worked at the Royal Academy of Turku, first as a professor of physics, then as a professor of theology and then as Bishop of Turku. He was a student of Carl von Linné, a world-renowned scholar in the natural sciences and an active researcher who was interested in questions in many different scholarly fields. Church history in Finland was a particular topic of interest to Mennander, and due to the positions he held, he had the opportunity to thoroughly familiarise himself with source of materials that shed light on the subject. He accumulated rare books and manuscripts, and he had a copy of Juusten's chronicle of bishops in his possession, depicting the main features of the progression of the Reformation and Agricola's groundbreaking work. Mennander understood the translation history of the Finnish Bible well, and while he was serving as bishop, he himself wrote the preface to the third edition of the Bible which was revised by Anders Lizelius and published in 1758. (Puukko 1946.)

Mennander had a large group of active students. One of them was Henrik Gabriel Porthan who developed into the greatest expert of Finnish literature after his teacher (V. Tarkiainen 1971). Porthan worked as a librarian at the Royal Academy of Turku and later as a professor, and it was evidently thanks to Mennander that he focused attention on Agricola and his status as the founder of Finnish-language literature. In 1778, Porthan wrote a series of articles for the newspaper *Tidningar Utgifne Af et Sällskap i Åbo* (later known as *Åbo Tidningar*) which briefly discussed the history of translating the Bible into Finnish. In this context, he expounded upon those works of Agricola which included translations of parts of the Bible, in other words, the New Testament, the Psalter and the Prophetic Books of the Old Testament.

Porthan began to publish Juusten's chronicle of bishops, furnished with comments, as a series of Doctoral dissertations in 1784, and its last – the 56th – part was published in 1800. Furthermore, he wrote an eight-part series of articles for the 1796 volume of *Åbo Tidningar*, which focused on the oldest published literature for the needs of the Finnish Church. Most of the parts in the series focused specifically on Agricola's output. *Rucouskiria*, *Se Wsi Testamenti* and *Psaltari* were the only works by Agricola noted in the chronicle of bishops, and Porthan could supplement this list on the basis of his own investigations.

Porthan was not actually a linguist, nor did he analyse Agricola's Finnish. He made the names of Agricola's works known and depicted their content, commenting especially on what their non-Finnish exemplary works were. He also surmised that in addition to preserved works, there would have also been Finnish-language primers and catechisms early during the Reformation even though there was no one preserved copy of such works. In this case, he referred to a chronicle in verse composed by Johannes Messenius and the preface in *Psaltari* in which Agricola himself described the works he published in Finnish. As we noted in chapter 3, the preserved parts of *Abckiria* were not found until much later than Porthan's time. There is also a part in the introductory poem in *Abckiria* which was earlier presumed to refer to a Finnish catechism. Messenius had indeed said that it was Luther's catechism that Agricola translated into Finnish, but this cannot be deemed historically reliable information because no one, including Messenius, admitted to have laid eyes upon such a book. Luther's catechism was indeed one of the exemplars to *Abckiria*, but not the only one, nor even the most important.

Agricola's role as the founder of literary Finnish was known and recognised at the end of the 18th century, but true research on Agricola did not begin until the latter half of the 19th century. In the meantime, the country became the Grand Duchy of Finland – an autonomous part of the Russian Empire – Helsinki became the capital and the university was transferred there. Nationalism began to have an effect in Finland as in other European countries, and there was a rise in patriotism by researching the country's history, culture and traditions. It was important to find and name a group of national notables as symbols of Finnishness in this process: Johan Ludvig Runeberg, who wrote in Swedish, was raised to national poet status and native Swedish speaker Johan Vilhelm Snellman became the national philosopher. The indisputable notable in the field of Finnish-language culture was native Finnish speaker Elias Lönnrot, compiler of Finnish folklore and publisher of *Kalevala*. The position of a notable in the history of Finnish language and literature fell upon the founder of literary Finnish, Mikael Agricola. Since Agricola was additionally a Finnish Reformer and the first Lutheran bishop of the Turku diocese, he was an exceptionally interesting figure also from the perspective of Church history and the history of the Finnish Bible.

Around the mid-19th century, Finnish literature was still quite scarcely available, if we omit spiritual literature. Rare textbooks and reference books were usually translated from foreign languages and superficially discussed matters concerning Finland. The first Finnish writer to begin making Agricola known to the common people was Gustav Erik Eurén, a teacher, textbook writer, journalist and book publisher from Hämeenlinna. He published a small booklet in 1858 entitled *Mikael Agrikola. Suomen pispa, uskonopin oikasia Suomessa, Suomen kielen ensimmäinen harjoittaja kirjoissa* ('Mikael Agricola. Finnish bishop, reviser of dogmatics in Finland, the first Finnish language specialist in books'). Eurén drew its content from both earlier literature and his own imagination. Without true evidence, he revealed that Agricola's father had worked as a fisher at Särkilahti Manor. The same unfounded claim was then repeated in later literature up until the early 20th century. Eurén ended his book with the hope that the Finns would build a statue in their hearts commemorating Agricola. He did not venture to suggest an actual sculpted statue because at that time, Finland did not even have one erected public monument of any figure.

Eurén's suggestion of a monument received support to some extent. A fundraising campaign began, and for this, a biography was written in 1870 in both Finnish and Swedish geared towards children and young people by Ludvig Leonard Laurén, a teacher from Vaasa. The author's name was not noted in this book, but the title page showed that its proceeds were for the Agricola fund. *Kalastajan poika* or in Swedish *Fiskaresonen* – both meaning 'The fisher's son' – was a pedagogic narrative of the son of a poor fisher who became a great national figure and benefactor of all of the Finnish people. There were also two pictures in the booklet. One was a drawn copy of Robert Wilhelm Ekman's painting of Agricola presenting his translation of the Bible [sic!] to King Gustav Vasa. The other picture depicted Agricola as a little boy reading a book on the seashore near his father's fishing nets.

August Ahlqvist, professor of Finnish at the University of Helsinki, was the first to become familiar with Agricola's Finnish in detail. However, he was not able to acquire all of Agricola's works. Instead, *Rucouskiria*, *Se Wsi Testamenti* and *Psaltari*, those same works noted in Juusten's chronicle of bishops, formed his set of materials. Ahlqvist's study discussed orthography, phonology, morphology and the lexicon, but none of these quite thoroughly. In any event, as a pioneer in his field of research, he succeeded in presenting a considerable amount of noteworthy observations. He published them in an extensive article in the journal *Kieletär* in 1871. He utilised his results in his lectures regarding the structure and development of Finnish and in other publications of his research.

At the same time, research on Agricola had sprung up in Church history. In 1885, Vicar J. A. Cederberg of Uusikaupunki had his synodal dissertation on the history of the Finnish Bible printed. It included a chapter on Agricola's literary output, especially in regard to the structure and translation of his works. Cederberg's study also covered the Finnish translations of the whole Bible.

The research started by Ahlqvist was soon continued in the field of linguistics. The Society for the Study of Finnish (*Kotikielen Seura*), a scholarly association founded in 1876 in connection with the University of Helsinki, published a special collection of articles entitled *Virittäjä* in honour of Ahlqvist's 60th birthday. The collection had an article on Agricola's Finnish by Arvid Genetz, Ahlqvist's student and successor. In addition to orthography, phonetics, morphology as well as the lexicon and observations regarding its special features, Genetz reported that he had also taken notes on syntax, but he said he would cover this in another context. Later on, however, he became first a lyceum teacher and then a researcher of the Balto-Finnic languages, so he no longer continued his research in the field of old literary Finnish.

Moreover, Ahlqvist's younger student Emil Nestor Setälä was inspired by old literary Finnish. His main target of interest, however, was neogrammarian phonetic history. Thus, he used the phonetic features of Agricola's Finnish as his material when he investigated Proto-Finnic phonetic history. Setälä never got to delve deep into old literary Finnish as such, but he was, however, merited with being a producer of source literature. Together with his Swedish colleague K. B. Wiklund, Setälä initiated a series concerning a commemoration of the Finnish language entitled *Suomen kielen muistomerkkejä* which would have difficult-to-get old literature published for the needs of researchers. The purpose was to focus, above all, on manuscripts, but as it became clear that the then known 16th century manuscripts had translations of the same texts which Agricola translated, the series began by publishing the texts alongside each other. Setälä had his students cut out words from published works for a future study, but these cutouts remained untouched amongst the piles of paper left behind as a collection of materials that can today be found in the Finnish National Archives. In 1896, Setälä initiated a great plan for a dictionary which included making one section a dictionary of old literary Finnish. This, however, was not seen as an urgent project, and so its implementation was put on hold for a few decades.

Not only were linguists interested in Agricola's works but also theologians. Arthur Hjelt examined the total number of parts of the Bible Agricola translated and published an article regarding this in the 1908 *Lännetär* album of Varsinaissuomalainen osakunta (the so-called student nation of Finland Proper). The same year, Jaakko Gummerus published a biographical description of Agricola, which, at the same time, was a special edition for the unveiling of a statue commemorating Agricola in Vyborg. The book was brimming with pictures furnished by Väinö Blomstedt. There were also a considerable number of language samples at the end of the book, and Agricola's text in most of them was given a contemporary form to make it easier to read. The linguistic form of these samples was revised by Heikki Ojansuu, who assisted Gummerus in the analysis of the special features found in old literary Finnish.

Gummerus later especially delved into analysing *Rucouskiria* and its sources, but this research was posthumously published as a three-volume study. It was edited by Aarno Maliniemi and Aarne Turkka and printed between 1941 and 1957. These volumes include a majority of text from *Rucouskiria* appearing alongside the non-Finnish source texts in two columns, which Gummerus found for it.

The first extensive monograph on old literary Finnish was written by Setälä's student Heikki Ojansuu. He became familiar with Agricola's

Finnish in writing his Doctoral dissertation on the phonetic history of the southwestern dialects (1901). After this, he gave many lectures on Agricola's Finnish at the University of Helsinki, starting with phonology and then his lexicon and syntax. The organisation of building up information is reflected directly from the structure of his 1909 monograph on Agricola's language entitled *Mikael Agricolan kielestä*. The book also includes a short, basic and non-academic review of Agricola as the founder of literary Finnish. Ojansuu's study takes all of Agricola's output into account, and the many sections of the book were collectively produced in such a way that they were discussed at university seminars before being published.

Ojansuu was also interested in language and literature older than Agricola. He searched for fragments from mediaeval documents, for instance, the medieval Church accounts of the Kalliala (Tyrvää) parish. Thousands of Finnish-language words, mainly personal and place names, were indeed found in these accounts. On the basis of the materials he found, Ojansuu was able to illustrate a mediaeval division of dialects and pre-literary phonetic changes. He lectured on these subjects after becoming the first professor of Finnish at the Finnish-language university founded in Turku in 1920. He did not, however, complete his research because he became ill and died in January 1923.

The most significant researcher of Agricola in the field of literary research was Viljo Tarkiainen, professor of Finnish literature at the University of Helsinki. He too was one of Setälä's students and began his scholarly career as a researcher of Finnish dialects, and then switched over to literary research. He had diverse philological education, thus he was able to cover a corpus spanning language, literature and cultural history. For well over 20 years, Tarkiainen published many small studies on the works of Agricola as well as their literary and historical background and planned on writing a complete exposition on Agricola's life and works. Tarkiainen did not, however, complete his work, as he died in 1951. The elements were finally compiled, supplemented and updated into one book by his grandson Kari Tarkiainen in 1985. In his preface, Kari Tarkiainen estimated that about half of the book was straight from Viljo Tarkiainen's manuscript and half from a set of materials edited on the basis of the manuscript or supplemented according to newer research. Kari Tarkiainen later researched Agricola from a historic perspective by specifically analysing the documents of his last official task – the peace delegation to Moscow (K. Tarkiainen 2008).

After Ojansuu, Martti Rapola was elevated to the status of leading researcher of old literary Finnish. Rapola's first studies touched upon Finnish dialects and old legal Finnish. However, it was impossible to sidestep Agricola when overviews or complete expositions on the development of literary Finnish and literature had to be written. Conducting research on Agricola's Finnish became essentially easier in 1931 when all of Agricola's Finnish-language works were put out as a three-volume reproduction.

In addition to phonetic history, vocabulary especially interested Rapola, and he wrote an abundant of overviews on the lexicon and also conducted research touching upon the development of a certain word or word family. He compared Agricola's vocabulary to the lexicon of manuscripts of the same time and in this way attempted to create a picture of what words were used in standard literary Finnish in Agricola's time. Rapola also composed a simple, basic textbook on old literary Finnish entitled *Vanha kirjasuomi*. Agricola's Finnish was given a major role in the book. In 1956, Rapola started up the editing work of the dictionary of old literary Finnish, *Vanhan kirjasuomen sanakirja*, which was originally planned by Setälä decades earlier, but not one part of it was completed during Rapola's lifetime.

Niilo Ikola was also one of Rapola's contemporary linguists who studied Agricola's output, but more from the perspective of the history of books than content. Ikola clarified, for example, the stages of the New Testament printing. He continued Hjelt's work, recounting, and in more detail than before, how large a share of the Bible Agricola succeeded in translating overall. This calculation was painstakingly done by hand, and could not be mechanically done for many reasons. Agricola did not always translate whole chapters of the Old Testament and actually a few passages and lengthier whole parts could be omitted. Smaller divisions were here and there selected for *Rucouskiria*, and their sources were not always reliably noted. A few sections were translated many times for the needs of different works. As the translated sections were uncovered, there still had to be a study on the breadth of those sections, in other words, a concrete measurement of how much text there was in which section. The final result was that Agricola translated 36.9 per cent of the whole Bible: he translated the New Testament in full, 21.7 per cent of the canonical books of the Old Testament, but only 6 per cent of the apocryphal books.

In theology, significant, fundamental research was conducted by Kauko Pirinen (1962) whose subject was the operation and economy of the cathedral chapter of Turku at the end of the Middle Ages and during the Reformation. In the same study, Pirinen went through its evidence in detail, which revealed the beginning stages of literary Finnish and the first literary outputs. He clarified the different ages between them on the basis of both contextual facts and documents on publishing activities. Pirinen summarised his perception of the birth of Finnish-language liturgical literature in his 1988 article geared especially towards linguists.

Pirinen's student Simo Heininen developed into a true Agricola specialist. Heininen began his research career on 17th century ecclesiastical notables but then switched over to examine Agricola and his contemporaries. Since the 1970s, he published a great deal of special research concerning Agricola and his works. He analysed the basis of the sources for the summaries and marginal notes in Agricola's texts and examined his translation techniques. He also furnished a study on those figures that, in one way or another, had an influence on Agricola's work or its evaluation. These figures include, for example, Erasmus and Juusten. In 2007, Heininen published an extensive, attractively illustrated complete exposition on Agricola's life and works entitled *Mikael Agricola. Elämä ja teokset*. This is a one of the definitive works used in contemporary research on Agricola.

In theology, Agricola has been examined as a reviser of ecclesiastical ceremonies and liturgical practices. Jyrki Knuutila's Doctoral dissertation analysed in what way marriage developed in Finland as a legal institution from the Middle Ages until the end of the Reformation (Knuutila 1990). In addition, he researched the instructions Agricola provides in his agenda on being wed and living in matrimony (Knuutila 1988). Agricola's code was not translated directly from any known source. Instead, they evidently were formed independently on the basis of discussions and disputes amongst his contemporaries. The code was written in the form of legal sections, thus Agricola's "regulations" can be seen as the first legal text printed in Finnish. Later, together with Anneli Mäkelä-Alitalo, Knuutila analysed and published the notes taken by Agricola on the income of the cathedral chapter and the clergy in Turku (2007). Knuutila also reconstructed the episcopal visitation routes Agricola took when he was bishop.

The work Gummerus and Heininen did in analysing the sources of *Rucouskiria* was continued by Juhani Holma. His Doctoral dissertation was completed in 2008. The study discussed the role of a prayer book (*Bekantnus der sünden mit etlichen betrachtungen und nützlichen gebetten*) as a source for *Rucouskiria*. The prayer book was used in a religious movement built around German mystic Caspar Schwenkfeld, and Holma's study has shown that Agricola used the whole book for *Rucouskiria* with the exception of the preface and the closing text. Choosing this specific book as a source for *Rucouskiria* is interesting because the Schwenkfelders were not considered dogmatic supporters of the Lutheran reforms, and their teachings were dismissed at the Schmalkaldic Convention in 1540. Evidently, the cathedral chapter of Turku had no knowledge of the theological problems of Schwenkfelderism, nor did doctrinal disputes come forth in prayers so clearly that they would have caught the translator's attention. The prayers of the Schwenkfelders were also accepted in German prayer books after the movement was condemned as heresy at the Schmalkaldic Convention.

After Niilo Ikola, research on the printing history of Agricola's works was continued by Anna Perälä (2007). She analysed how the printing of books generally got started in Sweden at the turn of the Middle Ages and the modern era and examined the way in which printing matters were arranged in Agricola's time at the Stockholm royal printing house at the hand of Amund Laurentsson. On this foundation, she went through all of Agricola's works in great detail and analysed the typefaces and woodcuts used in them as well as the themes in their ornamentation. Moreover, the picture sources and their presence in other products of the same printing house were highlighted. Perälä's research includes a complete list of pictures, ornamental patterns and ornamented initials.

Research projects regarding Agricola also started up in the field of archaeology. An excavation was carried out at Agricola's childhood homestead in Pernå in the summers of 2002 and 2007. The excavation work brought the foundation of his childhood home to light and further confirmed the understanding of Agricola's rustic background and the wealth of his homestead. There were excavations carried out in Vyborg at the old cathedral where Agricola's burial place is assumed to be located. Docent Aleksandr Saksa of the Russian Academy of Sciences in St Petersburg has mainly been in charge of archaeological research regarding the urban history of Vyborg, but there have been Finnish researchers and funders participating as well. For a long time, there had already been a great deal known about Agricola's environment in Turku: for example, the building history of Turku Cathedral and its surroundings have been examined for over a century. A complete exposition representative of these projects is a book published in 2003 entitled *Kaupunkia pintaa syvemmältä* ('A city from far beneath the surface'). There has recently been a study especially on the location of the school building and the trail the school's activities left behind in the cathedral environment (Harjula 2012b).

Linguistic research on Agricola has branched off into many directions in the late 20th and early 21st century. The most industrious of those going down the traditional philological line has been Silva Kiuru, conducting special research on many of Agricola's phonological and morphological features, lexicological details as well as the relationship between literary and colloquial Finnish. Osmo Nikkilä (1988, 1994) has conducted a study on apocope in old literary Finnish and made valuable observations on the language of Agricola and his contemporaries as well as its dialectical background. Nikkilä, as a specialist in the study of loanwords, has also conducted shorter special studies discussing the origins of the words used by Agricola.

Noteworthy research findings on Agricola's translation methods have been achieved by Marie-Elisabet Schmeidler (1969) and Marja Itkonen-Kaila (1997) who have proven his text to be a great puzzle. Agricola was accustomed to following multiple exemplary texts simultaneously, and he could even switch source texts in the middle of a sentence. Heininen (1992, 1993, 1994, 2008) has made similar observations on the summaries and glosses in Agricola's works. Itkonen-Kaila has taken syntactic constructions characteristic to Agricola's text into account, for example agentive constructions and non-finite clauses that show the influence of the source text.

In addition to studies specifically on Agricola, there have also been important observations made regarding Agricola's language together with studies regarding the history of Finnish. For example, Osmo Ikola (1949) investigated modal and temporal inflection of verbs in *Biblia* in his Doctoral dissertation and its supplementary research, and regarding all the features of what he studied, he also made complete comparisons to Agricola. While researching imperative forms in the Balto-Finnic languages, Heikki Leskinen (1970) also conducted a thorough analysis on the imperatives in Agricola. In a similar fashion, Ilkka Savijärvi (1977, 1988) examined the expression of negation both in Finnish dialects and in Agricola.

The editing for *Vanhan kirjasuomen sanakirja* begun by Rapola was continued at the Institute for the Languages of Finland, an organisation established in 1976. As trial entries were first made for the dictionary, it became clear that the materials had deficiencies even for ordinary words. What often happens in the collection of materials in manual work is that compilers and researchers focus their attention on special features, but common and even general issues are often overlooked because they can seem too obvious. To correct the matter, Agricola's works were written as a textbase, resulting in a complete list of word appearances taken from the books. This is the *Index Agricolaensis*, published in 1980: it includes all word appearances, printed in uppercase letters, in alphabetical order and provides numeric references to the book, page and line where the word form in question is found. The first volume of *Vanhan kirjasuomen sanakirja* (covering A through I) was published in 1985.

Since the late 20th century, dictionaries and archives began to be put into digital form. In this way, it is possible to handle rather large corpuses and compare them automatically. In 1987, the Institute for the Languages of Finland started to build a lexical database with Ruhr University Bochum. The purpose was to code comparable information on, for example, word length, syllabic count, word stress, word class, semantics, frequency and etymology, taken from the vocabularies of various languages. Moreover, one subject of analysis was the age of words in a literary language. Raimo Jussila headed the project for Finnish at the Institute for the Languages of Finland, and as a substudy of the project, compiled a list of first appearances of words in literary Finnish (Jussila 1998). This list and a special study based on it (Jussila 2000) illustratively elevated the importance of Agricola's works as the foundation of literary Finnish.

The 2000s marked the start of analysing Agricola's texts with the use of contemporary tools of information technology. A research project led by Kaisa Häkkinen creating a critical edition of Agricola's works and a morphosyntactic database (*Mikael Agricolan teosten kriittinen editio ja morfosyntaktinen tietokanta*) was started in 2004. This project analysed and digitally coded all of Agricola's works in regard to both morphological and syntactic features with researcher Nobufumi Inaba overseeing its IT needs. Its model was the Syntax Archives (*Lauseopin arkisto*) at the University of Turku, founded by Osmo Ikola, which includes a similarly analysed corpus of Finnish dialects. A book version on several of Agricola's works was published under the Agricola project, furnished with introductory articles and explanations. The book version was normalised with orthography for contemporary reading, but its original linguistic structure was preserved. Two of the younger workers in the project wrote their Doctoral dissertations on Agricola's Finnish: Heidi Salmi discussed Agricola's adpositions in 2010 and Kirsi-Maria Nummila wrote about Agricola's agentive suffixes in 2011.

The most recent stage of research on Agricola in linguistics is represented by a systematic comparison of Agricola's works to manuscripts of the same time. The first comparative subject was the Codex Westh, a manuscript including both a liturgical agenda and a missal, whose critical edition was published in 2012. As regards the same works, other comparative materials are available too, such as the Kangasala Missal and the Uppsala Codex B 28, both of which are currently being researched. The oldest Finnish manuscripts have recently been catalogued and detailed (Keskiaho 2013), and the next stage will be making them digitally available for the research community under the *Codices Fennici* research project established for this.

21st century research on Agricola has been carried out as interdisciplinary cooperative work as well. In order to understand the Finnish and the content in his books, it is important to also know the time and environment in which they were produced. Many subjects, objects, circumstances and events noted in Agricola are alien to the modern-day person, thus they must be examined and explained separately. Without background information, the modern-day person could not imagine what the world was like in Agricola's time, what was new then and what was old, what was common and what was rare, what people were able to do and with what sort of instruments. The doors to Agricola's world have been opened up in quite a new way, as not only linguists, theologians and Church history researchers, but also researchers in archaeology, cultural history, religious studies, literature, medicine and botany (Häkkinen & Lempiäinen 2007, 2011) have participated in the analysis of his era and the legacy it left behind. A multifaceted picture of these new lines of research is provided by a collection of articles entitled *Agricolan aika* ('Agricola's time') published in 2007, the year marking the 450th anniversary of Agricola's death. This book showcases representatives of various disciplines discussing questions on Agricola from the perspective of their own areas of expertise.

6.3 Mikael Agricola as a National Figure

Agricola is today, without a doubt, one of the greatest of all Finnish figures. In 2004, the television channel Yle TV1 conducted an audience poll to vote for the greatest Finns of all time. The winner was Marshal of Finland Carl Gustaf Emil Mannerheim who served as chief of the Finnish army and President in the early 1900s, and after him, there were certain other 20th century statesmen found at the top of the list. There were also a few prominent cultural figures that made it to the top ten. Generally speaking, 20th century figures and those from no earlier than the 19th century were voted to the top. The only exception from the 16th century was Agricola. He was voted in at number eight.

We have already shown in section 6.2 that the life's work of Agricola began to be introduced to a larger audience in the 19th century in non-scholarly depictions and in textbooks especially for children and young people. They introduced Agricola through historical documents that shed light upon his literary life's work and era because very little is known about him as a person. Fictive accounts have nevertheless been partly written on many significant individuals of the past: the author's imagination gets to fill in the gaps found in historical information. Agricola too was given literary coverage, but he was not the favourite of any author. The Reformation and Lutheranism as well as the foundation of literary Finnish were dry, factual themes which did not especially captivate writers or readers. Agricola as a figure in fiction has been studied by Päivi Lappalainen (2007).

The same acts and events that were known from scholarly research on Agricola were also highlighted in fictive works on him. The oldest biographical depictions categorised as non-fiction were already presented in section 6.2. The first clear piece of fiction on Agricola was Rafael Hertzberg's 1882 Swedish poem *Michael Agricola i Wittenberg* which described Agricola's period at the University of Wittenberg, the centre of the Reformation and Lutheranism. Moreover, Arvid Mörne's Swedish two-part poem *Mikael Agricola*, immediately published one year after Finnish independence in 1918, conveyed that Agricola's mother tongue was Swedish and he got to learn Finnish only after he left for school in Vyborg. The poem can be seen as a statement to the then topical language strife between the Finns and the Finland Swedes that manifested in scholarly, cultural and social aspects of life in the early 1900s.

Agricola was not chosen as a main character for any novel. There were only minor narratives written about him or he was mentioned only as a supporting character in more extensive works set in the 16th century. The most famous of these is the 1884 story *Gossen från Pernå*, written by Finland's beloved storyteller Zachris Topelius, originally published in Swedish in a collection of children's stories entitled *Läsning för barn*, later translated as *Lukemisia lapsille* ('Readings for children'). The story was released slightly thereafter in Finnish with the translated title *Pernajan poika* ('A boy from Pernå'). It describes how Mikael as a little boy goes to church and listens to the ceremonies in Latin and wonders why one cannot speak to God in the same language people speak amongst each other. Mikael would like to go to school and study to become a priest, but his father wants him to become a soldier. However, Mikael's wish comes true when a compassionate priest is able to talk his father into letting him go and Johannes Erasmi, headmaster of the school in Vyborg, promises to take Mikael as his student, without any payment in return.

Some novels have addressed the Reformation, such as Kyösti Wilkuna's 1912 *Viimeiset luostariasukkaat* ('The last abbey residents'). It depicts the last stages of the Birgittine Abbey in Naantali, whereupon Agricola went to carry out the last episcopal visitation. Wilkuna also wrote a group of nationally spirited, historical narratives which somewhat fictively depict certain stages in Agricola's life, for example how he stayed with Luther when he was in Wittenberg and began to translate the New Testament into Finnish. Wilkuna also described the final stages of Agricola's life upon his return from the Russo-Swedish peace negotiations. Santeri Ivalo's novel *Kuningas Suomessa* ('A king in Finland') describes King Gustav Vasa's 1551 mission in Finland. The king, according to the evidence found in historical sources, also visited Agricola in Turku while on this journey.

In terms of fiction, the most significant depiction of Agricola may be Paavo Haavikko's 1968 play *Agricola ja kettu* ('Agricola and the fox'). It starts with the cathedral chapter of Turku assembly in 1555 and ends with Agricola's burial in Vyborg in 1557. In addition to Agricola, King Gustav Vasa has an important role, as it is through him the importance of money and power comes forth as a feature that steers people's lives and actions. As Agricola does not humbly submit to the monarch's decisions, the King gets him out of the way by sending him to the strenuous Moscow peace negotiations, which is a foreshadowing of his fate. The Swedish delegation brings an assortment of gifts to the Russian tsar Ivan the Terrible who is especially pleased with a fox pelt. In the play, the fox symbolises cunning and a lust for power. In his youth, Agricola killed a helpless little fox, and this troubles him throughout his life the same way as the smouldering lust for power he has inside.

Not one portrait was painted of Agricola in his time nor is there any narrative description of his appearance in existence. When there was a desire to show Agricola through the visual arts, artists had to resort to using nothing more than their imaginations. There is, however, reliable information on clerical clothing typical of the period of the Reformation, and it is because of this that the pieces of art featuring Agricola resemble each other: a long cape and a hat covering his ears. Agricola is thus recognised because of his characterisation.

The first painting featuring Agricola was by Robert Wilhelm Ekman in the 1850s. The painting shows Agricola dressed as the bishop, presenting his translated Bible to King Gustav Vasa. The piece is, in many respects, unhistorical. Agricola did not translate the whole Bible, only the New Testament; nor was he an ordinary when the translation was published, only a member of the cathedral chapter and the bishop's secretary. After he assumed the leading position in the Turku diocese in 1554, Agricola held an episcopal mass in full formalwear, and let us remember that this angered the King to no end. Ekman's painting can be seen in the chancel in Turku Cathedral.

An especially widely used image of Agricola is the 1907 woodcut by internationally known Finnish artist Albert Edelfelt (see Plate 4 on page 161). This graphically clear and easily duplicated picture was originally published as an illustration for Topelius' *Lukemisia lapsille* series. The woodcut shows Agricola at his writing desk, deeply involved in his translation work. The top of the picture has the salutation *Michael Agricola Christiano Salutem* from the cover of the second printing of *Abckiria*, and the bottom has a few lines from the *Abckiria* introductory poem.

Attempts at getting projects started for erecting a statue commemorating Agricola were made from the late 19th century by a number of quarters. The newspaper *Suomalainen* reported in 1889 that the local reading circle provided the Finnish Literary Society of Vyborg with a donation for the initial funding of a statue to be erected in Vyborg. There was an aspiration to have the statue specifically in Vyborg because that is where Agricola's gravesite was located. In 1864, the matter of a statue was discussed at the clerical assembly of the Kuopio diocese. The assembly decided to start promoting the matter by calling upon the other dioceses in Finland – Turku and Porvoo – to partake in the statue venture. Thus, the project became public and included the whole of Finland of the time. The erecting of a statue commemorating H. G. Porthan in the Old Great Square in Turku that same year evidently sped up the process. However, rather little money was collected for the statue, and so there was time to complete a few other works of art showcasing Agricola before there was a statue in Vyborg.

In 1877, a small statue designed by Carl Eneas Sjöstrand was completed and placed in the chamber of the cathedral chapter of Turku. The first statue of Agricola erected in a public space was by Ville Vallgren. Its unveiling was in Helsinki Cathedral in 1887. The Koivisto Youth Society erected a memorial stone in 1900 at Agricola's assumed place of death in the rural district of Kuolemajärvi. It is an unassuming natural stone with text reminiscent of Agricola. Later, the stone disappeared but it was found and re-erected. Today, the stone is decoratively fenced in, and a small cabin that was built next to it operates as a museum on Agricola. As Pernå was Agricola's place of birth, an obelisk-like memorial stone was erected near its church in 1914, but it was later transferred to the yard of his childhood home, the Sigfrids homestead.

1908 marked the 400th anniversary of Agricola's assumed birth year, and a bust of him, sculpted by Emil Wikström, was finally erected at the façade of Vyborg Cathedral. Agricola was shown reading aloud, with a book before him, which was reminiscent of the role of literacy and literary Finnish. The statue was placed on a high base, reminiscent of a pulpit. At the bottom, in front of the base, there were statues of an elderly person and a child that symbolised the circle of life. A copy of the statue was commissioned for Turku Cathedral where it was erected on an unassuming base in the entrance.

1917 commemorated the 400th anniversary of the Reformation. At that time, the cathedral chapter of Turku organised a competition to design a public monument in Turku in memory of Agricola. Around a dozen sketches were submitted, and even though prizes were given out, none of the proposals were ever considered feasible enough. Instead, a portion of the funds collected were used to publish a facsimile of Agricola's works. The books were published in 1931 by Werner Söderström Corporation in three hefty volumes. The project for erecting a statue in Turku was temporarily put on hold but it was reconsidered in 1947, three years after Vyborg and a part of eastern Finland were lost to the Soviet Union as a result of the Continuation War. Some sculptors were commissioned to submit a few sketches, and finally, Oskari Jauhiainen's proposal was chosen for the project. The nearly three-metre high bronze statue was erected at the outside wall of Turku Cathedral in 1952.

The original statue in Vyborg met hard times as it went missing nearing the end of the Winter War in 1940. When the Finns wound up ceding Vyborg to the Russians, the city was evacuated and the statue of Agricola was either destroyed or was taken to such good safe keeping that regardless of searches, it has never been found. However, the copy at Turku Cathedral was in one piece, and two new casts of the bust were made in the 1950s: one was erected in Lahti and the second next to the church in Pernå.

With Agricola 2007 – the 450th anniversary of Agricola's death – drawing near, a project for a statue in Vyborg was reopened as a Finnish–Russian joint venture. There was only a damaged impost left over from the original statue, but as a result of co-operation between the City of Vyborg and a special monument committee, a new cast of Wikström's bust was able to be erected atop the impost and the new granite base in 2009. A plaque with information on Agricola and the monument was placed next to the statue. The earlier stages of the Agricola monuments were especially analysed by former parliamentary minister Jaakko Numminen (2004) who served as chair of the monument committee.

There have been many associations and organisations established to uphold the memory of Agricola and study his life's work. Two of them are genuine scholarly organisations. The Luther-Agricola Society was founded

Plate 4: Edelfelt's woodcut and Donald Duck as Agricola. Drawing: Kari Korhonen, © Disney.

in 1940 for supporting research on the Reformation and the theological and ecclesiastical tradition that originated from the movement. It has two publication series which releases studies discussing theology as well as writings on ecumenics and missiology, mostly in German and English. The interdisciplinary Mikael Agricola Society was founded in 2006. As of yet, it does not do any publishing but has compiled materials for its website on Agricola 2007 as well as links for research touching upon Agricola and his contemporaries. The Mikael Agricola Society organises Agricola-related talks and trips and also organises research projects on Agricola with outside funding.

Non-academic information on Agricola has been available to the Finns as well. The national public service broadcasting company Yle produced a three-part television documentary for Agricola 2007 entitled *Agricolan jalanjäljillä* ('In Agricola's footsteps'). Repeats were aired multiple times both in 2007 and afterwards. The series showcased Agricola as a Church Reformer, a translator and a diplomat. The Finnish National Board of Education and the Central Administration of the Evangelical Lutheran Church of Finland have compiled information on Agricola for their websites to be used in schools and in church services. The Central Administration of the Church has also published a reconstruction of Agricola's missal, enabling the possibility to organise church services today in the style of Agricola's era.

Lighter forms of popular literature are represented by a playful dictionary published in multiple languages entitled *Agricola tunnissa* ('Agricola in One Hour') compiled by author Roope Lipasti. Agricola has even reached *Aku Ankka*, a comic book featuring its eponymous character: Donald Duck in Finnish. There was a special issue for Agricola 2007 which had one story translated into an adapted form of Agricola. Moreover, Donald Duck himself was drawn to look like the portrait by Edelfelt (see Plate 4 on page 161). Activities on Agricola have comprehensively been presented in the Agricola 2007 report (Report 2008).

Today, Mikael Agricola is a well-known name in Finland. It has been used in many contexts, for example in names of organisations, learning institutions, projects, products and websites. Some of these quarters wish to be associated with literature and learning, but far from every project and business carrying Agricola's name has a true connection to him. There are streets and buildings named after Agricola and many postage stamps have been issued in honour of him. Since 1960, his date of death has been an established day of observance and flag day on 9 April. In addition to the fact that Mikael Agricola is known and recognised as the founder of literary Finnish and as a Reformer, he has become a Finnish brand, and there is an aspiration to utilise his good reputation in education, culture and even in business life.

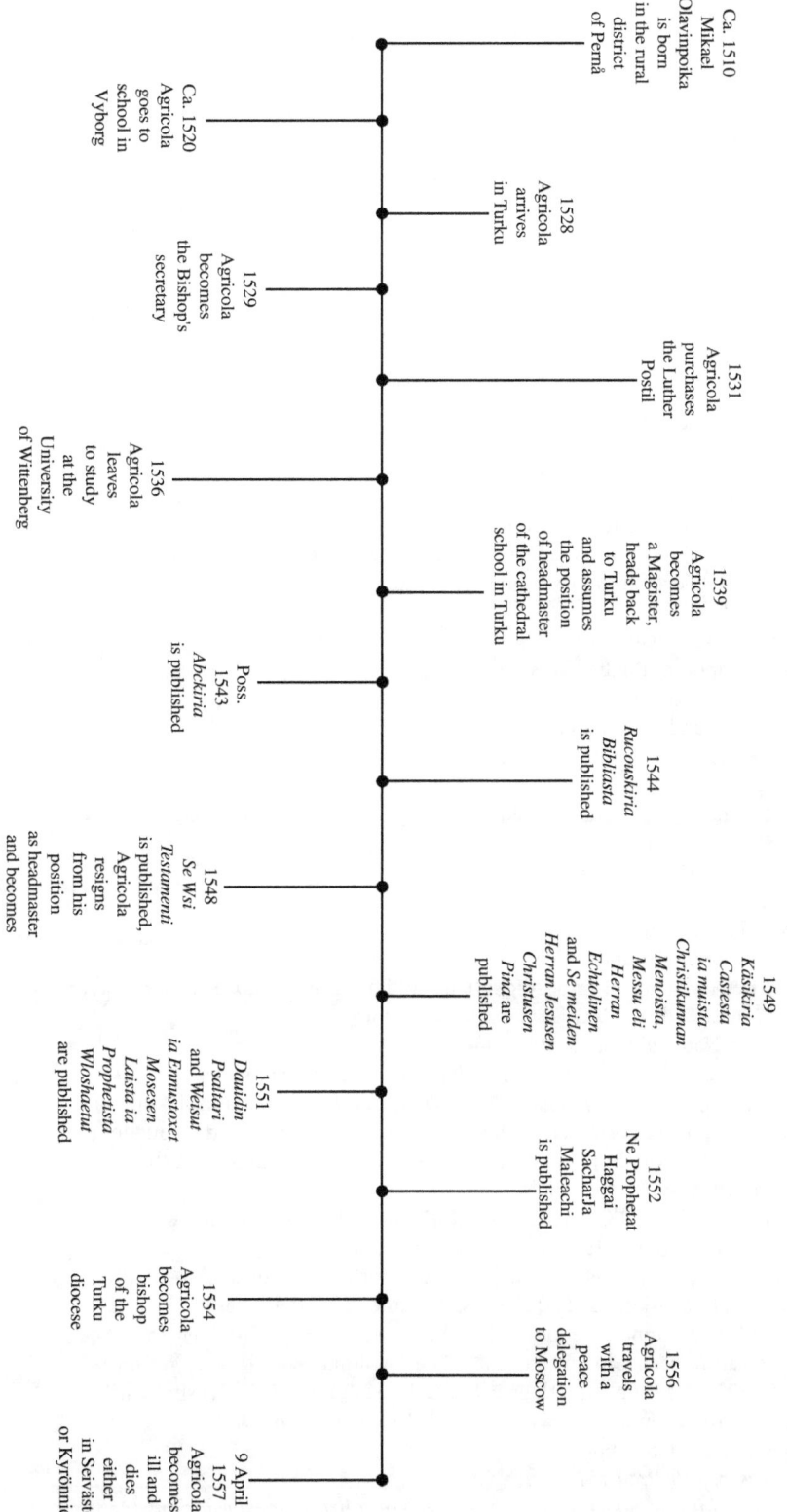

Timeline of Events in the Life of Mikael Agricola

Bibliography

Source Materials

Agricola, Mikael see MAT. Retrieved from: http://kaino.kotus.fi/korpus/vks/meta/agricola/agricola_coll_rdf.xml

Bibles in English. Retrieved from: www.biblegateway.com
  AMP = Amplified Bible
  CEB = Common English Bible
  CEV = Contemporary English Version
  ERV = Easy-to-Read Version
  ESV = English Standard Version
  GNV = 1599 Geneva Bible
  KJV = King James Version
  KJ21 = 21st Century King James Version
  LEB = Lexham English Bible
  NET = New English Translation
  NIV = New International Version
  NLT = New Living Translation
  NRSV = New Revised Standard Version

Åbo Tidnigar. Retrieved from: http://digi.lib.helsinki.fi/sanomalehti/secure/browse.html?action=year&id=1457-4772&name=Åbo Tidningar

Codex Westh. The National Library of Finland, C III 19.

Ericus Erici 1621, 1625: *Postilla, Eli Ulgostoimitus, nijnen Ewangeliumitten päälle cuin ymbäri aiastaian, saarnatan Jumalan Seuracunnasa. I–II.* Stockholmis. [Postil, or an explanation to these gospels, preached in the congregation of God throughout the year. I–II. In Stockholm.] Facsimile. Ed. Martti Parvio. Helsinki, Finnish Literature Society 1988, 1990.

Index Agricolaensis I–II. Esko Koivusalo (ed.). Kotimaisten kielten tutkimuskeskuksen julkaisuja 11. Helsinki: Institute for the Languages of Finland.

MAT = *Mikael Agricolan teokset I—III.* [The works of Mikael Agricola I—III.] [I. Abckiria 1543; Rucouskiria 1544; II Se Wsi Testamenti 1548; III Käsikiria Castesta ja muista Christikunnan menoista 1549; Messu eli Herran Echtolinen 1549; Se meiden Herran Iesusen Christusen Pina 1549; Dauidin Psaltari 1551; Weisut ia Ennustoxet 1551; Ne Prophetat. Haggaj. SacharIa. Maleachi 1552.] Facsimile with contemporary transcriptions. WSOY, Porvoo – Helsinki – Juva 1987.

Messan på Swensko 1541. Stocholm.

Messan på Swensko, förbettrad 1548. Stocholm.

Missale Aboense = Missale Aboense secundum ordinem fratrum praedicatorium 1488. Facsimile, ed. Martti Parvio. Porvoo 1971.

Münster, Sebastian 1544: *Cosmographia.* Basel.
Raamattu. Uusi ja vanha suomennos. [The Bible. New and old Finnish translations.] Retrieved from: http://www.evl.fi/raamattu/
SKM I = Setälä, E. N. & Wiklund, K. B. (eds.) (1893): *Mikael Agricolan käsikirja ja messu.* [Mikael Agricola's agenda and missal.] Suomen kielen muistomerkkejä I. Finnish Literature Society, Helsinki.
SKM II = *Kristoffer kuninkaan maanlaki, herra Martin suomeksi kääntämä.* [King Christopher's Law of the Realm, translated by Lord Martti.] Suomen kielen muistomerkkejä II. Finnish Literature Society, Helsinki.
Suomalainen. Sanomia Sydän-Suomesta. [Suomalainen. News from the heart of Finland.] Retrieved from: http://digi.kansalliskirjasto.fi/sanomalehti/secure/browse.html?action=year&id=1457-4632&mnemonic=Suomalainen
Tidningar utgifne af et Sällskap i Åbo. Retrieved from: http://digi.lib.helsinki.fi/sanomalehti/secure/browse.html?action=year&id=1457-4756&name=Tidningar Utgifne af et Sällskap i Åbo
Turun tuomiokirkon musta kirja – Registrum Ecclesiae Aboensis [1229–1515]. [Black Book of Åbo Cathedral [1229–1515].] Art House, 1996.

Literature

Agricolan aika. [Agricola's time.] Eds. Kaisa Häkkinen & Tanja Vaittinen. Helsinki: BTJ Kustannus oy 2007.
Ahlqvist, August 1871: Mikael Agricolan kieli. [The language of Mikael Agricola.] – *Kieletär* 1 pp. 1–24. Helsinki.
Antell, Kurt 1956: *Pernå sockens historia I. Tiden till år 1700.* Helsingfors: Akademiska bokhandeln.
Arffman, Kaarlo 1997: *Die Reformation und die Geschichte der Kirche.* Helsinki: Finnische Gesellschaft für Kirchengeschichte.
Arffman, Kaarlo 2008: Olaus Petri – syrjäytetty reformaattori. [Olaus Petri – a displaced Reformer] – Joona Salminen (ed.): *Reformaatio. Henkilökuvia ja tutkimussuuntia.* Suomen kirkkohistoriallisen seuran toimituksia 208. Helsinki: Finnish Theological Literature Society and Finnish Society of Church History.
Cameron, Euan 2012: *The European reformation.* 2nd ed. Oxford; New York, NY: Oxford University Press.
Cederberg, A. J. 1885: *Suomalaisen Raamatun Historia Gezeliusten aikoihin saakka.* [The history of the Finnish Bible up to the time of the Gezeliuses.] Turku: Wilén & Co.
Erkamo, V. 1983: Pärnä-*sanasta ja sen merkityksistä.* [On the word *pärnä* and its semantics.] Suomi 124:4. Helsinki: Finnish Literature Society.
Eurén, G. E. 1858: *Mikael Agrikola. Suomen pispa, uskonopin oikasia Suomessa, Suomen kielen ensimmäinen harjoittaja kirjoissa.* [Agricola. Finnish bishop, reviser of dogmatics in Finland, the first Finnish language specialist in books.]
Genetz, Arvid see Jännes, Arvi
Grell, Peter (ed.) 1995: *The Scandinavian Reformation: from evangelical movement to institutionalization of reform.* Cambridge: Cambridge University Press.
Gummerus, Jaakko 1908: *Mikael Agricola. Elämäkerrallinen kuvaus.* [Mikael Agricola. A bibliographical description.] Jyväskylä: Gummerus.
Gummerus, Jaakko 1941–1955: *Mikael Agricolan Rukouskirja ja sen lähteet.* [Mikael Agricola's *Rucouskiria* and the sources for it.] Eds. Aarno Maliniemi & Aarne Turkka. Suomen kirkkohistoriallisen seuran toimituksia 44. Helsinki: Finnish Society of Church History.

Haavikko, Paavo 1968: *Agricola ja kettu*. [Agricola and the fox.] Play. [Published 1971, no publisher information.]

Häkkinen, Kaisa 2010: Suomen kieli Michael Bartholdi Gunnæruksen introituskokoelmassa. [Finnish in Bartholdi Gunnærus' collection of introits.] – Jorma Hannikainen (ed.) *Facultas ludendi. Erkki Tuppuraisen juhlakirja* pp. 115–133. Kuopio: Sibelius Academy, Kuopio unit.

Häkkinen, Kaisa 2012a: Johdatus Mikael Agricolan runoihin. [An introduction to the poems of Mikael Agricola.] – Kaisa Häkkinen (ed.): *Mikael Agricolan runokirja*. Wanhan suomen arkisto 6. Turku, University of Turku.

Häkkinen, Kaisa 2012b: Westhin koodeksin suhde Mikael Agricolan teoksiin. [The Codex Westh in relation to the works of Mikael Agricola.] – Kaisa Häkkinen (ed.) *Tutkimuksia Westhin koodeksista* pp. 9–48. Publications of the Department of Finnish and Finno-Ugric Languages of the University of Turku 2. Turku.

Häkkinen, Kaisa 2013: Kansanrunouden aineksia vanhimmassa suomalaisessa kirjallisuudessa. [Folk poetry elements in the oldest period of Finnish literature.] – Tuomas Hovi, Kirsi Hänninen, Merja Leppälahti & Maria Vasenkari: *Viisas matkassa, vara laukussa. Näkökulmia kansanperinteen tutkimukseen* pp. 56–75. Folkloristiikan julkaisuja 3. Turku: Turun yliopisto.

Häkkinen, Kaisa (ed.) 2007: *Mikael Agricolan Aapiskirja*. [Mikael Agricola's primer.] Helsinki: Kirjapaja.

Häkkinen, Kaisa (ed.) 2012a: *Codex Westh. Westhin koodeksin tekstit*. [Codex Westh texts.] Wanhan suomen arkisto 5. University of Turku School of Languages and Translation Studies, Finnish Language. Turku.

Häkkinen, Kaisa (ed.) 2012b: *Tutkimuksia Westhin koodeksista*. [Studies on the Codex Westh.] Publications of the Department of Finnish and Finno-Ugric Languages of the University of Turku 2. Turku.

Häkkinen, Kaisa (ed.) 2012c: *Mikael Agricolan runokirja*. [A book of Mikael Agricola's poetry.] Wanhan suomen arkisto 6. University of Turku School of Languages and Translation Studies, Finnish Language. Turku.

Häkkinen, Kaisa & Lempiäinen, Terttu 2007: *Agricolan yrtit. Mikael Agricolan rukouskirjan terveyttä tuovat kasvit ja niiden käyttö*. [Agricola's herbs. The appearance and use of health-giving plants in Mikael Agricola's *Rucouskiria*.] Turku: Kirja-Aurora.

Häkkinen, Kaisa & Lempiäinen, Terttu 2011: *Aaloesta öljypuuhun. Suomen kielellä mainittuja kasveja Agricolan aikana*. [From *aaloe* 'aloe' to *öljypuu* 'olive'. Finnish plant names appearing in Agricola's time.] Helsinki: Teos.

Hakulinen, Lauri 1964: Vanhan kirjasuomen uskonnolliset ja juridiset termit *luhdata, luhtia*. [The religious and legal terms *luhdata* and *luhtia* ('to defend, to prove innocent') in old literary Finnish.] – *Virittäjä* 1964 pp. 233–237.

Hannikainen, Jorma 2006: *Suomeksi suomalaisten tähden. Kansankielisen tekstin ja sävelmän suhde Michael Bartholdi Gunnæruksen suomenkielisessä Officia Missæ -introituskokoelmassa (1605)*. [In Finnish for the Finns. The relationship between vernacular text and melody in Bartholdi Gunnærus' Finnish-language collection of introits Officia Missæ (1605).] Studia musica 29. Kuopio: Sibelius Academy.

Harjula, Janne 2012a: Alustavia ajatuksia Turun tuomiokirkon tuohikirjeestä. [Preliminary thoughts on the birch bark letter from the Cathedral Square excavation in Turku.] *SKAS* 1–2 pp. 3–21. Turku: Society for Medieval Archaeology in Finland.

Harjula, Janne 2012b: Sulkakynillä ja kirjoituspuikoilla. Arkeologi kirjallistumisen jäljillä. [With quills and writing sticks. An archaeologist on the trail of literalisation.] – *Bibliophilos* 71 2012/4 pp. 4–11.

Harviainen, Tapani & Heininen, Simo & Huhtala, Aarre 1990: *Opi nyt vanha ja nuori*. [Take a lesson now old and young.] Helsinki: Otava.

Heikkilä, Tuomas 2009: *Piirtoja ja kirjaimia. Kirjoittamisen kulttuurihistoriaa keskiajalla*. [Strokes and letters. Cultural history of writing in the Middle Ages.] Finnish Literature Society Publications 1208. Helsinki: Finnish Literature Society.

Heininen, Simo 1976: *Nuori Mikael Agricola*. [A young Mikael Agricola.] Suomi 120:3. Helsinki: Finnish Literature Society.
Heininen, Simo 1979: Mikael Agricolan Passio. [Mikael Agricola's Passion.] – *Suomen kirkkohistoriallisen seuran vuosikirja 68–69* pp. 17–30. Helsinki: Finnish Society of Church History.
Heininen, Simo 1980: *Die finnischen Studenten in Wittenberg 1531–1552*. Schriften der Luther-Agricola-Gesellschaft A 19. Helsinki: Luther-Agricola-Gesellschaft.
Heininen, Simo 1992: *Mikael Agricolan psalmisummaariot*. [Mikael Agricola's summaries of the Psalms.] Suomi 166. Helsinki: Finnish Literature Society.
Heininen, Simo 1993: *Mikael Agricolan Vanhan testamentin summaariot*. [Mikael Agricola's summaries of the Old Testament.] Suomi 169. Helsinki: Finnish Literature Society.
Heininen, Simo 1994: *Mikael Agricolan Psalttarin reunahuomautukset*. [Mikael Agricola's glosses in *Psaltari*.] Suomi 174. Helsinki: Finnish Literature Society.
Heininen, Simo 1996: Mikael Agricolan kirjasto. [Mikael Agricola's personal library.] *Mundus librorum* pp. 59–67. Helsinki.
Heininen, Simo 2006: *Mikael Agricola ja Erasmus Rotterdamilainen*. [Mikael Agricola and Erasmus of Rotterdam.] Suomi 192. Helsinki: Finnish Literature Society.
Heininen, Simo 2007: *Mikael Agricola. Elämä ja teokset*. [Mikael Agricola. His life and works.] Helsinki: Edita.
Heininen, Simo 2008: *Mikael Agricolan Vanhan testamentin reunahuomautukset*. [Mikael Agricola's glosses of the Old Testament.] Suomi 196. Helsinki: Finnish Literature Society.
Heininen, Simo 2012: *Agricolan perintö. Paulus Juustenin elämä*. [The legacy of Mikael Agricola. The life of Paulus Juusten.] Helsinki: Edita.
Heininen, Simo & Heikkilä, Markku 1996: *Suomen kirkkohistoria*. [The Church history of Finland.] Helsinki: Edita.
Hiekkanen, Markus 2004: Piispa Mikael Agricolan hautapaikka ja mahdollisuudet sen arkeologiseen tutkimukseen. [The gravesite of Bishop Mikael Agricola and the possibilities for archaeological research.] – Ossi Tuusvuori (ed.): *Agricola-symposiumi. Turku 20.–21.9.2004* pp. 15–25. Turku: Agricola working group.
Hiekkanen, Markus 2007: *Suomen keskiajan kivikirkot*. [Mediaeval stone churches in Finland.] Finnish Literature Society Publications 1117. Helsinki: Finnish Literature Society.
Hjelt, Arthur 1908: Kuinka paljon on Agricola Vanhaa Testamenttia suomentanut tai suomeksi toimittanut. [How much of the Old Testament Agricola translated or produced in Finnish.] – *Lännetär I*. Helsinki: Varsinais-Suomalainen Osakunta.
Holma, Juhani 2008: *Sangen ialo Rucous. Schwenkfeldläisten rukouskirja Mikael Agricolan lähteenä*. [Quite a noble prayer. The Schwenkfelder prayer book as a source for Mikael Agricola.] Helsinki [self-published].
Holma, Juhani 2010: Luterilaisen jumalanpalvelusmusiikin juurilla. [At the roots of Lutheran worship music.] – Jorma Hannikainen (ed.) *Facultas ludendi. Erkki Tuppuraisen juhlakirja* pp. 43–78. Kuopio: Sibelius Academy, Kuopio unit.
Huizinga, Johan 1953: *Erasmus*. Porvoo: WSOY.
Ikola, Niilo 1966: Mikael Agricolan Uuden testamentin painatusvaiheita. [Stages of the printing of Mikael Agricola's New Testament.] – *Sananjalka* 8 pp. 117–128. Turku.
Ikola, Niilo 1988: Mikael Agricolan suomentamat Raamatun kohdat ja niiden osuus koko Raamatusta. [Biblical sections translated by Mikael Agricola and their percentage of the whole Bible.] – Esko Koivusalo (ed.): *Mikael Agricolan kieli*. Tietolipas 112 pp. 229–248. Helsinki: Finnish Literature Society.
Ikola, Osmo 1949: *Tempusten ja modusten käyttö ensimmäisessä suomalaisessa raamatussa verrattuna vanhempaan ja nykyiseen kieleen. I*. [The use of tense and mood in the first Finnish Bible in comparison to older and contemporary Finnish. I.] Publications of the University of Turku, series B, vol. XXXII. Turku: University of Turku.

Ikola, Osmo 1988: Agricolan äidinkieli. [Agricola's mother tongue.] – Esko Koivusalo (ed.): *Mikael Agricolan kieli*. Tietolipas 112 pp. 25–68. Helsinki: Finnish Literature Society.

Ikola, Osmo & Palomäki, Ulla & Koitto, Anna-Kaisa 1989: *Suomen murteiden lauseoppia ja tekstikielioppia*. [Syntax and text grammar in Finnish dialects.] Finnish Literature Society Publications 511. Helsinki: Finnish Literature Society.

Itkonen, Erkki 1955: Onko itämerensuomessa jälkiä duaalista? [Is there a trace of the dual in Balto-Finnic?] – *Virittäjä* 51 pp. 161–175. Helsinki.

Itkonen-Kaila, Marja 1992: "Ja Jerusalem pite tallattaman pacanoilda". Ablatiiviagentti ja sen perilliset Agricolasta uuteen raamatunsuomennokseen. ["Ja Jerusalem pite tallattaman pacanoilda" ('And Jerusalem shall be trodden down by the Gentiles'). The ablative agent and its beneficiaries from Agricola to the new Finnish translation of the Bible.] – *Virittäjä* 96 pp. 137–164.

Itkonen-Kaila, Marja 1997: *Mikael Agricolan Uusi testamentti ja sen erikieliset lähtötekstit*. [Mikael Agricola's New Testament and its source texts from different languages.] Suomi 184. Helsinki: Finnish Literature Society.

Ivalo, Santeri 1919: *Kuningas Suomessa*. [A king in Finland.] Historical novel. Porvoo: Söderström.

Jännes, Arvi 1886: Jälkileikkuuta Mikael Agricolan kielestä. [New aspects on Mikael Agricola's language.] – *Virittäjä* 1886 pp. 145–183.

Jussila, Raimo 1998: *Vanhat sanat*. [Old words.] Helsinki: Finnish Literature Society.

Jussila, Raimo 2000: Vanhan kirjasuomen sanaston kasvu. [The growth of the lexicon in old literary Finnish.] – *Pipliakielestä kirjakieleksi*. Eds. Matti Punttila, Raimo Jussila, Helena Suni. Kotimaisten kielten tutkimuskeskuksen julkaisuja 105 pp. 279–292. Helsinki: Kotimaisten kielten tutkimuskeskus.

Jussila, Raimo 2009: *Kalevalan sanakirja*. [Kalevala dictionary.] Helsinki: Otava.

Juusten, Paulus 1575: *Se Pyhä Messu*. [The holy Mass.] Facsimile. Edited and postscripted by Martti Parvio. Helsinki: Finnish Literature Society 1978.

Karlsson, Fred 1999 [1983]: *Finnish: an essential grammar*. New edition, Andrew Chesterman (trans.). Routledge: London and New York.

Kaupunkia pintaa syvemmältä: arkeologisia näkökulmia Turun historiaan 2003. [A city from far beneath the surface: archaeological perspectives on the history of Turku.] Ed. Liisa Seppänen; [Turku]: TS Group and Society for Medieval Archaeology in Finland.

Kepsu, Saulo 2005: *Uuteen maahan. Helsingin ja Vantaan vanha asutus ja nimistö*. [Into a new land. Old settlement and nomenclature of Helsinki and Vantaa.] Helsinki: Finnish Literature Society.

Keskiaho, Jesse 2013: Codices Fennici. Kartoitus Suomessa ennen vuotta 1600 valmistetuista tai käytetyistä käsikirjoituksista. [Codices Fennici. A survey of manuscripts prepared or used in Finland before 1600.] Retrieved from: http://www.finlit.fi/tutkimus/codices_handlist.pdf

Kettunen, Lauri 1940: *Suomen murteet III. Murrekartasto*. [Finnish dialects III. Dialect atlas.] Finnish Literature Society Publications 188. Helsinki: Finnish Literature Society.

Kiuru, Silva 1988: Agricolan teonnimijohdosten erikoispiirteitä. [Special features of Agricola's derived action nouns.] – Esko Koivusalo (ed.): *Mikael Agricolan kieli*. Tietolipas 112 pp. 133–177. Helsinki: Finnish Literature Society.

Knuutila, Jyrki 1987: Liturgisen yhdenmukaistamisen toteutuminen Suomen reformaatiokaudella 1537–1614. [The realisation of liturgical standardisation during the Reformation in Finland between 1537 and 1614.] – *Suomen kirkkohistoriallisen seuran vuosikirja* 77 pp. 9–40. Helsinki: Finnish Society of Church History.

Knuutila, Jyrki 1988: Regulat ia oienuxet. Vuonna 1549 annetut ohjeet avioliiton solmimisesta ja siinä elämisestä. [Regulations and guidelines. Instructions provided in 1549 on marriage and living in matrimony.] – *Teologinen aikakauskirja 93* pp. 282–292. Helsinki.

Knuutila, Jyrki 1990: *Avioliitto oikeudellisena ja kirkollisena instituutiona Suomessa vuoteen 1629.* [Marriage as a juridical and ecclesiastical institution in Finland up to 1629.] Suomen kirkkohistoriallisen seuran toimituksia 151. Helsinki: Finnish Society of Church History.

Knuutila, Jyrki 2007: Selvitys Turun tuomiokirkon ja sen papiston tuloista. [An account on the earnings of Turku Cathedral and its clergy.] – Jyrki Knuutila & Anneli Mäkelä-Alitalo (eds.): *Mikael Agricola: Turun tuomiokirkon ja papiston tulot 1541–1542.* Finnish Literature Society Publications 1129 pp 13–73. Helsinki: Finnish Literature Society.

Knuutila, Jyrki 2010: Tukholman suomalaisen seurakunnan "messukirja" ja jumalanpalveluselämän muuttuminen evankeliseksi 1500-luvulla. [The "missal" of the Finnish parish in Stockholm and the change to Evangelical church services in the 16th century.] – Jorma Hannikainen (ed.) *Facultas ludendi. Erkki Tuppuraisen juhlakirja* pp. 79–113. Kuopio: Sibelius Academy, Kuopio unit.

[Kovalenka, Nina] 2004: Liite. Jäljennös Venäjän ja Ruotsin välirauhansopimuksesta, joka solmittiin 40 vuodeksi ja jonka allekirjoittivat Novgorodin käskynhaltijat ja ruotsalaiset lähettiläät Novgorodissa 25. maaliskuuta 1557. [Appendix. A copy of the Russo-Swedish peace treaty for a truce of 40 years, signed by the Novgorod stadtholders and Swedish envoys in Novgorod on 25 March 1557.] – Ossi Tuusvuori (ed.): *Agricola-symposiumi. Turku 20.–21.9.2004* pp. 79–111. Turku: Agricola working group.

Kurvinen, P. J. I. 1929: *Suomen virsirunouden alkuvaiheet v:een 1640.* [The beginning stages of Finnish hymnal poetry up to 1640.] Helsinki: Finnish Literature Society.

Lahtinen, Anu 2007: Mikael Agricola aatelisvallan verkostoissa. [Mikael Agricola in the networks of noble authority.] – Kaisa Häkkinen & Tanja Vaittinen (eds.): *Agricolan aika.* Helsinki: BTJ Kustannus oy.

Lappalainen, Päivi 2007: Mikael Agricola kaunokirjallisuudessa. [Mikael Agricola in fiction.] – Kaisa Häkkinen & Tanja Vaittinen (eds.): *Agricolan aika* pp. 183–200. Helsinki: BTJ Kustannus oy.

Larson, James L. 2010: *Reforming the North: the kingdoms and churches of Scandinavia, 1520–1545.* Cambridge; New York: Cambridge University Press.

[Laurén, L. L]. 1870: *Kalastajan poika. Suomen ijäti muistettawa hywäntekiä.* [The fisher's son. An eternally remembered benefactor of Finland.] [Turku: Frenckell.]

Lavery, Jason 2006: *The history of Finland.* Westpoint, Conn.: Greenwood Press.

Lehtinen, Tapani 2007: *Kielen vuosituhannet. Suomen kielen kehitys kantauralista varhaissuomeen.* [Centuries of a language. The development of Finnish from Proto-Uralic to Early Finnish.] Tietolipas 1. 3. painos. Helsinki: Finnish Literature Society.

Leskinen, Heikki 1970: *Imperatiivin muodostus itämerensuomalaisissa kielissä. I. Suomi.* [The formation of the imperative in the Balto-Finnic languages. I. Finnish.] Suomi 115:2. Helsinki: Finnish Literature Society.

Leskinen, Juha 1990: *Suomen kielen inkongruentit instruktiivirakenteet ja niiden tausta.* [Finnish incongruent instructive structures and their background.] Finnish Literature Society Publications 536. Helsinki: Finnish Literature Society.

Mäkelä-Alitalo, Anneli 2007: Mikael Agricolan veroluettelot. [Mikael Agricola's tax lists.] – Jyrki Knuutila & Anneli Mäkelä-Alitalo (eds.): *Mikael Agricola: Turun tuomiokirkon ja papiston tulot 1541–1542.* Finnish Literature Society Publications 1129 pp. 74–95 Helsinki: Finnish Literature Society.

Maliniemi, Aarno 1933: *Opillinen ja kirjallinen kulttuuri keskiaikana.* [A doctrinal and literary culture in the Middle Ages.] Helsinki [no publisher information].

Mark, Julius 1925: *Die Possessivsuffixe in den uralischen Sprachen.* Mémoires de la Société Finno-Ougrienne LIV. Helsinki: Finno-Ugrian Society.

Marshall, Peter 2009: *The Reformation: a very short introduction*. Oxford; New York: Oxford University Press.
Meinander, Henrik 2011: *A history of Finland*. New York: Columbia University Press.
Montagu, Jeremy 2004: *Musical instruments of the Bible*. Lanham, Md.; London: Scarecrow Press.
Murray, Robert 1954: *Finska församlingen i Stockholm*. Stockholm: Svenska kyrkans diakonistyrelses förlag.
Nikkilä, Osmo 1988: Agricolan kieli ja teokset loppuheiton valossa. [The Finnish and works of Agricola in light of apocope.] – Esko Koivusalo (ed.): *Mikael Agricolan kieli*. Tietolipas 112 pp. 94–110. Helsinki: Finnish Literature Society.
Nikkilä, Osmo 1994: *Loppuheitto ja vanha kirjasuomi. Suomen kielen i:n loppuheiton historiaa*. [Apocope and old literary Finnish. The history of apocope of the Finnish *i*.] Opera Fennistica & Linguistica 8. Tampere: Department of Finnish Language and General Linguistics, University of Tampere.
Nordberg, Henric 1963: Mikael Agricolan käsikirjan lähteitä. [Sources for Mikael Agricola's agenda] – *Suomen Kirkkohistoriallisen Seuran vuosikirja* 48–51 pp. 20–38. Helsinki: Finnish Society of Church History.
Nummila, Kirsi-Maria 2011: *Tekijännimet Mikael Agricolan teosten kielessä. Henkilötarkoitteisten johdosten merkitykset, funktiot ja rakenteet* [Agent nouns in the language of Mikael Agricola's works. The meanings, functions and structures of derivatives referring to persons.] Annales Universitatis Turkuensis Ser. C Tom. 328. Turku: University of Turku.
Numminen, Jaakko 2004: Mikael Agricolan muistomerkkigalleria ja sen kehittäminen Agricolan 450-vuotisjuhlaksi 2007. [A collection of Mikael Agricola memorials and its development for Agricola 2007, the 450th celebratory year.] – Ossi Tuusvuori (ed.): *Agricola-symposiumi. Turku 20.–21.9.2004* pp. 61–70. Turku: Agricola working group.
Nuorteva, Jussi 1999: *Suomalaisten ulkomainen opinkäynti ennen Turun akatemian perustamista 1640*. [Finns studying abroad before the foundation of the Royal Academy of Turku.] Helsinki: Finnish Historical Society and Finnish Society of Church History.
Nuorteva, Jussi 2012: Petrus Särkilahti. *Kansallisbiografia*, retrieved from http://www.kansallisbiografia.fi/kb/artikkeli/290/
Ojansuu, Heikki 1901: *Suomen lounaismurteiden äännehistoria. Vokaalioppi*. [The phonetic history of southwestern Finnish dialects. Vowels.] – Suomi 3:19. Helsinki.
Ojansuu, Heikki 1904: Vanhimmat Isämeidän rukoukset suomen kielellä. [The oldest versions of the Lord's Prayer in Finnish.] *Virittäjä* 8 pp. 130–134.
Ojansuu, Heikki 1909: *Mikael Agricolan kielestä*. [On the language of Mikael Agricola.] Suomi IV:7:1. Helsinki: Finnish Literature Society.
Ojansuu, Heikki 1923: Millaista suomea puhuttiin keskiaikana. [How Finnish was spoken in the Middle Ages.] – Heikki Ojansuu: *Suomen kielen tutkimuksen työmailta 1* pp. 24–43. Jyväskylä: Gummerus.
Ojansuu, Heikki 1926: Lisiä keskiajan suomen tuntemukseen. [Additions to the understanding of Finnish in the Middle Ages] – *Satakunta VI* pp. 37–56.
Paarma, Jukka 1980: *Hiippakuntahallinto Suomessa 1554–1604*. [Diocesan administration in Finland from 1554 to 1604.] Helsinki: Finnish Society of Church History.
Paarma, Jukka 1999: Martinus Skytte. *Kansallisbiografia*, retrieved from: http://www.kansallisbiografia.fi/kb/artikkeli/332/
Palola, Ari-Pekka 2002: Petrus Sild. *Kansallisbiografia*, retrieved from: http://www.kansallisbiografia.fi/kb/artikkeli/282/
Pantermöller, Marko 2010: *Der finnische Abessiv. Ein Kasus zwischen spontanem Wandel und gezielter Sprachplanung*. Veröffentlichungen der Societas Uralo-Altaica. Wiesbaden: Harrassowitz.

Parvio, Martti 1978: Paavali Juusten ja hänen messunsa. Liturgianhistoriallinen tutkimus. [Paavali Juusten and his missal. A liturgical-historical study.] *Suomi 122:3*. Helsinki: Finnish Literature Society.

Paunonen, Heikki 1975: *Monikon genetiivin muodostus suomen kielessä I: Johdanto: Yksivartaloisten kaksitavujen monikon genetiivi suomen murteissa*. [The formation of the genitive plural in Finnish I: an introduction: the genitive plural of single-stem, two-syllable words in Finnish dialects.] Finnish Literature Society Publications 317. Helsinki: Finnish Literature Society.

Pellinen, Hanna-Maria 2007: Arkeologit Mikael Agricolan jalanjäljillä Pernajassa. [Archaeologists in the footsteps of Agricola in Pernå.] – Kaisa Häkkinen & Tanja Vaittinen (eds.): *Agricolan aika* pp. 201–211. Helsinki: BTJ Kustannus oy.

Penttilä, Aarni 1931: *Upsalan suomenkielisen (1500-luvulta polveutuvan) evankeliumikirjan fragmentin kielestä*. [On the langauge of the fragment of the Finnish-langaue Upsala Evangelion (from the 16th century).] Suomi V:13. Helsinki: Finnish Literature Society.

Penttilä, Aarni 1942: *Upsalan suomenkielisen (1500-luvulta polveutuvan) evankeliumikirjan katkelma*. [An excerpt from the Finnish-langaue Upsala Evangelion (from the 16th century).] Suomi 101: 95–120. Helsinki.

Perälä, Anna 2007: *Mikael Agricolan teosten painoasu ja kuvitus*. [Typography and illustration in the works of Mikael Agricola.] Helsinki: Finnish Literature Society.

Pirinen, Kauko 1956: *Turun tuomiokapituli keskiajan lopulla*. [The cathedral chapter of Turku at the end of the Middle Ages.] Suomen kirkkohistoriallisen seuran toimituksia 58. Helsinki: Finnish Society of Church History.

Pirinen, Kauko 1962: *Turun tuomiokapituli uskonpuhdistuksen murroksessa*. [The cathedral chapter of Turku in the turning point of the Reformation.] Suomen kirkkohistoriallisen seuran toimituksia 62. Helsinki: Finnish Society of Church History.

Pirinen, Kauko 1988: Suomenkielisen liturgisen kirjallisuuden synty. [The birth of Finnish liturgical literature.] – Esko Koivusalo (ed.): *Mikael Agricolan kieli*. Tietolipas 112 pp. 9–24. Helsinki: Finnish Literature Society.

Puukko, A. F. 1946: *Suomalainen Raamattumme Mikael Agricolasta uuteen Kirkkoraamattuun*. [Our Finnish Bible from Mikael Agricola to the new Church Bible.] Helsinki: Otava.

Rapola, Martti 1962: *Agricolan apajalla*. [At the fishing ground of Agricola.] Tietolipas 28. Helsinki: Finnish Literature Society.

Rapola, Martti 1963: *Henrik Hoffman, puristinen kielenkorjaaja*. [Henrik Hoffman, a puristic proofreader.] Suomi 110:3. Helsinki: Finnish Literature Society.

Rapola, Martti 1969: *Vanha kirjasuomi*. [Old literary Finnish.] Tietolipas 1. 3. painos. Helsinki: Finnish Literature Society.

Report 2008 = Agricola 2007. Oma kieli, oma mieli – Mikael Agricolan juhlavuosi 2007. [Agricola 2007. Oma kieli, oma mieli ('our own language, our own thoughts') – 2007, the celebratory year of Mikael Agricola.] Opetusministeriön julkaisuja 2008: 29. Helsinki: Ministry of Education and Culture. Retrieved from: http://www.minedu.fi/OPM/Julkaisut/2008/Agricola_2007_Oma_kieli_oma_mieli

Salmi, Heidi 2010: *Mikael Agricolan teosten kielen ala-, ylä- ja pää-vartaloiset adpositiot*. [Adpositions with the stems *ala*, *ylä* and *pää* in the language of Mikael Agricola's works.] Annales Universitatis Turkuensis Ser. C Tom. 307. Turku: University of Turku.

Santesson, Lillemor 2002: Nordic language history and religion/ecclesiastical history III: Luther's Reformation. – Oskar Bandle (main editor): *The Nordic Languages*. Vol. 1. pp. 412–424. Handbücher zur Sprach- und Kommunikationswissenschaft 22.2. Berlin – New York: Walter de Gruyter.

Sarajas, Annamari 1956: *Suomen kansanrunouden tuntemus 1500–1700-lukujen kirjallisuudessa*. [Understanding of Finnish folk poetry in literature between the 16th and 18th centuries.] Helsinki [no publisher information].

Saukkonen, Pauli & Haipus, Marjatta & Niemikorpi, Antero & Sulkala, Helena 1979: *Suomen kielen taajuussanasto. A Frequency Dictionary of Finnish.* Helsinki: WSOY.
Savijärvi, Ilkka 1977: *Itämerensuomalaisten kielten kieltoverbi. I. Suomi.* [The negative verb in the Balto-Finnic languages. I. Finnish.] Finnish Literature Society Publications 333. Helsinki: Finnish Literature Society.
Savijärvi, Ilkka 1988: Agricolan kieltolause. [The negative clause in Agricola.] – Esko Koivusalo (ed.): *Mikael Agricolan kieli.* Tietolipas 112 pp. 69–93. Helsinki: Finnish Literature Society.
Schalin, Olav D. 1946–1947: *Kulthistoriska studier till belysande av reformationens genomförande i Finland I–II.* Helsingfors: The Society of Swedish Literature in Finland.
Schmeidler, Marie-Elisabeth 1969: Zur Analyse der Übersetzung des Neuen Testaments durch Michael Agricola (1948). – *Studia Fennica XIV* pp. 41–56. Helsinki: Finnish Literature Society.
Suojanen, Matti K. 1977: *Mikael Agricolan teosten indefiniittipronominit: totalitiivit.* [Indefinite pronouns in the works of Mikael Agricola: totalitives.] Finnish Literature Society Publications 334. Helsinki: Finnish Literature Society.
Suomi, Kari & Toivanen, Juhani & Ylitalo, Riikka 2008: *Finnish sound structure: phonetics, phonology, phonotactics and prosody.* Studia Humaniora Ouluensia 9. Oulu: University of Oulu.
Taavitsainen, Jussi-Pekka 2007: Mikael Agricolan Viipuri – Viipurin Mikael Agricola? [Mikael Agricola's Vyborg – Vyborg's Mikael Agricola?] – Kaisa Häkkinen & Tanja Vaittinen (eds.): *Agricolan aika* pp. 212–232. Helsinki: BTJ Kustannus oy.
Tarkiainen, Kari 2004: Mitä tiedämme vuoden 1557 rauhansopimusneuvotteluista Ruotsin ja Venäjän välillä? [What do we know about the 1557 Russo-Swedish peace negotiations?] – Ossi Tuusvuori (ed.): *Agricola-symposiumi. Turku 20.–21.9.2004* pp. 15–25. Turku: Agricola working group.
Tarkiainen, Kari 2007: *Ruotsin ja Venäjän rauhanneuvottelut 1557: Mikael Agricola Ruotsin lähetystön jäsenenä.* [The 1557 Russo-Swedish peace negotiations: Mikael Agricola as a member of the Swedish delegation.] Finnish Literature Society Publications 1104. Helsinki: Finnish Literature Society.
Tarkiainen, Kari 2008: *Finlands svenska historia. 1, Sveriges Österland: från forntiden till Gustav Vasa.* Skrifter utgivna av Svenska litteratursällskapet i Finland 702:1. Helsingfors: The Society of Swedish Literature in Finland; Stockholm: Atlantis.
Tarkiainen, Viljo 1948: Mikael Agricolan kirjastosta. [On the personal library of Mikael Agricola.] *Kirjastolehti.* [Reprinted in Viljo Tarkiainen 1958: *Mikael Agricola. Tutkielmia*, pp. 69–78. Helsinki: Finnish Literature Society.]
Tarkiainen, Viljo 1971: *Henrik Gabriel Porthan.* Tietolipas 6. Helsinki: Finnish Literature Society.
Tarkiainen, Viljo & Tarkiainen, Kari 1985: *Mikael Agricola, Suomen uskonpuhdistaja.* [Mikael Agricola, Finnish Reformer.] Otava, Helsinki.
Topelius, Zachris 1884: Gossen från Pernå. – Zachris Topelius: *Läsning för barn* 6 pp. 135–141. Stockholm: Bonnier.
Tuppurainen, Erkki 2007: Mikael Agricolan virret. [Mikael Agricola's hymns.]Retrieved from: http://evl.fi/agricola2007.nsf/sp3?open&cid=Content18831
Tuppurainen, Erkki (ed.) 2012: *Codex Westh. Westhin koodeksin kirkkolaulut.* [Codex Westh litugical songs.] DocMus-tohtorikoulun julkaisuja 2. Helsinki: Sibelius Academy.
Tuppurainen, Erkki & Hannikainen, Jorma 2010: *Suomenkielisiä kirkkolauluja 1500–1600-luvuilta.* [Finnish liturgical songs from 1500 to 1600.] Kirkkomusiikin osaston ja Kuopion osaston julkaisuja 33. Kuopio: Sibelius Academy.
Urponen, Jenni 1999: "Passio meidän Herran Jesuxen Christuxen." Johannes Urnoviuksen muokkaama Melchior Vulpiuksen Matteus-passio luterilaisen passioperinteen esimerkkinä. ["Passio meidän Herran Jesuxen Christuxen" '[The Passion

of our Lord Jesus Christ'. Melchior Vulpius' *Matteus-passio* adapted by Johannes Urnovius as an example of the Lutheran tradition of the Passion.] Project work (unpublished). Kuopio: Sibelius Academy.

Vartiainen, Ritva 1988: Agricolan kielen keskeiset hengelliset laatusanat. [Essential spiritual adjectives in Agricola's Finnish.] – Esko Koivusalo (ed.): *Mikael Agricolan kieli*. Tietolipas 112 pp. 180–202. Helsinki: Finnish Literature Society.

Virrankoski, Pentti 1956: *Suur-Kalajoen historia 1. Esihistorian ajasta isoonvihaan.* [The history of Suur-Kalajoki 1. From prehistory to the Greater Wrath.] Kokkola: Suur-Kalajoen historiatoimikunta.

Wilkuna, Kyösti 1912: *Viimeiset luostariasukkaat*. [The last abbey residents.] Porvoo: WSOY.

Wulf, Christina 1982: Zwei finnische Sätze aus dem 15. Jahrhundert. *Ural-Altaische Jahrbücher*, Neue Folge 2 pp. 90–98.

Historical Personal Names

Historical personal names used for this book	Historical, Fennicised personal names in other literature
Amund Laurentsson	Amund Lauritsanpoika
Canutus Johannis	Knut Johanneksenpoika
Carl	Kaarle
Christian	Kristian
Christopher	Kristoffer
Erasmus of Rotterdam	Erasmus Rotterdamilainen
Eric (Prince)	Erik, Eerikki
Ericus Erici	Eerik Sorolainen
Finno, Jacobus	Finno, Jaakko, Suomalainen, Jaakko
Frederick	Fredrik
Frederick the Wise	Fredrik Viisas
Galen	Galenos
Genetz, Arvid	Jännes, Arvi
Gustav Vasa	Kustaa Vaasa
Henry, Bishop	Henrik, piispa
Ivan IV Vasilyevich, Ivan the Terrible	Iivana Julma

Historical personal names used for this book	Historical, Fennicised personal names in other literature
St Jerome, Church Father	Hieronymos, Hieronymus
Johannes Erasmi	Johannes Erasmuksenpoika
John	Juhana
Juusten, Paulus	Juusten, Paavali
Keijoi, Thomas Francisci	Keijoi, Tuomas Fransiskuksenpoika
Laurentius	Lauri, Lauritsa
Lizelius, Anders	Lizelius, Antti
Luther, Martin	Luther, Martti
Magnus II Tavast	Maunu Tavast
Michael Stefani	Mikael Tapaninpoika
Lord Martti	Martti, Herra Martti, Mårten
Nicolaus Magni, Nils Månsson	Nikolaus Maununpoika, Nikolaus Magni
Norman, Georg	Norman, Yrjö
Petraeus, Aeschillus	Petraeus, Eskil
Pliny	Plinius
Särkilax, Petrus	Särkilahti, Pietari
Sild, Petrus	Sild, Pietari, Silta, Pietari
Simon Henrici Wiburgensis	Simo Viipurilainen
Skytte, Martinus	Skytte, Martti
Teit, Martinus	Teitti, Martti
Thomas	Tuomas
Topelius, Zachris	Topelius, Sakari

Place Names in Past and Present Finland

Naming in Finland

Since contemporary Finland is officially a bilingual country (90% Finnish, 5.4% Swedish – and to some extent Sámi 0.03% as a recognised regional language), place names (i.e. cities, towns and villages, and other municipalities and districts) are dependent on the mother tongue population. The language majority of a bilingual municipality is the deciding factor on its name. If the municipality has a Finnish-speaking majority, it will have a common, internationally used Finnish name and a Swedish counterpart used only in Swedish (e.g. the common name *Turku* in Finnish is *Åbo* in Swedish). If the municipality has a Swedish-speaking majority, it is the opposite (e.g. the common name *Jakobstad* in Swedish is *Pietarsaari* in Finnish). Unilingual municipalities have no counterpart in the other language (e.g. the Finnish name *Jyväskylä* and the Swedish name *Korsnäs*).

Below is a list of names used in this book that have a common name used internationally and a counterpart used in the other official language in Finland. In a historic context, for example, a Swedish name is used even though the common name is in Finnish (e.g. *County of Nyslott*).

Common	Counterpart
Naantali (Fin.)	Nådendal (Swe.)
Närpes (Swe.)	Närpiö (Fin.)
Nöteborg (Swe.)	Pähkinäsaari (Fin.)
Pernå (Swe.)	Pernaja (Fin.)
Tartu (Est.)	Tartto (Fin.), Dorpat (Ger.)
Turku (Fin.)	Åbo (Swe.)
Savonlinna (Fin.)	Nyslott (Swe.)
Shlisselburg (Rus.)	Pähkinälinna (Fin.)
Vyborg (Swe./Rus.)	Viipuri (Fin.)

Historical Provinces

The historical provinces of Finland were administrative entities when the region of Österland – or Finland – was a part of the Swedish Realm. Because of the lack of literary Finnish, their original names in official, administrative use were at first in Swedish. The provinces were dissolved in 1634 when new provinces were set up, and the province system lasted until 2010. Nowadays, Finland is divided into 19 regions.

Some of the names of the historical provinces in English are based on their Latin variants. Nowadays, most of the Latin-based names are no longer in use in English for the regions: for example, *Häme*, *Savo* and *Lapland* are used for these respective regions in official, English administrative texts (e.g. *Regional Council of Häme*). The name *Southwest Finland* is today officially used when speaking of Varsinais-Suomi. However, the Latin-based names *Karelia* and *Ostrobothnia* are still in use in English today, as are the remaining Finnish names *Satakunta* and *Uusimaa* and Swedish *Åland*.

Swedish	Finnish	English
Egentliga Finland	Varsinais-Suomi	Finland Proper
Karelen	Karjala	Karelia
Lappland	Lappi	Laponia
Österbotten	Pohjanmaa	Ostrobothnia
Satakunda	Satakunta	Satakunta
Savolax	Savo	Savonia
Tavastland	Häme	Tavastia
Nyland	Uusimaa	Uusimaa
Åland	Ahvenanmaa	Åland

Inflectional Paradigms in Finnish

Nominal Inflection

	Singular	Plural	Singular	Plural	Singular	Plural
Nominative	talo 'house'	talot	vesi 'water'	vedet	taivas 'sky, heaven'	taivaat
Genitive	talon	talojen	veden	vesien	taivaan	taivaiden
Partitive	taloa	taloja	vettä	vesiä	taivasta	taivaita
Essive	talona	taloina	vetenä	vesinä	taivaana	taivaina
Translative	taloksi	taloiksi	vedeksi	vesiksi	taivaaksi	taivaiksi
Inessive	talossa	taloissa	vedessä	vesissä	taivaassa	taivaissa
Elative	talosta	taloista	vedestä	vesistä	taivaasta	taivaista
Illative	taloon	taloihin	veteen	vesiin	taivaaseen	taivaisiin
Adessive	talolla	taloilla	vedellä	vesillä	taivaalla	taivailla
Ablative	talolta	taloilta	vedeltä	vesiltä	taivaalta	taivailta
Allative	talolle	taloille	vedelle	vesille	taivaalle	taivaille
Abessive	talotta	taloitta	vedettä	vesittä	taivaatta	taivaitta
(Comitative	taloine-px	taloine-px	vesine-px	vesine-px	taivaine-px	taivaine-px)
Instructive	–	taloin	–	vesin	–	taivain

Possessive Suffixes

First-person singular	taloni	veteni	taivaani
Second-person singular	talosi	vetesi	taivaasi
Third-person singular	talonsa	vetensä	taivaansa
First-person plural	talomme	vetemme	taivaamme
Second-person plural	talonne	vetenne	taivaanne
Third-person plural	talonsa	vetensä	taivaansa

Nominal Inflection with Possessive Suffixes (shown here in the first-person singular)

	Singular	Plural	Singular	Plural	Singular	Plural
Nominative	taloni	taloni	veteni	veteni	taivaani	taivaani
Genitive	taloni	talojeni	veteni	vesieni	taivaani	taivaitteni
Partitive	taloani	talojani	vettäni	vesiäni	taivastani	taivaitani
Essive	talonani	taloinani	vetenäni	vesinä	taivaanani	taivainani
Translative	talokseni	taloikseni	vedekseni	vesikseni	taivaakseni	taivaikseni
Inessive	talossani	taloissani	vedessäni	vesissäni	taivaassani	taivaissani
Elative	talostani	taloistani	vedestäni	vesistäni	taivaastani	taivaistani
Illative	talooni	taloihini	veteeni	vesiini	taivaaseeni	taivaisiini
Adessive	talollani	taloillani	vedelläni	vesilläni	taivaallani	taivaillani
Ablative	taloltani	taloiltani	vedeltäni	vesiltäni	taivaaltani	taivailtani
Allative	talolleni	taloilleni	vedelleni	vesilleni	taivaalleni	taivailleni
Abessive	talottani	taloittani	vedettäni	vesittäni	taivaattani	taivaittani
Comitative	taloineni	taloineni	vesineni	vesineni	taivaineni	taivaineni
Instructive	–	–	–	–	–	–

This paradigm applies to all possessive suffixes.

Personal Pronoun Inflection

	minä 'I'	sinä 'you'	hän 'he/she'	me 'we'	te 'you (pl./form.)'	he 'they'
Nominative	minä	sinä	hän	me	te	he
Genitive	minun	sinun	hänen	meidän	teidän	heidän
accusative	minut	sinut	hänet	meidät	teidät	heidät
Partitive	minua	sinua	häntä	meitä	teitä	heitä
Essive	minuna	sinuna	hänenä	meinä	teinä	heinä
Translative	minuksi	sinuksi	häneksi	meiksi	teiksi	heiksi
Inessive	minussa	sinussa	hänessä	meissä	teissä	heissä
Elative	minusta	sinusta	hänestä	meistä	teistä	heistä
Illative	minuun	sinuun	häneen	meihin	teihin	heihin
Adessive	minulla	sinulla	hänellä	meillä	teillä	heillä
Ablative	minulta	sinulta	häneltä	meiltä	teiltä	heiltä
Allative	minulle	sinulle	hänelle	meille	teille	heille
Abessive						
Comitative		} N/A				
Instructive						

Verbal Inflection

Indicative

	Affirmative			Negative		
	sanoa 'to say'	ottaa 'to take'	hakata 'to chop'			

Present active

First-person singular	sanon	otan	hakkaan	en sano	en ota	en hakkaa
Second-person singular	sanot	otat	hakkaat	et sano	et ota	et hakkaa
Third-person singular	sanoo	ottaa	hakkaa	ei sano	ei ota	ei hakkaa
First-person plural	sanomme	otamme	hakkaamme	emme sano	emme ota	emme hakkaa
Second-person plural	sanotte	otatte	hakkaatte	ette sano	ette ota	ette hakkaa
Third-person plural	sanovat	ottavat	hakkaavat	eivät sano	eivät ota	eivät hakkaa

Present passive

	sanotaan	otetaan	hakataan	ei sanota	ei oteta	ei hakata
Past active						
First-person singular	sanoin	otin	hakkasin	en sanonut	en ottanut	en hakannut
Second-person singular	sanoit	otit	hakkasit	et sanonut	et ottanut	et hakannut
Third-person singular	sanoi	otti	hakkasi	ei sanonut	ei ottanut	ei hakannut
First-person plural	sanoimme	otimme	hakkasimme	emme sanoneet	emme ottaneet	emme hakanneet
Second-person plural	sanoitte	otitte	hakkasitte	ette sanoneet	ette ottaneet	ette hakanneet
Third-person plural	sanoivat	ottivat	hakkasivat	eivät sanoneet	eivät ottaneet	eivät hakanneet

Past passive

	sanottiin	otettiin	hakattiin	ei sanottu	ei otettu	ei hakattu

Perfect active

First-person singular	olen sanonut	olen ottanut	olen hakannut	en ole sanonut	en ole ottanut	en ole hakannut
Second-person singular	olet sanonut	olet ottanut	olet hakannut	et ole sanonut	et ole ottanut	et ole hakannut
Third-person singular	on sanonut	on ottanut	on hakannut	ei ole sanonut	ei ole ottanut	ei ole hakannut
First-person plural	olemme sanoneet	olemme ottaneet	olemme hakanneet	emme ole sanoneet	emme ole ottaneet	emme ole hakanneet
Second-person plural	olette sanoneet	olette ottaneet	olette hakanneet	ette ole sanoneet	ette ole ottaneet	ette ole hakanneet
Third-person plural	ovat sanoneet	ovat ottaneet	ovat hakanneet	eivät ole sanoneet	eivät ole ottaneet	eivät ole hakanneet

Perfect passive

	on sanottu	on otettu	on hakattu	ei ole sanottu	ei ole otettu	ei ole hakattu

Pluperfect active

First-person singular	olin sanonut	olin ottanut	olin hakannut	en ollut sanonut	en ollut ottanut	en ollut hakannut
Second-person singular	olit sanonut	olit ottanut	olit hakannut	et ollut sanonut	et ollut ottanut	et ollut hakannut
Third-person singular	oli sanonut	oli ottanut	oli hakannut	ei ollut sanonut	ei ollut ottanut	ei ollut hakannut
First-person plural	olimme sanoneet	olimme ottaneet	olimme hakanneet	emme olleet sanoneet	emme olleet ottaneet	emme olleet hakanneet
Second-person plural	olitte sanoneet	olitte ottaneet	olitte hakanneet	ette olleet sanoneet	ette olleet ottaneet	ette olleet hakanneet
Third-person plural	olivat sanoneet	olivat ottaneet	olivat hakanneet	eivät olleet sanoneet	eivät olleet ottaneet	eivät olleet hakanneet

Pluperfect passive

	oli sanottu	oli otettu	oli hakattu	ei ollut sanottu	ei ollut otettu	ei ollut hakattu

Conditional

Present active

First-person singular	sanoisin	ottaisin	hakkaisin	en sanoisi	en ottaisi	en hakkaisi
Second-person singular	sanoisit	ottaisit	hakkaisit	et sanoisi	et ottaisi	et hakkaisi
Third-person singular	sanoisi	ottaisi	hakkaisi	ei sanoisi	ei ottaisi	ei hakkaisi
First-person plural	sanoisimme	ottaisimme	hakkaisimme	emme sanoisi	emme ottaisi	emme hakkaisi

Second-person plural	sanoisitte	ottaisitte	hakkaisitte	ette sanoisi	ette ottaisi	ette hakkaisi
Third-person plural	sanoisivat	ottaisivat	hakkaisivat	eivät sanoisi	eivät ottaisi	eivät hakkaisi

Present passive

	sanottaisiin	otettaisiin	hakattaisiin	ei sanottaisi	ei otettaisi	

Perfect active

First-person singular	olisin sanonut	olisin ottanut	olisin hakannut	en olisi sanonut	en olisi ottanut	en olisi hakannut
Second-person singular	olisit sanonut	olisit ottanut	olisit hakannut	et olisi sanonut	et olisi ottanut	et olisi hakannut
Third-person singular	olisi sanonut	olisi ottanut	olisi hakannut	ei olisi sanonut	ei olisi ottanut	ei olisi hakannut
First-person plural	olisimme sanoneet	olisimme ottaneet	olisimme hakanneet	emme olisi sanoneet	emme olisi ottaneet	emme olisi hakanneet
Second-person plural	olisitte sanoneet	olisitte ottaneet	olisitte hakanneet	ette olisi sanoneet	ette olisi ottaneet	ette olisi hakanneet
Third-person plural	olisivat sanoneet	olisivat ottaneet	olisivat hakanneet	eivät olisi sanoneet	eivät olisi ottaneet	eivät olisi hakanneet

Perfect passive

	olisi sanottu	olisi otettu	olisi hakattu	ei sanottaisi	ei otettaisi	ei hakattaisi

Potential

Present active

First-person singular	sanonen	ottanen	hakannen	en sanone	en ottane	en hakanne
Second-person singular	sanonet	ottanet	hakannet	et sanone	et ottane	et hakanne
Third-person singular	sanonee	ottanee	hakannee	ei sanone	ei ottane	ei hakanne
First-person plural	sanonemme	ottanemme	hakannemme	emme sanone	emme ottane	emme hakanne
Second-person plural	sanonette	ottanette	hakannette	ette sanone	ette ottane	ette hakanne
Third-person plural	sanonevat	ottanevat	hakannevat	eivät sanone	eivät ottane	eivät hakanne

Present passive

	sanottaneen	otettaneen	hakattaneen	ei sanottane	ei otettane	ei hakattane

Perfect active

First-person singular	lienen sanonut	lienen ottanut	lienen hakannut	en liene sanonut	en liene ottanut	en liene hakannut
Second-person singular	lienet sanonut	lienet ottanut	lienet hakannut	et liene sanonut	et liene ottanut	et liene hakannut
Third-person singular	lienee sanonut	lienee ottanut	lienee hakannut	ei liene sanonut	ei liene ottanut	ei liene hakannut
First-person plural	lienemme sanoneet	lienemme ottaneet	lienemme hakanneet	emme liene sanoneet	emme liene ottaneet	emme liene hakanneet
Second-person plural	lienette sanoneet	lienette ottaneet	lienette hakanneet	ette liene sanoneet	ette liene ottaneet	ette liene hakanneet
Third-person plural	lienevät sanoneet	lienevät ottaneet	lienevät hakanneet	eivät liene sanoneet	eivät liene ottaneet	eivät liene hakanneet

Perfect passive

	lienee sanottu	lienee otettu	lienee hakattu	ei liene sanottu	ei liene otettu	ei liene hakattu

Imperative

Present active

First-person singular	–	–	–	–	–	–
Second-person singular	sano	ota	hakkaa	älä sano	älä ota	älä hakkaa
Third-person singular	sanokoon	ottakoon	hatkatkoon	älköön sanoko	älköön ottako	älköön hakatko
First-person plural	sanokaamme	ottakaamme	hakatkaamme	älkäämme sanoko	älkäämme ottako	älkäämme hakatko
Second-person plural	sanokaa	ottakaa	hakatkaa	älkää sanoko	älkää ottako	älkää hakatko
Third-person plural	sanokoot	ottakoot	hakatkoot	älkööt sanoko	älkööt ottako	älkööt hakatko

Present Passive

	sanottakoon	otettakoon	hakattakoon	älköön sanottako	älköön otettako	älköön hakattako

Perfect active

First-person singular	–	–	–	–	–	–
Second-person singular	ole sanonut	ole ottanut	ole hakannut	älä ole sanonut	älä ole ottanut	älä ole hakannut
Third-person singular	olkoon sanonut	olkoon ottanut	olkoon hakannut	älköön olko sanonut	älköön olko ottanut	älköön olko hakannut
First-person plural	olkaamme sanoneet	olkaamme ottaneet	olkaamme hakanneet	älkäämme olko sanoneet	älkäämme olko ottaneet	älkäämme olko hakanneet
Second-person plural	olkaa sanoneet	olkaa ottaneet	olkaa hakanneet	älkää olko sanoneet	älkää olko ottaneet	älkää olko hakanneet
Third-person plural	olkoot sanoneet	olkoot ottaneet	olkoot hakanneet	älkööt olko sanoneet	älkööt olko ottaneet	älkööt olko hakanneet
Perfect passive						
	olkoon sanottu	olkoon otettu	olkoon hakattu	älköön olko sanottu	älköön olko otettu	älköön olko hakattu

Infinitive (Non-Finite) Forms

First infinitive = A infinitive

| Nominative | sanoa | ottaa | hakata |
| Translative | sanoakse-PX | ottaakse-PX | hakatakse-PX (e.g. sanoakseni, sanoaksesi, sanoaksensa etc.) |

Second infinitive = E infinitive

Active inessive	sanoessa	ottaessa	hakatessa
Passive inessive	sanottaessa	otettaessa	hakattaessa
Instructive	sanoen	ottaen	hakaten

Third infinitive = MA infinitive

Inessive	sanomassa	ottamassa	hakkaamassa
Elative	sanomasta	ottamasta	hakkaamasta
Illative	sanomaan	ottamaan	hakkaamaan
Adessive	sanomalla	ottamalla	hakkaamalla
Abessive	sanomatta	ottamatta	hakkaamatta
Active instructive	sanoman	ottaman	hakkaaman
Passive instructive	sanottaman	otettaman	hakattaman

Fourth infinitive

sanominen	ottaminen	hakkaaminen
sanomista	ottamista	hakkaamista

First participle = VA participle

Active	sanova	ottava	hakkaava
Passive	sanottava	otettava	hakattava

Second active participle = NUT participle

sanonut	ottanut	hakannut

Second passive participle = TU participle

sanottu	otettu	hakattu

Agent participle

sanoma	ottama	hakkaama

Abstract

Kaisa Häkkinen

Spreading the Written Word
Mikael Agricola and the Birth of Literary Finnish

Translated by Leonard Pearl

The Protestant Reformation began in Germany in 1517, and the adoption of Lutheranism was the decisive impetus for literary development in Finland. As the Reformation required the use of the vernacular in services and ecclesiastical ceremonies, new manuals and biblical translations were needed urgently.

The first Finnish books were produced by Mikael Agricola. He was born an ordinary son of a farmer, but his dedication to his studies opened up the road to leading roles in the Finnish Church. He was able to bring a total of nine works in Finnish to print, which became the foundation of literary Finnish.

The first chapter outlines the historical background necessary to understand the life's work of Mikael Agricola. The second chapter describes Agricola's life. Chapter three presents the Finnish works published by Agricola. The fourth chapter is a depiction of Agricola's Finnish. Agricola carried out his life's work as part of a network of influential connections, which is described in chapter five. The sixth chapter examines the importance of Agricola's work, research on Agricola and Agricola's role in contemporary Finnish culture. The book mainly focuses on language and cultural history, but in terms of Church history, it also provides a review on the progression and arrival of the Reformation to Finland.

Finnish is a Uralic language but the source languages of Agricola's translations – Latin, German, Swedish and Greek – were all Indo-European languages. Thus, the oldest Finnish texts were strongly influenced by foreign elements and structures. Some of those features were later eliminated whereas others became essential constituents of standard Finnish. To illustrate this development, the Finnish in Agricola's works has systematically been compared with the standard contemporary language.

Index

Note: Boldface page numbers indicate definitions or major discussions.

Abckiria 40, 43, **53–57,** 58, 61, 74, 77, 90, 111, 140, 149, 159, 163
Åberg, Åke 57
abessive 12, 87, 89, **93**, 104, 178
ablative 12, **92**, 96, 111, 178
accusative 89, 90, **91**, 94, 110, 120, 146, 179
action nouns (nomen actionis) 123
active voice **96**, 104, 105, 106, 107, 120, 180, 181, 182, 183, 184, 185
adessive 12, **92–93**, 94, 101, 104, 105, 112, 124, 178, 179, 184
agent nouns (nomen agentis) 123
agent participle see participles
Agricola (etymology) 34
Agricola, Christian 48, 71, 159
Agricola, Laurentius 43
Agricola 2007 (anniversary) 137, 160, 161, 162
Ahlqvist, August 150, 151,
Aku Ankka see Donald Duck
allative 12, 91, **92–93**, 178, 179
alphabet 11, 54, 55, **76–84**, 121
Amund Laurentsson 28, 48, 53, 57, 111, 133, 154, 174
Aristotle 40, 135, 141
Augustine (Church Father) 37, 40, 71
Angelic Salutation 20, 54, 55, 139
apocope **87–88**, 91, 92, 93, 107, 146, 155
Apostles' Creed 54, 67
assimilation (phonetic) 87, **88**
Ave Maria, see Angelic Salutation

Banér, Nils Axelsson 42, 43
Basil the Great (Saint) 71
Bertil (frälseman) 138
Bertil (Vicar of Pernå) 33, 34, 130–131, 135

Bible
Biblia: Se on: Coco Pyhä Ramattu Suomexi 146, 147, 148, 155
Gustav II Adolf Bible 146
Gustav Vasa Bible 24, 54, 72
Lutheran Bible 24, 38, 72, 73
Vanha kirkkoraamattu 147
Vulgate 21, 61, 72
Bielke, Hogenskild 42, 43, 48
Bielke, Nils 42, 45, 60, 132
birch bark letters 16
Birgit (Saint) 50
Birgittine (Order) 15, 16, 50, 63, 158
Birgitta Olavintytär (Agricola's wife) 48, 52
Bishop of Finland 16, 135
Bishop of Turku 8, 16, 18, 31, 50, 131, 135, 138, 146, 148
Black Book of Åbo Cathedral 17
Block, Johannes 26, 35, 131
Blomstedt, Väinö 151
Book of Psalms 48, **69–72,** 133
Botvid Suneson 49–50, 136
boundary lengthening 98, **102**, 103
bridal Mass 64
Brunfels, Otto 58, 72
Budde, Jöns 15
Bugenhagen, Johannes 23, 40, 68, 69, 70, 72

calendar 16, 30, 47, 49, 58–59, 77, 79, 129, 140, 141
calls to prayer 54
Canutus Johannis Braumensis 26, 38, 39, 47, 50, 51, 52, 132, 136, 137
caritive (derivation)107, 123
Carl (Prince of Sweden) 41
cathedral chapter of Turku 16, 26, 27, 31,

187

38, 40, 41, 42, 45, 46, 48, 49, 50, 133, 136, 153, 154, 158, 159, 160
cathedral school of Turku 8, 15, 31, 34, 35, 38, 39, 41–45, 51, 71, 132, 146, 163
Cato, Marcus 140
Cederberg, J. A. 150
Chato see Cato
Christian II of Denmark 23, 24, 38
Christopher III (of Sweden) 29, 64
Chronicon Episcoporum Finlandensium (chronicle of bishops) 27, 32, 34, 35, 35, 38, 43, 49, 50, 52, 62, 71, 136, 141, 148, 149, 150
clitics 12, 99, 101, 102, 112, 113, 114
codex 15
Codex Aboensis 47
Codex B 28 63, 64, 156
Codex Kalmar 47
Codex Westh 29, 63, 64, 66, 68, 122, 123, 127, 156
collects 66
comitative 12, 89, **93**, 178, 179
comparative (degree) **124–125**
compounds 11, 79, 102, 122, 123, 124, 126
compound verbs 124
conditional 96, **97**, 99, 100, 181–182
Confiteor 66
consonant-final stem **89**
Cranach, Lucas 23
Credo (creed) 20, 54, 67
Cruciger, Caspar 40

Dauidin Psaltari 48, **69–72**, 102, 117, 129, 145, 149, 150, 163
Decalogue see Ten Commandments
Decius, Nicolaus 67
degrees of comparison 124
demonstrative pronouns 94, **95**
derivation 81, 86, 95, 97, 101, 104, 105, 107, 122, 123–126, 127
dialects 8, 18, 19–20, 32, 62, 76, 80, 81, 84, 85, 86, 87, 88, 91, 93, 94, 96, 97, 101, 102, 103, 105, 106, 107, 112, 116, 118, 121, 122, 123, 124, 125–126, 143, 145, 146, 152, 155, 156
Dietrich, Veit 72
dissimilation 88
Divine Service 66
Donald Duck 161, 162

Edelfelt, Albert 159, 161, 162
Ekman, Robert Wilhelm 150, 159

elative 12, **92**, 96, 104, 111, 178, 179, 184
Epiphanius of Salamis 63
episcopus 50, 136
Erasmus of Rotterdam 21–22, 35, 38, 49, 61, 133–134, 140, 141, 142, 153
Eric (Prince of Sweden) 39, 40, 136
Ericus Erici 66, 146
Eskil (son of Vicar Bertil) 33
essive 12, 87, **91**, 178, 179
etymology
  of *Agricola* 34
  of *Pernaja* 32
  of *psalmi* 70
  of *psalttari* 70
Eucharist 54, 64, 65, 67
Eurén, Gustav Erik 150
Europaeus, Daniel 122
Evangelical Lutheran Church of Finland 25, 145, 161
Exhortation 66, 67

Fincke, Gustaf 47
Finland vs. Finland Proper 14, 18, 19, 20, 62, 76, 121, 177
Finnish folklore 30, 149
Finno, Jacobus 145
Finno-Ugric 10, 87, 101, 103, 106, 108, 121
Finno-Ugric transcription 83
Fleming, Erik 132
fraktura 54
Frederick I (of Denmark) 23
Frederick the Wise 22, 23, 37
future (tense) **98**, 104, 105, 113

Galen 141
Ganander, Christfrid 122
Genetz, Arvid 151, 174
genitive 12, 88, 89, **90–91**, 92, 93, 94, 95, 106, 109, 112, 118, 120, 124, 127
genitive plural **90**
Ghotan, Bartholomeus 16
Gradual 66
Granit-Ilmoniemi, E. 57
Gummerus, Jaakko 58, 151, 154
Gunnaerus, Michael Bartholdi 145
Gustav I Vasa 24, 30, 35, 38, 39, 40, 41, 46, 50, 51, 60, 133, 134, 136, 137, 138, 139, 150, 158, 159, 174

Haavikko, Paavo 158
Hail Mary see Angelic Salutation
Häkkinen, Kaisa 145, 156
Hannes Ingenpoika 30

Hanseatic League 19
Härkäpää, Erik 73
Heininen, Simo 10, 52, 69, 140, 153, 154, 155
Hemming (Bishop) 16
Hemminki of Masku (Hemmingus Henrici) 122
Henry (Bishop) 16, 174
Hertzberg, Rafael 157
Hessus, Eobanus 72
Hjelt, Arthur 151, 153
Hoffman, Henrik 62, 146
Hogenskild, Anna 42, 132
Holma, Juhani 58, 154
Holy Communion 66
Huberinus, Caspar 63
humanism 21, 35, 37, 38, 133, 141
humanists 21, 22, 34, 72, 141
Hyckerström, P. J. 57
hymnal 30, 59, 122, 145

Ikola, Niilo 153, 154
Ikola, Osmo 98, 146, 155, 156
illative 11, 12, **92**, 104–105, 107, 178, 179, 184
illative plural **92**, 178, 179
illuminated manuscript 15, 47
imperative 12, 74, 86, 88, 95, 96, **97**, 98–100, 101, 102, 147, 155, 183
Inaba, Nobufumi 156
incongruency 112
indefinite pronouns **95–96**
Index Agricolaensis 120, 155
indicative 96, **97**, 99–100, 180
inessive 12, **91–92**, 104, 178179, 184
infinitives 12, 62, **103–105**, 107, 184–185
  first infinitive **103–104**, 110
  second infinitive **104**
  third infinitive 85, 88, **104–105**, 106, 113
  fourth infinitive **105**
inflectional stem **89**
interrogative pronouns 89, **95**
instructive (case) 12, 85, 89, **93**, 104, 113, 127, 178, 179, 184
Itkonen, Erkki 107
Itkonen-Kaila, Marja 98, 155
Ivalo, Santeri 158
Ivan the Terrible, Ivan IV Vasilyevich 51, 137, 158, 174

Jännes, Arvi see Genetz, Arvid
Jauhiainen, Oskari 160
Jerome St (Church Father) 21

Johannes Erasmi 34, 35, 131, 158, 175
Johannes Petri 45
John (Prince of Sweden, later King John III) 29, 41, 64
John of Hoya and Bruchhausen 26, 35
Jonas, Justus 23, 40
Juslenius, Daniel 122,
Jussila, Raimo 122, 156
Juusten, Paulus 27, 32, 34, 35, 36, 38, 39, 41, 43, 45, 49, 50, 52, 71, 136, 141, 145, 148, 149, 150, 153, 175

Kalevala 71, 96, 121, 149
Kalevala metre 30
Kalliala church accounts 18, 152
Kalmar Union 23
Kangasala Missal 28, 156
Käsikiria Castesta ia muista Christikunnan Menoista 28, 47, **62–65**, 163
Katedralskolan i Åbo see cathedral school of Turku
Keijoi, Thomas Francisci 26, 38–39, 41, 45, 175
Kiuru, Silva 10, 155
knittelvers 59
Knuutila, Jyrki 153–154
Kotikielen Seura 150
Kristoffer (King) see Christopher
Krook, Klemet 48, 131
Kuninkaantie 33
Kurki, Arvid 135

Lappalainen, Päivi 157
Laurén, Ludvig Leonard 150
Laurentius Andrae 24, 38, 133
Laurentius Canuti 25
Laurentius Petri 49, 51, 52, 64, 133, 136, 137, 138
Laurentsson see Amund Laurentsson
leisi 21
Lejonhufvud, Sten Eriksson 137
Leskinen, Heikki 97, 155
Leskinen, Juha 93
Linné, Carl von 148
Lipasti, Roope 161
Lönnrot, Elias 149
Lord Martti 29–30, 64, 127
Lord's Prayer 20, 54, 67, 108, 142–143
Luther, Martin 21, 22, 23, 27, 35, 36, 37, 38, 39, 40, 45, 54, 57, 60, 61, 64, 66, 68, 69, 71, 72, 73, 134, 140, 149, 158
Luther-Agricola Society 160–161
Luther Postil 34, 36, 66, 134, 140, 163

Magnus II Tavast 18, 175
Major, Georg 72
Mäkelä-Alitalo, Anneli 154
Maliniemi, Aarno 151
Månsson, Nils see Nicolaus Magni
Mannerheim, Carl Gustaf Emil 157
Mark, Julius 108
Martti see Lord Martti
Matteus-passio see St Matthew Passion
Mela, Pomponius 142
Melanchton, Philipp 22, 37, 40, 45, 54, 134–135, 140, 141,
Mennander, Carl Fredrik 148
Messenius, Johannes 149
Messu eli Herran Echtolinen 28, 47, **65–68**, 70, 163
Mikael Agricola Society 161
Mikael Stefani 61
Mikkelsen, Hans 38
Missale Aboense 16–17, 28, 36, 58, 67
mood 96, **97–98**, 99, 101, 103
Mörne, Arvid 157
Münster, Sebastian 72, 73, 127, 142

negative verb 12, 74, 86, 96, **101–103**, 109, 112, 113,
Ne Prophetat Haggai SacharJa Maleachi **74–75**, 102, 129, 163
New Testament 21, 22, 25, 27, 40, 44, 68, 142, 147, 148, 149
   Agricola's New Testament see *Se Wsi Testamenti*
   King Christian's New Testament 24, 38
   Swedish New Testament 24, 28, 38, 44, 61
Nicolaus Magni 39, 41
Nikkilä, Osmo 10, 87, 155
Ninety-Five Theses 21, 22, 37
nominative 81, 87, 88, 89, **90**, 95, 105, 107, 110, 178, 179, 184
Norman, Georg 27, 39, 41, 44, 60, 132, 133, 134, 136, 137, 142, 143, 175
Nummila, Kirsi-Maria 156
Numminen, Jaakko 160

Ojansuu, Heikki 10, 151, 152
Olaus Petri 22, 24, 25, 29, 38, 62, 63, 64, 66, 67, 132, 133
Old Testament 40, 48, 70, 72, 73, 74, 147, 149, 153
ordinarius 50, 136
Osiander, Andreas 54

Pantermöller, Marko 93
participles 12, 103, **105–107**, 117–118, 119–120, 185
   first participle **105–106**
   second participle **106**, 111
   agent participle **106**, 111
   negative participle **107**
partitive 12, 81, **91**, 93, 105, 113, 178, 179
passive voice 12, 85, 92, **96**, 99, 100, 104, 105, 106, 107, 110–111, 119, 180–181, 182, 183, 184, 185
past (tense) 88, 96, 97, **98**, 99, 100, 106, 111, 118, 180
Pater Noster see Lord's Prayer
Paunonen, Heikki 90
Perälä, Anna 57, 61, 69, 133, 154
perfect (tense) 96, 97, **98**, 106, 181, 182, 183, 184
personal pronouns 89, **94**, 107, 111,
Petraeus, Aeschillus 146, 175
Petrus Ragvaldi 136
Piae cantiones 43
Pirinen, Kauko 153
Plato 140
Plautus 40
Pliny the Elder 141, 175
Pliny the Younger 142, 175
pluperfect (tense) 96, **98**, 106, 181
Porthan, Henrik Gabriel 52, 148–149, 159
potential (mood) 12, 96, **97–98**, 99, 101, 182
prebend 40, 42, 45, 46
preface 30, 36, 38, 42, 43, 48, 49, 57, 59, 62, 64, 67, 68, 69, 70, 71, 76, 131, 133, 139, 142, 144, 148, 149, 152, 154
present (tense) 96, 97, **98**, 99, 100, 101, 102, 105, 118, 120, 180, 181, 182, 183
protestant Reformation 8, 13, 18, 21, 37, 186
psalm 40, 48, 58, 66, 69, 70–72, 133, 145
   etymology 70
Psaltari see *Dauidin Psaltari*
Puukko, A. F. 147

Rapola, Martti 10, 146, 152–153, 155
reflexive 94, 95, **96–97**, 110, 111
regalia parishes 50
Reinhold, Erasmus 141
relative pronoun **95**, 114
Richolff, Jürgen 28, 38, 53, 57
Royal Academy of Turku 148

Rucouskiria Bibliasta 30, 36, 43, 49, 54, **58–59,** 60, 61, 63, 66, 67, 68, 70, 71, 72, 77, 79, 103, 119, 128, 129, 140, 141, 145, 149, 150, 151, 153, 154, 163
    calendar section 30, 58–59
Runeberg, Johan Ludvig 149
Russo-Swedish peace negotiations 51, 137, 158

Saksa, Aleksandr 154
Salmi, Heidi 109, 156
Särkilax, Petrus 25–26, 35, 38, 175
Savijärvi, Ilkka 102, 103, 155
Schalin, Olav D. 29,
Schmeidler, Marie-Elisabet 155
schwabacher 23, 54
Schwenkfeld, Caspar 154
Se meiden Herran Jesusen Christusen Pina 28, 47, **68–69,** 74, 118, 163
Se Wsi Testamenti 27, 29, 38, 40, 43, 47, 54, **59–62,** 69, 70, 73, 76, 118, 121, 132, 133, 135, 137, 142, 146, 153, 158, 159
Sermon 25, 35, 36, 42, 53, 66, 68, 74, 132, 134
Service of the Sacrament 67
Setälä, Emil Nestor 29, 151, 152, 153
Shlisselburg 51, 176
Sigfrid Månsson 32
Sigfrids 32, 160
Sild, Petrus 25, 38, 175
Simon Henrici Wiburgensis 27, 39, 41, 45, 60, 175
Sjöstrand, Carl Eneas 159
Skytte, Martinus 35–36, 37, 41, 47, 48, 131–132, 136, 175
Smith, Henrik 38
Snellman, Johan Vilhelm 149
Solinus, Julius 142
Soroi, Petrus 26
Sorolainen, Erik see Ericus Erici
Spalatin, Georg 22, 37
St Matthew Passion 147
Strabo 40, 142
Suojanen, Matti 96
superlative **124–125**

Tarkiainen, Kari 10, 152
Tarkiainen, Viljo 10, 140, 152
Teit, Martinus 27, 33, 34, 39, 40, 41, 60
Ten Commandments 54, 66, 74
tense 69, 96–97, **98,** 99, 101, 102, 103, 106

textualis 15
theuerdank 54, 55
Topelius, Zachris 158, 159
Torsbius, Torsby 31, 48, 71, 131
Tott, Anna 42, 48, 132
translative 12, 87, **91,** 104, 124, 178, 179, 184
Treaty of Nöteborg (Oreshek) 17, 51, 176
trivium 34, 43, 44
Turkka, Aarne 151
typeface 23, 54, 55, 154

University of Bochum 156
University of Greifswald 37
University of Helsinki 149, 150, 152
University of Leipzig 37
University of Leuven 25, 35
University of Paris 16, 37
University of Rostock 25, 27, 37
University of Turku 10, 152, 156
University of Uppsala 44
University of Wittenberg 22–23, 27, 35, 37, 39, 40, 60, 68, 131, 134, 141, 157, 163
Uppsala Agenda (B 28) 29, 63, 64, 156
Uppsala Evangelion, Uppsala Gospel Book 29, 122, 123
Uppsala Missal (included in *Uppsala Agenda*) 123

Vadian, Joachim 142
Valerius Maximus 142
Vallgren, Ville 159
Vasa see Gustav Vasa
Vasilyevich see Ivan IV Vasilyevich
Vinter, Christiern 38
Virittäjä 150
Virsikirja 145
vowel-final inflectional stem **89**

Weisut ia Ennustoxet Mosesen Laista ia Prophetista Wloshaetut 48, 70, **72–74,** 102, 163
Westh see *Codex Westh*
Wiklund, Karl Bernhard 29, 151
Wikström, Emil 160
Wilkuna, Kyösti 158
word formation **123–124,** see also compounds and derivation

Ziegler, Jacob 142

Studia Fennica Ethnologica

Memories of My Town
The Identities of Town Dwellers and Their Places in Three Finnish Towns
Edited by Anna-Maria Åström, Pirjo Korkiakangas & Pia Olsson
Studia Fennica Ethnologica 8
2004

Passages Westward
Edited by Maria Lähteenmäki & Hanna Snellman
Studia Fennica Ethnologica 9
2006

Defining Self
Essays on emergent identities in Russia Seventeenth to Nineteenth Centuries
Edited by Michael Branch
Studia Fennica Ethnologica 10
2009

Touching Things
Ethnological Aspects of Modern Material Culture
Edited by Pirjo Korkiakangas, Tiina-Riitta Lappi & Heli Niskanen
Studia Fennica Ethnologica 11
2008

Gendered Rural Spaces
Edited by Pia Olsson & Helena Ruotsala
Studia Fennica Ethnologica 12
2009

Laura Stark
The Limits of Patriarchy
How Female Networks of Pilfering and Gossip Sparked the First Debates on Rural Gender Rights in the 19th-century Finnish-Language Press
Studia Fennica Ethnologica 13
2011

Where is the Field?
The Experience of Migration Viewed through the Prism of Ethnographic Fieldwork
Edited by Laura Hirvi & Hanna Snellman
Studia Fennica Ethnologica 14
2012

Laura Hirvi
Identities in Practice
A Trans-Atlantic Ethnography of Sikh Immigrants in Finland and in California
Studia Fennica Ethnologica 15
2013

Eerika Koskinen-Koivisto
Her Own Worth
Negotiations of Subjectivity in the Life Narrative of a Female Labourer
Studia Fennica Ethnologica 16
2014

Studia Fennica Folkloristica

Pertti J. Anttonen
Tradition through Modernity
Postmodernism and the Nation-State in Folklore Scholarship
Studia Fennica Folkloristica 15
2005

Narrating, Doing, Experiencing
Nordic Folkloristic Perspectives
Edited by Annikki Kaivola-Bregenhøj, Barbro Klein & Ulf Palmenfelt
Studia Fennica Folkloristica 16
2006

Mícheál Briody
The Irish Folklore Commission 1935–1970
History, ideology, methodology
Studia Fennica Folkloristica 17
2008

Venla Sykäri
Words as Events
Cretan Mantinádes in Performance and Composition
Studia Fennica Folkloristica 18
2011

Hidden Rituals and Public Performances
Traditions and Belonging among the Post-Soviet Khanty, Komi and Udmurts
Edited by Anna-Leena Siikala & Oleg Ulyashev
Studia Fennica Folkloristica 19
2011

Mythic Discourses
Studies in Uralic Traditions
Edited by Frog, Anna-Leena Siikala & Eila Stepanova
Studia Fennica Folkloristica 20
2012

Studia Fennica Historica

Medieval History Writing and Crusading Ideology
Edited by Tuomas M. S. Lehtonen & Kurt Villads Jensen with Janne Malkki and Katja Ritari
Studia Fennica Historica 9
2005

Moving in the USSR
Western anomalies and Northern wilderness
Edited by Pekka Hakamies
Studia Fennica Historica 10
2005

DEREK FEWSTER
Visions of Past Glory
Nationalism and the Construction of Early Finnish History
Studia Fennica Historica 11
2006

Modernisation in Russia since 1900
Edited by Markku Kangaspuro & Jeremy Smith
Studia Fennica Historica 12
2006

SEIJA-RIITTA LAAKSO
Across the Oceans
Development of Overseas Business Information Transmission 1815–1875
Studia Fennica Historica 13
2007

Industry and Modernism
Companies, Architecture and Identity in the Nordic and Baltic Countries during the High-Industrial Period
Edited by Anja Kervanto Nevanlinna
Studia Fennica Historica 14
2007

CHARLOTTA WOLFF
Noble conceptions of politics in eighteenth-century Sweden (ca 1740–1790)
Studia Fennica Historica 15
2008

Sport, Recreation and Green Space in the European City
Edited by Peter Clark, Marjaana Niemi & Jari Niemelä
Studia Fennica Historica 16
2009

Rhetorics of Nordic Democracy
Edited by Jussi Kurunmäki & Johan Strang
Studia Fennica Historica 17
2010

Fibula, Fabula, Fact
The Viking Age in Finland
Edited by Joonas Ahola & Frog with Clive Tolley
Studia Fennica Historica 18
2014

Novels, Histories, Novel Nations
Historical Fiction and Cultural Memory in Finland and Estonia
Edited by Linda Kaljundi, Eneken Laanes & Ilona Pikkanen
Studia Fennica Historica 19
2015

JUKKA GRONOW & SERGEY ZHURAVLEV
Fashion Meets Socialism
Fashion industry in the Soviet Union after the Second World War
Studia Fennica Historica 20
2015

Studia Fennica Anthropologica

On Foreign Ground
Moving between Countries and Categories
Edited by Marie-Louise Karttunen & Minna Ruckenstein
Studia Fennica Anthropologica 1
2007

Beyond the Horizon
Essays on Myth, History, Travel and Society
Edited by Clifford Sather & Timo Kaartinen
Studia Fennica Anthropologica 2
2008

Studia Fennica Linguistica

Minimal reference
The use of pronouns in Finnish and Estonian discourse
Edited by Ritva Laury
Studia Fennica Linguistica 12
2005

Antti Leino
On Toponymic Constructions as an Alternative to Naming Patterns in Describing Finnish Lake Names
Studia Fennica Linguistica 13
2007

Talk in interaction
Comparative dimensions
Edited by Markku Haakana, Minna Laakso & Jan Lindström
Studia Fennica Linguistica 14
2009

Planning a new standard language
Finnic minority languages meet the new millennium
Edited by Helena Sulkala & Harri Mantila
Studia Fennica Linguistica 15
2010

Lotta Weckström
Representations of Finnishness in Sweden
Studia Fennica Linguistica 16
2011

Terhi Ainiala, Minna Saarelma & Paula Sjöblom
Names in Focus
An Introduction to Finnish Onomastics
Studia Fennica Linguistica 17
2012

Registers of Communication
Edited by Asif Agha & Frog
Studia Fennica Linguistica 18
2015

Kaisa Häkkinen
Spreading the Written Word
Mikael Agricola and the Birth of Literary Finnish
Studia Fennica Linguistica 19
2015

Studia Fennica Litteraria

Women's Voices
Female Authors and Feminist Criticism in the Finnish Literary Tradition
Edited by Päivi Lappalainen & Lea Rojola
Studia Fennica Litteraria 2
2007

Metaliterary Layers in Finnish Literature
Edited by Samuli Hägg, Erkki Sevänen & Risto Turunen
Studia Fennica Litteraria 3
2008

Aino Kallas
Negotiations with Modernity
Edited by Leena Kurvet-Käosaar & Lea Rojola
Studia Fennica Litteraria 4
2011

The Emergence of Finnish Book and Reading Culture in the 1700s
Edited by Cecilia af Forselles & Tuija Laine
Studia Fennica Litteraria 5
2011

Nodes of Contemporary Finnish Literature
Edited by Leena Kirstinä
Studia Fennica Litteraria 6
2012

White Field, Black Seeds
Nordic Literacy Practices in the Long Nineteenth Century
Edited by Anna Kuismin & M. J. Driscoll
Studia Fennica Litteraria 7
2013

Lieven Ameel
Helsinki in Early Twentieth-Century Literature
Urban Experiences in Finnish Prose Fiction 1890–1940
Studia Fennica Litteraria 8
2014

The most important places throughout Mikael Agricola's life

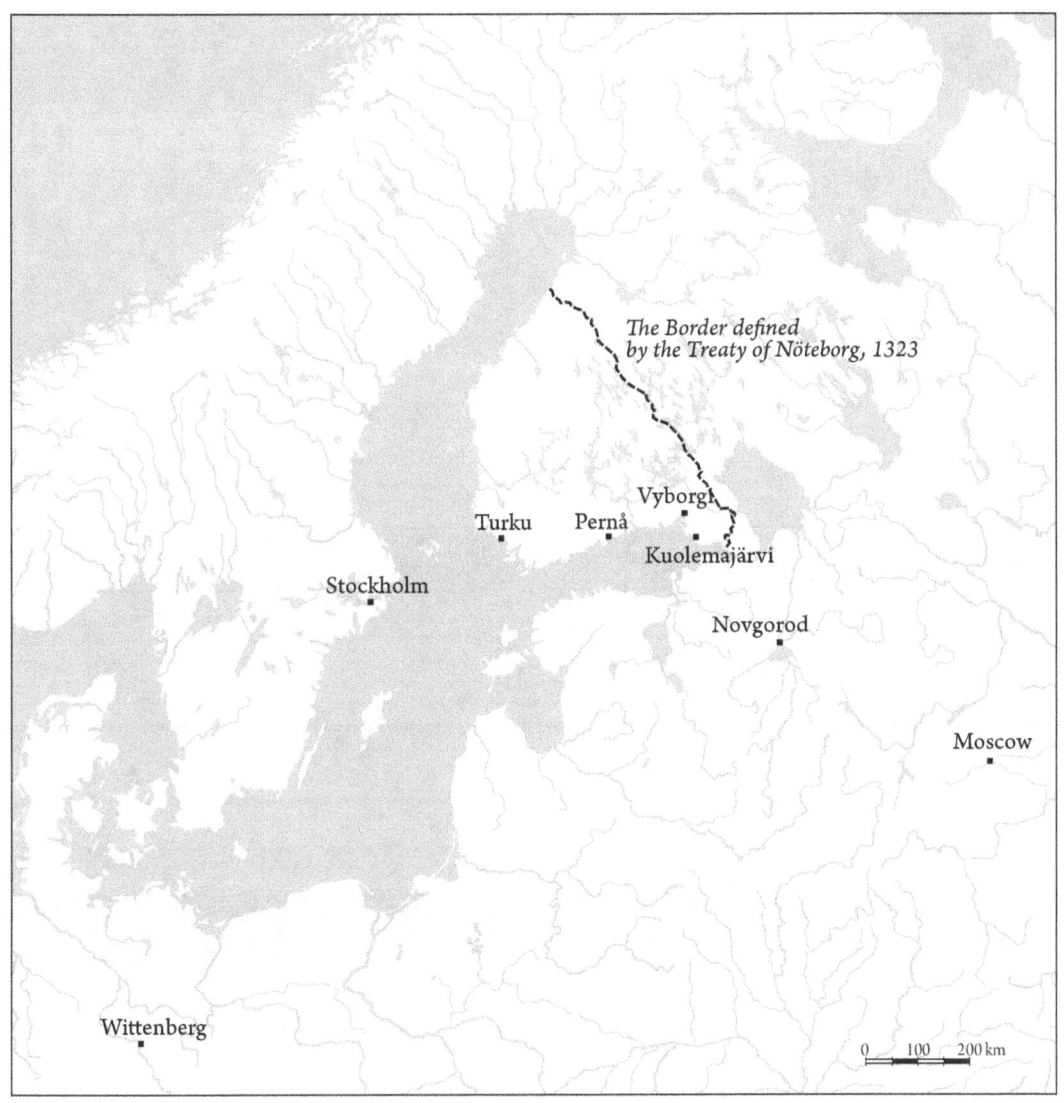

195

www.ingramcontent.com/pod-product-compliance
Lightning Source LLC
Chambersburg PA
CBHW080806300426
44114CB00020B/2843